"Packed full of information, juxtaposed with ...   ...nan
who has spent her life nurturing filmmakers.'
— Barbara Trent, Academy Award w   ...ic *Panama Deception*

"This book is the most intelligent, insightful and comprehensive guide to finding
the money that I have ever read. Carole Dean is the independent filmmaker's best
friend!"
— Christopher Ward, award-winning independent filmmaker

"Carole Dean has years of experience both as a producer and a funder, and her new
book is full of nuts-and-bolts information from both sides of the fence, told in a
conversational and heart-felt manner. Of special interest to filmmakers will be the
in-depth interviews with experts in the field, and an extensive appendix chock full of
references. A great new addition to the filmmaker's lexicon."
— Morrie Warshawski, consultant and author of *Shaking the Money Tree*

"Carole is your mentor throughout the book. She leads wary filmmakers through the
dark, daunting forest of 'no's' to the green-light power of 'yes.' The sensitive artist as
successful producer is a rare commodity. That's about to change. There are myriad,
alternative ways to finance a film without selling your soul, and Carole Lee Dean
knows them all."
— Judi Jordan, editor-at-large, *Latin Style Magazine*

"In *The Art of Film Funding*, Carole Dean has assembled insights and wisdom that will
prove immensely useful to filmmakers in their search for funding."
— Mark Litwak, attorney and author

"Carole Dean is well known in the motion picture industry for her innovations and
creative genius. In her book, *The Art of Film Funding*, she has created a superb bible
that will serve the novice as well as the seasoned filmmaker. Carole has utilized her
experience in the industry and her talent to create a masterpiece — a concise roadmap
for financing a film which reads like a novel. This book is a major contribution and
is bound to be the catalyst for valuable film production that the public and scholars
would otherwise miss."
— S. G. Fassoulis, film producer

"This book is a good start toward seeing the world of funding through the eyes of
experienced funders like Carole Dean and her colleagues. We need to master the
techniques outlined here so we can create not just one or two films, but an ongoing
body of work which will bring years of provocative insights to the public."
— Patric Hedlund, author and filmmaker

"My hat's off to Carole Dean for writing *The Art of Film Funding*. Written with a spiritual perspective and trust for your intuition, she not only acknowledges these creative forces, but rightfully honors the business process as an art in itself! What a joyful journey into filmmaking."

— Wendy De Rycke, indie producer

"Carole Dean's book successfully bridges the gap between the vision of the project and the realities of the market for the serious filmmaker."

— Louise Levison, author of
Filmmakers and Financing: Business Plans for Independents

"There's a saying in Spanish: 'There are two ways of spreading light; to be the candle; or the mirror that reflects it.' Carole, you are both!"

— Efrem Logreira, producer

"Carole Lee Dean knows the secrets of how to catch the attention of the people who can write the checks that enable you to make (or finish) your film. Her book offers an excellent overview of what you need to know to get started raising the funding for your dream project."

— Catherine Clinch, Associate Publisher, *Creative Screenwriting* Magazine

THE ART OF
FILM FUNDING
ALTERNATIVE FINANCING CONCEPTS

CAROLE LEE DEAN

Published by Michael Wiese Productions
3940 Laurel Canyon Blvd.# 1111
Studio City, CA 91604
tel. 818.379.8799
fax 818.986.3408
mw@mwp.com
www.mwp.com

Cover Design: Kevin Capizzi
Book Layout: Gina Mansfield Design
Editor: Paul Norlen

Printed by McNaughton & Gunn, Inc., Saline, Michigan
Manufactured in the United States of America
Printed on recycled paper

Library of Congress Cataloging-in-Publication Data

Dean, Carole Lee.
  The art of film funding : alternative financing concepts / Carole Lee Dean.
      p. cm.
  Includes bibliographical references and index.
  ISBN 10: 1932907319
  ISBN 13: 9781932907315
  1. Motion picture industry--United States--Finance. I. Title.
  PN1993.5.U6D35 2007
  384'.830973--dc22
                                          2007013945

This book is dedicated to my exceptional children,
Rick Dean & Carole Joyce

TABLE OF CONTENTS

FOREWORD

Independent films and filmmakers are the new paradigm, a bona fide revolution. As studios over the last two decades have begun to act more and more like independents rather than the other way around, film funding has evolved also. Over the last seven years, the extraordinary success of such low-budget indie films as *The Blair Witch Project*, *My Big Fat Greek Wedding* and *Napoleon Dynamite* has brought an increasing number of "average citizens" into film funding. In addition, a score of billionaires have entered the fray, sponsoring features both fictional and non-fictional. As documentary films have entered the mainstream, so has the art of funding them.

Prior to the start of the 21st century, there weren't enough theatrical docs that had earned significant revenues to make the discussion interesting. During the 1980s and '90s, there was a smattering of documentary box office triumphs. The success of *Roger and Me* in 1989 began the reemergence of the nonfiction film as a credible theatrical release. After a few successful films in the intervening years, 1994's *Hoop Dreams* attracted a lot of attention by accumulating North American box office receipts of $7.8 million on a budget of $800,000. The same year, *Crumb* reached a total of $3 million on a budget of $300,000. In 1997, a Best Documentary Oscar nominee, *Buena Vista Social Club*, scored almost $7 million at the box office and spun off a best-selling soundtrack album.

Nielsen Media Research has estimated that 85% of U.S. television households watch documentaries. Apparently much of this audience was no longer willing to wait for television rollouts and began going in larger numbers to see them in movie theaters first. At the same time, documentaries, influenced by Ken Burns and others bringing more creativity to the format, made films that would draw a movie theater audience. In addition, analysts feel that reality television has given viewers a taste for true-life stories, and thus helped the growth of the theatrical audience. As attendance figures for those crucial first weekends grew, distributors had the marketing ammunition to increase the attendance for succeeding screenings. The resulting box office revenues helped drive the value of docs to the video/DVD buyers and television programmers.

Critics and analysts proclaimed 2004 "the year of the documentary." At first many thought that the success of the films was tied to the turbulent elections of 2000 and 2004 — that perhaps Michael Moore was an anomaly as a documentarian and had managed to find a quirky loophole for making theatrical hits with *Bowling for Columbine* and *Fahrenheit 9/11*, and that succeeding political docs had snuck in through the same opening. However, when non-political films, such as *Spellbound*, *Mad Hot Ballroom* and the no-budget *Super Size Me*, also became successful, it became clear that docs of varying genres could compete with fiction features. Then in 2005 came *March of the Penguins*. Made for $3 million by the original French company and revised by Warner Independent Pictures and National Geographic Films with an English narration and Hollywood-type musical score for another $4 million, the film earned an estimated $224 million worldwide. Peter Bart, editor-in-chief of *Variety*, gives it credit, along with *Brokeback Mountain*, for convincing the studios that "there's gold in what used to be called art movies."

Now nonfiction films are made for and sold through every outlet that we know today — theatrical, television, direct-to-DVD, direct-to-foreign — and will be for the new technologies. Docs come in long form and short form. They are shown at every festival in the world. Filmmakers in every country make documentaries in every language. They cover every topic and genre.

With their growing potential to bring back profits to private investors, feature documentaries have reached another plateau. There is now enough information to create traditional business plans for them. The target markets for documentaries are the same as those for fiction films, save one group. Documentary audiences themselves are the first target audience. Every documentary has a subject, be it political, economic, inspirational, historic, sports-related, etc. These market segments often can be quantified or at least described. Unlike those financed by networks, docs financed with equity have their distribution streams open. As these films reach the festivals, distributors — both indie and studio — can bid for them, creating higher sales figures and the all-important "buzz factor."

With emerging technologies, more sales paths are likely to open up for non-fiction films. While users may not want to watch Superman Returns in ten-minute blocks on their cell phones or iPods while waiting in line at the bank, they may have a different attitude toward documentaries. Purveyors of content and equipment see the viability of the format on these platforms. It is too early to tell the value of nonfiction content in digital downloads, nor are the navigation systems mature yet, nor do we know what payouts are likely. Whatever retailing outlets become financially viable, however, the funders will be there along with the filmmakers to reap the rewards.

Louise Levison

Author, *Filmmakers and Financing: Business Plans for Independents*

ACKNOWLEDGMENTS

Janeva Hornbaker did a marvelous job of editing the book. She is a talented writer and filmmaker with extraordinary skills in research and a great sense of humor.

The chapters by Xackery Irving, Robert Mastronardi, Corky Kessler, Craig Ellefsen, Britt Penrod, Craig Ellefsen, Jilann Spitzmiller, Fernanda Rossi, Morrie Warshawski, Mark Litwak, and Dan Sherrett are all gifts for your guidance in funding your films. You could not have better mentors.

It's my grant sponsors that deserve the most credit. From 1992 when I started the Roy W. Dean film grants I have been graciously supported by the top people in our industry. One woman who was a finalist for the grant said it for me: "I want to win for the contacts. The donors to the grant are the top people in the film industry!" If you are ready to shoot your film please know that this list is the top of the industry and represents people who sincerely care for and nurture their clients. These companies donate to my grants because they want to give back to filmmakers. You could not find a better production list than on my website. Go to *www.fromtheheartproductions.com* and see the left-hand side for sponsors.

I have a special thanks to my friend Branwen Edwards who became my life coach and supported me weekly. Believe me, this is a wonderful way to write a book. Having someone to monitor you and to encourage you is a great asset for writers.

Phyllis Roth encouraged me to write back in 2000 when I sold my film business; her weekly contacts gave me constant support.

"Rickydidit" was the first word my daughter learned to say, even before Daddy. No matter what happened, if she broke something or her toys were left outside, she would just point and say Rickydidit. Well this time she's right, Rick Dean was a major catalyst for me in writing the book, so thanks Rick. Life *is a bowl of cherries* if only you will live it.

INTRODUCTION

You are a filmmaker because you are an artist and a visionary. Where else are you going to find a job that encourages you to create something based on your ideas and thoughts, then get to see it all dance across a 25-foot screen? What other career gives you the opportunity to design something that has the potential to inspire so many people? Filmmaking is a passion that infuses every fiber of your being. It challenges you to reach beyond your potential and allows you to observe the world from a unique perspective.

Film production is also one of the most demanding careers you could choose. During the course of your career you will be required to make an endless number of artistic decisions that will ultimately affect the final outcome of your film. Each stage of production is paved with potential pitfalls. If you screw something up in production, you'll pay dearly for it in post. Of course the upside to the frenetic pace of your chosen career is that you will never be bored. Filmmakers seem to thrive on all the twists and turns that come with the job, and they love to talk about their latest war stories.

Just grab a toffee-nut latte and a table at Starbucks over on Hollywood Boulevard and you will hear it all, from passionate debates over the best format and the latest editing equipment, to a broad range of esoteric criticism on some rogue director's bizarre shooting style. What you probably won't hear is the excited banter of filmmakers discussing the latest in funding.

There is more to filmmaking than stepping behind a camera. A film's life does not begin with production and end with postproduction. There is another stage that is equally important. I'll give you a few hints: Decisions made during this stage will determine the very essence of your film, including where it will go, who will see it, what it will say, and whether or not it will survive. It is a stage that occurs long before you dust off your camera, and it requires just as much artistic skill as directing and editing.

You were probably going to take a wild stab based on the title of this book and guess preproduction funding, only the part about it requiring as much artistic skill as directing and editing threw you, right?

Always go with your first answer. Preproduction funding is the most critical stage of your film's life. If you don't learn the latest funding techniques and marketing trends you will not survive in this industry. Your future career as a filmmaker and the integrity of your film are both on the line. Do you still want to set this book down and get right to the art of directing?

If you do you're not unlike the majority of those filmmakers over at Starbucks. By the way, have you ever wondered why there are so many filmmakers sitting around drinking coffee in the middle of the day when they could be out there making movies? Maybe it's because they don't happen to have a couple hundred thousand dollars lying around to support their film habit.

If you don't have funding you don't have a film. You might be able to pull off a small project with the help of your little plastic buddies, Visa and Master-Card (along with whatever you can manage to squeeze out of good old mom and dad), but if you do not learn the art of funding, your film career is going to be very short.

Believe me: I know what I'm talking about. I've watched too many talented filmmakers pack up their cars and leave town because they were hocked up to their eyeballs. It's not easy to produce a film when you're working all day at Kinko's and tending bar on the weekends so you can pay off the debt from your last project.

There is another reason why the funding stage is so critical. The very heart of your film begins with the funding process. The tasks you complete during the funding stage will take you deeper into your project than ever before. Your project will start to come together and will take on a whole new perspective as you explore and write about the background of your story, the style and structure you will use to tell the story, and all the other elements that go into your proposal. Dov S-S Simens of *HollywoodU.com* thinks funding is such an important part of the filmmaking process that he gave it its own special category, which he calls the "pre-preproduction" stage.

Too many filmmakers think the process of funding their films is going to be a long uphill battle that is going to suck the creative juices right out of their veins. Maybe this is because they can hear the dull echo of doors slamming before they even get started.

The money is out there. You just have to know how to find it. No, I haven't been living in a cave. I know times are tough. I have heard the grim economic forecasts. I have sat through meetings where board members drone on and on about how the economy has dramatically affected funding for the arts. Okay, so let's take a look at the figures and see just how bad things really are.

According to the Foundation Center:

1. Overall, foundation giving reached an estimated $33.6 billion in 2005, up from $31.8 billion in 2004. Accounting for inflation, growth in 2006 giving is likely to be modest.

2. For the close to 68,000 U.S. grant-making foundations, estimated giving increased 5.5 percent to a new milestone of $33.6 billion (in 2005).

This does not say funding will go down, it says it will go modestly upwards. Did you have any idea of the amount of money given to art in this country? I think it is astonishing.

A report by David Rockefeller's foundation, Business Committee for the Arts, says: *Nearly 90% of the record $33.2 billion that business gave to the arts in 2003 came from small (49%) and midsize (40%) companies, according to a recent national survey commissioned by the Business Committee for the Arts, Inc. (BCA) — a national not-for-profit organization that brings business and the arts together — and conducted by Shugoll Research, Bethesda, MD. The margin of error is + or − 4 percent.*

This means that the donations went up even after the 9/11 terror attack.

Business Committee for the Arts states: *Factors most important in a company's decision to support specific arts organizations were offering arts education initiatives (72%), offering arts programs to the underserved (72%), tying the arts to social causes such as hunger, violence or homelessness (61%), and offering a company recognition opportunities (61%). In 2005, 19% of respondents project an increase in support to the arts.*

If your films fit these concepts you may find it even easier than you thought to get funding.

Now, how much did you say it was going to take to get your film made and distributed? We are talking billions of dollars here! Individuals and corporations are giving away billions of dollars to support the arts. The amount you need to make your film represents a tiny drop in the bucket, so what's stopping you from going out there and getting your piece of the "funding pie"?

If you believe your film is worth the effort and the money that it is going to take to produce it, and if you believe that you have what it takes to become a great filmmaker, then you owe it to yourself to take the journey toward discovering the art of funding your films. Along the way I will introduce you to ideas and concepts that I have picked up after more than 30 years in the film industry.

Throughout this book you will also hear from successful industry professionals who will share insights and strategies that will help you make your filmmaking dreams a reality.

Just one more thing before we take off. I travel light. There's no room for negativity on this train, so you are going to have to leave your excess baggage at the station!

Note: We cannot guarantee the legitimacy of the claims made by any of the entities listed in this book and strongly advise that you obtain legal counsel before you discuss any specific agreements regarding your project with any online or off-line entity.

CHAPTER 1

COMMIT OR BE COMMITTED

*The guideposts or books will only tell you the road or the direction
for the destination. You must make the journey and experience the
joy and the victory.*

— Sai Baba

You've got an idea for a film. Great! So does my neighbor's daughter, the man who sold me this crummy computer, and the pizza delivery boy. My plumber pitched a film that will gross ten times more than *E.T.* while he unclogged my sink!

So what sets your idea apart from the rest of the naked city's untold stories? What makes your story so special that investors and grantors are going to want to hand you their hard earned money and let you take it to Tinseltown to produce a film?

I've read grant applications that start off, "I am thinking of making a film about the secret lives of moths. What do you think?" Even if the concept was crackerjack, the filmmaker's lack of confidence and commitment to the project makes me (along with every funder I know) nervous enough to pass.

With that in mind, I have devised a list of questions that every potential filmmaker should answer before committing to a project. This is not one of those *Cosmo* quizzes where you add up all the "A's" and "B's" and subtract all the "C's" to get some arbitrary score. If you answer each question honestly your answers will reveal your level of commitment to the film.

List three compelling reasons why this film should be made.

Describe your connection to the story and explain why you are the one who should make this film.

Who will benefit from this film? If your primary purpose in making the film is to prove that you can do it, then that's what you should put down. Just be honest.

Are you willing to quit your job for the next three years and accept the financial consequences that will accompany this decision?

If not, can you produce the film in your spare time?

How many hours a week can you put into this film?

Are you willing to give up your family time to do this film? (I don't recommend this)

Are you willing to forgo the Gap and wear the same clothes for the next 3 years?

How long can you drive your car? Will it last the next 3 years with minor repairs?

Why is this film important to you?

You should now have a healthy concept of the reality of filmmaking. If your answers tell you that this is not the film you are willing to make these sacrifices for, then don't do it. If, however, your answers reflect that you are willing to make the sacrifices necessary to make this film, that you are fully committed to your project and nothing can stop you, then read on. This book was written just for you.

Of course that doesn't mean this is going to be a cakewalk. Producing an independent film is a lot like draining an alligator pit. Most of the time you are so busy fighting off alligators that it's easy to forget why you went in there in the first place! That's why you're going to carry the answer to the last question with you wherever you go. When things get hairy take it out and read it again. Remember where you are coming from and focus on that energy.

SECRETS TO SUCCESS

The Soul never thinks without a mental picture.
— Aristotle

Two equally talented filmmakers set off to make their fortunes. One ends up securing a three-picture deal at Miramax while the other ends up parking cars in West Covina. What is the key ingredient that separates these two film-makers? Is it film school? I doubt it, since the majority of successful filmmakers out there did not graduate from film school. Is it wealth? Hardly.

Try creativity and vision.

"Cool, Carole! I've got creativity! I've got vision!"

I'm sure you do, grasshopper, but stay with me. Successful filmmakers know how to apply their creativity to the entire project, from the first spark of an idea, all the way through preproduction, production, distribution, and screening. Successful filmmakers understand that funding their project is as much an art as producing it.

My good friend Lynn Preston, who lives outside Sai Baba's compound in Puttaparthi, India, told me a beautiful story about the power of visualization. One afternoon while Sai Baba and several men were engaged in a planning meeting, Sai Baba pointed to a site on the map and announced that they would build a hospital with a new school and a new housing complex close by. When one of the men interrupted Sai Baba and asked him where the money would come from, Sai Baba looked at the man and simply said, "From wherever it is now."

That is such a simple way to manifest. Sai Baba did build the hospital, the school and the housing complex. He brought the money from wherever it was at that time into his coffers and created his dreams. This is a key element to manifesting money. Don't worry about where the money for your film will come from; just know that it will come to you from some bank, from some corporation, or "from wherever it is now." Once you make the decision that your film must be made and that you are the right person to make it, see and feel that money in your bank account and continue to focus on the finished film. See the film in your mind's eye as completed.

THE JOURNEY

It is our duty as men and women to proceed as though the limits
of our abilities do not exist.
— Pierre Teilhard de Chardin

The journey starts upstairs in your head. You must be ready to throw away any preconceived ideas about the funding process. The economic forecasters were right. Times have changed — there is more money than ever! You just have to learn to go outside the box and look for it. That is what this book is about. It is about adopting new ways of thinking when it comes to funding your film. It is about recreating some of the old methods and accepting new ones.

That's exactly what documentary filmmaker Nina Gilden Seavey did when she decided to do a documentary about seven Russian teenagers who formed a country western band called Bering Strait. Nina took her idea to PBS, which had embraced several of her films in the past. This time the execs at PBS sent her away without a dime, and Nina found herself out there dancing on a high wire without a net. She could have given up on her idea. She could have come up with another project that PBS would accept, but after some deep soul searching she knew that she had to make this film. Instead of accepting defeat, Nina decided PBS's rejection would be a new beginning. Once she came to this decision she started searching for alternative ways to make her dream a reality.

It didn't take long. While reading the trades one morning Nina discovered that Roland House had just taken a multi-million dollar leap into the HD arena. This gave her an idea. She needed equipment and backing, and she knew Roland House could use a documentary shot on HD as an effective marketing tool. But when Nina sat down to prepare her pitch, she realized that she had very little to offer. She wanted to shoot the film cinema verite style and knew this meant the project could take years to produce. Now this would have put most filmmakers off, but Nina came up with an approach.

She put together a proposal that was honest and realistic. She knew that she could not guarantee the success of her proposed venture so she offered Roland House what she had. She offered her full attention and commitment to the project along with her promise that she would keep their best interest in mind at all times. As a seasoned producer and director, Nina knew that her reliability throughout this project, and her reputation for reliability during past productions, was the best asset she had.

After Nina won support from Roland House, she took her creativity on location to Russia where she made cold calls to Russian oil companies in search of additional support. She didn't let the language barrier or the gruff foreigners on the other end of the line intimidate her; she kept at it until she found an oil baron who listened. When she finished her pitch he presented her with an unusual proposition. He would donate money for her film if she could get Bering Strait to play at his birthday party. Nina worked with the band's manager, delivered the band at the appropriate place and time, and true to the oil baron's word her check came in the mail. Nina also used more traditional methods to drawing attention to her work, which had some odd and unexpected results.

Bering Strait was selected for the No Borders Independent Feature Film Market sponsored by the IFP. There was a lot of interest, but no one was willing to help with the financing (at that time, or ever as it turned out). But oddly enough, the same weekend Nina was at No Borders, a 13-minute work-in-progress of her film was being screened at the Jackson Hold Digital Fusion Symposium.

There was so little hi-def material being shot at the time that the symposium organizers asked to screen her work even though the project wasn't finished. Nina couldn't attend the Jackson Hole Symposium as she was in New York at the IFP, but Barry Rebo, one of the pioneers of hi-def, was there. When he saw Nina's project he knew she would need financing for her doc, so he called her and offered to act as her agent and co-producer. Barry was able to negotiate an agreement with NHK in Japan, whose Hi-Vision service is at the forefront of broadcast distribution of HD material. So while nothing came out of the weekend at the IFP in New York as Nina had hoped, there were obviously other forces at work elsewhere to help her get this film made.

Nina carried her creativity all the way through to an unforgettable screening. The final credits rolled to an end and the screen went black, bathing the theatre in darkness. Suddenly the audience went wild. The same seven Russian teenagers they had just followed in Nina's 98-minute heart-tugging documentary walked out from behind the projection screen and started playing "The Ballad of Bering Strait." Nina won the Audience Award at the Washington DC Film Festival and won the Official Selection at the International Documentary Association Festival in Los Angeles, and *Bering Strait* was nominated for a Grammy.

But Nina wasn't out of the woods yet. She had wracked up a $250,000 debt in fees and services to Roland House and license fees from music publishers. Nina finished the film, but she obviously was going to need a large sale.

Barry introduced Nina to Ira Deutchman, famed founder and former president of Fine Line Features. Ira loved the project and, using a very carefully developed strategy, he proved all of the marketing gurus wrong who had predicted that no one would buy a movie about an unknown country music band from Russia. Emerging Pictures, Microsoft, Digital Cinema Solutions and Country Music Television sponsored the theatrical release of *Ballad*. The film sold to VIA-COM for VH1/CMT for broadcast, and the DVD rights were sold as the first release on the Koch-Lorber DVD Label of Koch Entertainment, plus the film is now represented by 3-DD Entertainment in London for foreign sales!

This film was also sold on second window to Rainbow Media's VOOM for their HD service.

Nina Seavey is a filmmaker who knows the art of filmmaking involves the entire filmmaking process. Once you move to this concept your natural creativity will open up a floodgate of fundraising ideas. For more interviews with filmmakers see my website: *www.fromtheheartproductions.com/interviews.shtml*.

When I was a kid I listened to a radio program called *Let's Pretend*. Every Saturday morning I would tune in my radio and take off on a wonderful exotic trip. I never left my home but you could never tell me that. As far as I was concerned I was right there alongside Miss Nila Mack and her cast of Pretenders on every one of their magical voyages.

I'm sure you have similar memories of playing make-believe. Remember how real it all seemed? To help fund your film, you want to recapture that child-like faith that will enable you to see, hear, and feel your goals.

When I want something I put it in writing first. This helps me clarify what it is I really want. Begin by writing down your goals. Describe exactly what you want to do and what the outcome will be. Draw pictures if you like, just include as much detail as you possibly can. You want to be able to see the money and feel the confidence that it brings to you knowing that others fully support you in the filmmaking process.

Once you have outlined your filming goals, get a mental picture of how you will fund it. Picture your bank account with a large balance and see the date. I once wanted a certain amount in my account by November and while I didn't get it that year, I had it the next year! This taught me that exact dates are very important.

See a check with a large amount of money and see yourself depositing it in your account. Visualize your dream by believing that the money is coming and do not be locked into any one grant or donation or investment from a specific person. Just know it will come from — wherever it is now. Believing will open your mind and allow you to continue without being blocked by fear.

Next, verbalize your dream. Discuss it at the beach or on a long walk with yourself. That's right, how does it feel when you verbalize your dream? Do you get a queasy stomach? If so, your body doesn't agree with your mind. You may be asking too much too quick. Keep talking until your body and mind are both able to accept your verbal description of your dream and especially with the dates when you intend to manifest them.

The more detail you use the better, because detail helps you visualize exactly what you want. Be sure to put a lot of passion in your visualization; passion manifests.

This is how you empower your dreams.

Start with an idea.

Write it down.

Visualize.

Emotionalize.

There are three books that will help you with this part of your journey. *Excuse Me, Your Life is Waiting for You: The Astonishing Power of Feelings* by Lynn Grabhorn, which gives you an idea of the power of your mind. My second book, *The Art of Manifesting: Creating Your Future* will help you master the art of clearly defining your goals and explain how to manifest using new concepts from quantum physics. *The Four Agreements: A Practical Guide to Personal Freedom*, by Don Miguel Ruiz, will help you deal with the rejection that is so common in this business.

Throughout my career in the industry I have witnessed the success of some very strange films while excellent projects fell by the wayside. This led me to the realization that there was a missing ingredient in filmmaking that was not spoken of in industry circles. I first believed the missing ingredient was passion; however, I looked deeper and saw that many filmmakers who found themselves blocked half-way through production had plenty of passion. Some were so dedicated they were working sixty hours a week so they could scrape together the funds to complete their film, but it still wasn't happening for them. No, passion is an important ingredient, but it is not the secret ingredient.

It soon became apparent that the missing ingredient is faith. You must have faith in yourself and faith in your film. The funding starts in your mind, you are the creator. We attract what we think. So, the very things we feel we can attract like fear of failure, insecurity, loss, self-doubt — you know, those issues that are usually foremost in a filmmaker's mind. "Did I choose the right format?" "Should I have gone with the more experienced editor?" "Am I going to be able to pull off the pitch of a lifetime when I walk through that door?" Your own self-confidence is the first thing you need to shore up.

These books will help you understand why many of your dreams have not materialized and they will give you the tools to change your life. They will help you be aware of the power of your mind and prepare you for the *Art of Film Funding*.

THE POWER OF SOUNDS AND WORDS

The thought that comes from your mind should be pure; the words you utter should be true and sweet and the work you do should be sacred.

— Sai Baba

It was a perfect day in the Bahamas. The air was clear and the 80-degree water below offered amazing visibility. As I dove off the platform of Martin Woolen's grand yacht, *The Mustard Seed*, I was greeted by a kaleidoscope of comical fish along with an amazing assortment of exotic creatures, all coexisting amid a spectacular coral garden. It was a sight that soothed the soul.

I was joyfully exploring this underwater wonderland when another guest from the yacht swam toward me, pointed out a giant lobster, then without warning, aimed his spear gun and sent his spear into the tail of the brightly colored creature. The lobster emitted an ear-piercing scream as it writhed about. I will never forget that sound; it taught me the awesome power of sound to convey emotions.

Many creatures emit sounds or change colors to express themselves. The octopus is one of the greatest underwater communicators. When they are hungry they change colors to disguise themselves from unsuspecting prey, when they feel sexy they change colors to attract a mate, and when threatened they change colors to confuse their enemy. It seems for the octopus every single thought is on display in living color! The octopus is so talented that he can even emit a cloud of black ink that resembles his own shape, a phenomenon called pseudomorph, meaning false body.

We also become what we believe. You are a very unique being. Look at the talents you possess and cherish your self. Never ever put yourself down. My father, Roy W. Dean, used to say, "If you can't say something nice about a person, don't say anything at all." This proverb also applies to what you say about yourself. You have been chosen to impart art, beauty, and knowledge to the rest of us. Everything you do is a reflection of you. If you put yourself down you also put down your film and reduce your image to your crew, so hold yourself in the highest esteem.

The words we use to describe our dreams and our aspirations hold an immense power to create and manifest. Think about the words you use to create things in your life. How many times have you made plans for the future and verbalized your plans? Once spoken, your plans are like a fait accompli. What you have said comes true even if you are not aware that you verbalized this plan in the past. Be responsible and choose your words carefully when verbalizing your hopes and dreams. Above all, be kind to yourself.

As an artist you also have a profound responsibility to choose the best sounds and words to project your message. Your audience will walk away from your film with images embedded in their senses. Once you show something as fact, many people will store this information forever and it will become part of their belief system.

Alison Landsberg coined the phrase 'prosthetic memory' to describe a phenomenon that occurs when memories that are not organically based, are nonetheless experienced with one's own body through various cultural technologies, such as film and television. According to Landsberg the experience of film "might actually install in individuals 'symptoms' through which they didn't actually live, but to which they subsequently have a kind of experiential relationship."

Landsberg's studies have shown that prosthetic memories derived from watching films can actually "become part of one's personal archive of experience." [1]

If you move to the concept that you are shaping minds and assigning emotions and beliefs with every picture, every word, and every sound, you will realize how important your words, sounds, and pictures are to humanity. This is especially true when pictures are enhanced with words, sounds, and music. You must be in control of your script and take great care during the edit if your audience is going to receive the message you want them to receive.

You should always be asking, "Do these words convey the message I want to impart to the world?" "Do the sounds convey the meaning and emotions I want my audience to remember?"

Sound is one of the most powerful tools you will use in your film. Sound can create and sound can destroy. It can shatter glass, and can even produce subtle patterns in sand. Sound can lower or increase blood pressure. When martial arts experts shout "KI-AI!" during impact, they are using sound to focus all of their internal energy. Kiai, also known as the spirit yell, literally means to concentrate one's life force or energy.

There is a scene in *Bobby Deerfield* when the film's terminally ill heroine waits for a noisy train before she releases the most unforgettable scream. The entire theatre can feel this woman's anger, grief, despair, and helplessness. I was so impressed that I went home and tried to do the same thing. I put on a CD, cranked it up full-blast, and I let it rip. It was very disappointing. All I could manage to come up with was a squeaky, stifled little shriek. I immediately went to work on improving my scream and can now go up against some of the best screamers out there. Sound strange? Try it! I find it amazingly therapeutic and frequently will use it to release all sorts of pent-up emotions. Of course this therapy should be used with caution as it can elicit some strange looks, not to mention a police officer or two at your front door!

Sound conveys energy and meaning to your audience. It is up to you to make sure it conveys the meaning you want to project.

A Conversation with Filmmaker Xackery Irving

Jack London once said, "*You can't wait for inspiration. You have to go after it with a club.*"

That is exactly how Xackery Irving made *American Chain Gang*, a documentary that explores the controversial revival of prison chain gangs in the South. Xackery is a hunter. He is always moving; always observing. He stalks the human condition with a camera and takes deliberate dead aim on his subjects to produce documentaries that make a difference.

In an interview I chatted with Xackery about how he captured the idea for *American Chain Gang*, how he raised the funds, and how he managed to stay focused while surrounded by such a hostile environment.

Xackery, I heard that after *American Chain Gang* was released, the practice of using chain gangs was actually outlawed in Alabama, so you now have an important historical document.

I would like to know where you got the idea for this film.

What sparked my interest was a photo essay on the chain gang in Alabama. There were beautiful black-and-white photos of the officers and the inmates and I really got hooked on the subject. I thought, "This is an experience that hasn't been around for years." I researched it thinking of making a film. I focused on prior works and found some short news stories on the subject.

During the research of the history of chain gangs I found horrible things that were done to inmates. Releasing them to coal mines and factories where they were forced to work under harsh conditions — no heat, chained to beds without mattresses, and no medical attention whatsoever.

I had an interesting perspective on this concept and I felt it was a very powerful subject. I took a trip to Alabama and received permission to spend time at the prison and meet people who would be in the film and then I was hooked. I knew this was a good story. I saw inmates that were white supremacists chained to and working with African Americans. I saw the resentment and hatred among the inmates that were chained together and I saw the resentment from the inmates to the officers. This seemed to be an emotionally charged environment. I felt I could tell the story.

It's an amazing process to watch the story unfold, isn't it?

When I was in Alabama, I called you Carole and you gave me some ideas on production. You said, "This film is alive. It has taken on its own life and as a good filmmaker; you must follow it because it will take its own path." You said, "You can contribute your own vision, but you have to catch this reality and it can be refreshing that you don't have control of some things."

And yes, I did have the luxury of catching these elements of reality with a net. It is like building a house versus building a prefab home or a skyscraper with your budget. You have a blueprint of what you want to build and it is very well planned. Next you get the things you need to build with, your script, your coverage, and you have a strong idea of the film based on the blueprint. Doc filmmaking in this analogy is finding trees to make a log cabin but in production you are gathering these logs and cutting them down and when you go to the edit suite, that's where you really make the film. These raw materials now exist and you can't design them. You have to put them together. You may think you have an idea, but once you get into the edit room your story is really what you have on the film.

How did you make your vision of the film into a reality?

The most important thing you need to do for the film is to be very organized. You need to have a good treatment, a solid pitch and a clear presentation of what you want to achieve in the film. Having a well-written treatment is most important. If you can get press clippings about the subject matter, and press about you making the film, it will be very helpful. Have all of this in a presentable book and include your budget information too. Being prepared to answer questions about the film in a clear and definitive way will show people that you are very close to the subject and are fully organized.

So the search for funding begins.

I applied for the Roy W. Dean grant in New York because I knew that I could make the film. Once I was chosen as one of the five finalists, I heard I had to pitch the film in front of an audience. Now I had to create a verbal pitch to give at the National Arts Club in front of filmmakers. This made me get even closer to the film.

(The night Xackery pitched his film at the National Arts Club, he and Ann Stern were neck and neck for first place. The judges were going back and forth, agonizing over the decision before finally awarding the grant to Stern.)

(Xackery did not walk away with first place that night but it was far from over for this tenacious filmmaker. His passion and dedication to his project really came through in his pitch, which is why I decided then and there to find a way to help him realize his dream. I dug some ASA 50 & ASA 400 16mm stock out of the vault and donated it to him so he could start shooting.)

It really does start with the concept and the pitch, doesn't it? What advice can you give filmmakers about pitching their projects?

It is good to practice your pitch. You will be asking a lot of people to help with your film, so learn how to pitch your film and ask for help so even if they say no it is a good use of your time. You can look at it as practice to help you to sharpen your pitch.

The other good thing about talking to people — pitching to people — is that it forces you to be very articulate about the direction of the film, as people ask questions on the film. It becomes a good process to listen to ideas from others and go over logistical problems. This prepares you mentally and creates new approaches for how and what to shoot.

What is the most difficult challenge when approaching potential donors?

You have to be very clear about what they are contributing to. If you are asking for time or money you have to have a clear, concise picture of what you want to do in your film so they are clear about what they are providing. You always want to know exactly what you want to ask for.

Documentaries are special in this way as they are usually films that have a social issue or they are something about people or the world that takes times to achieve. You are selling a film about something that you have to examine. You want to help change the world through this examination. This can be very powerful. When you communicate this with enthusiasm it can be contagious. You want to ignite the same spark in the donor.

So there you were with your vision and some donated raw stock. How did you keep the momentum moving forward?

I believe you must start shooting. Do what you have to do to get the resources together so you can start shooting. It is very effective to cut a five-minute piece to communicate the ideas of your film and what your story is about in a compressed format. This is also another way of making your pitch visually. You are communicating what your editorial style will be, who your characters are, and what your creative approach is.

You can put this on paper and send it out till the cows come home but you will have a much greater response when it is on film or video. It is a financial burden but it is the most effective way to get things off the ground. As soon as you are prepared mentally, just start shooting so you have visual material to present to your donors and grantors.

Another mentor of mine is George Stoney. He is a wonderful man who teaches documentary filmmaking at NYU. He has made several docs and is called the grandfather of public access. He is another great documentary pioneer filmmaker who has helped many documentary filmmakers develop their craft. When George read American Chain Gang's treatment he was the first one who impressed upon me that it is really tough to raise money with paper. You have to shoot something to show them your vision.

When you were filming *American Chain Gang*, you were one-on-one with some pretty tough characters. What advice can you offer other documentary filmmakers about how to approach the interview?

Your subjects are the people who communicate your story. It's great to have articulate people but you don't always have this luxury. There are times you have to use people that are not good communicators. This becomes a challenge. Know that everyone is an interesting person even if there may be lots of digging involved to find it. Look for interesting parts of their personality that work well with your story and makes them sympathetic to the viewer. This is a process of uncovering parts of a personality that at first glance may not read well on camera. Sitting down and getting to know them is a good way to find interesting elements for your film. Sometimes this means spending a lot of time talking to them while the camera is not out of its case.

How do you win your subjects' trust, especially inside a prison?

You need to get them used to the camera. They are in a very vulnerable position, putting themselves in your hands. Let them look through the viewfinder and roll some film or tape on them. Let the subject of the film be empowered to tell their own story. If you impose your storytelling on them too much they will feel this and you will not get an organic story. If they feel and know they have the ability to express themselves in their own words then you have opened the treasure chest and will find some gems you never considered.

What important lessons have you learned about the art of the interview?

Albert Maysles taught me that it is more effective to have someone communicate an idea to someone else in the film rather than to the camera. It allows the audience to see the information unfold between two people so it seems more organic and real.

Good docs are about people. Whether you are making a social issue film or one about a character, the most compelling thing to people is a story of someone's experience. The camera changes everything when it's there and it is a wonderful tool to gather your story with nothing between your subject and the lens. You have to be fast and open your mind and heart to tell the story as it unfolds.

If you had the opportunity to go back and do this film over again, what would you do differently?

I would have fewer subjects. I would spend more time with my subjects to get them comfortable with the camera. I would stay glued to them to get their story. I would get more interactions between the main character and other people. I would have communicated more conflicts between them, and I will do that in my next film.

You want a human face to tell your story. The most compelling thing in a film is people [overcoming] conflict and obstacles to get what they want.

As a documentary filmmaker you are constantly shooting life as it unfolds. What tips can you offer new filmmakers?

This is a great way to tell a story. It is like hunting; you get the shot or you don't. If you are not comfortable with shooting then hire someone. The wonderful thing about it is, the more you shoot and are in this environment you begin to anticipate how the action will come across and you can get into position.

Ask yourself these questions before each scene:

"Do I have the camera in the right position?" There may be more than one correct position. You have to think of yourself as a war photographer and get close to the action.

"Do I have depth of field?"

"Is my sound coming through clearly?"

"Is it more important to follow the action or is it more important to be in position to get the elements that are there?" You have to judge changing camera positions and the position of your mike while the scene is happening because there is no second take.

"Are the right questions being asked?"

"Is the objective of the scene being clearly communicated?"

"Am I getting the material that my editor and I will need in the editing suite to tell this story — a variety of angles, different camera positions, different focal lengths that will cut well together?"

If you are not a professional cinematographer, hold shots longer than you think you need to. We may know where to cut in our heads but you have to hold longer than you want to look at the shot. You may find something magical just when you were about to turn off; you might even find a good audio clip at the end.

Are you getting a beginning, middle and an end of each scene? Many times you will turn a camera on as the scene has begun. You need to think of how you can set that scene up. You may want your subject to enter the room. It is important to have a visual and audio for the beginning and get some options for the editor.

The end of the scene may be as easy as someone leaving the room or the frame or the conversation ending. Many times you can find other endings that you want so that you will have options in the editing room. It is important to keep this process in your mind as you are shooting. Keep asking yourself these questions and you will become a good shooter and editor.

Xackery, you really hit the mark with *American Chain Gang*. It's full of amazing contrasts like the drab colors of the prison against the rich colors of the surrounding countryside. As I watched this film I could feel myself being drawn into the subject's lives. I could feel the despair of being chained together and working while surrounded by such beauty.

I am so happy I shot *Chain Gang* on film. On a visual level the film needed that vibrant image of the gang chained together.

Yet you've said that your next film will probably be shot on digital.

My next documentary will definitely be shot on a digital format. HD handheld videography is so inexpensive and so accessible. You can tell a story with one person with a digital but it is very difficult to do a one-person film shoot. There are lots of advantages with a small crew. You can be mobile quickly and you don't affect the environment when you have one or two people in the crew. Also it is a great idea to look at your footage and listen to your audio as soon as you can. Video lets you do this immediately.

Film must be processed while on location. You need to see where you can improve while on location. Look for what is working and what did not work. It gives you confidence and you can pick up what you lost. Get a head start on the editing, if you see things you missed you can get them next time. Editing will always show you where the holes are. When you view your dailies you can see what your options are and what footage you have to tell the story. Give your editor options and you will have a great story.

I use a small DV camera on the television producing and shooting work I have been doing for TLC, Discovery, A&E for the past several years on such run-and-gun productions as *Trauma: Life in the ER*, *Paramedics*, and *Dallas SWAT* where you need flexibility to capture a story very quickly. You can monitor your audio and shoot at the same time. This gives you more intimacy with your subject and is the key to making you as close to invisible as possible. You can see how the subject reacts to your big crew versus a small crew. It changes the way you tell the story.

Xackery, what do you like best about being a documentary filmmaker?

I love the process of filmmaking. Making documentaries is terrific because it is hands-on. You can start anytime you want. It is as simple as picking up the tape and camera and following people around. You can light or not light, as you choose. You can bring material to editing and start your film immediately. I love storytelling and I love shooting, editing, and planning scenes. Ever since the first day in film school when I shot something and saw it on the screen this has stayed with me.

Is film school a must?

Film school is not imperative. What it does is give you a level of training and this can give you a false sense of confidence, thinking that you can make a film right away. But that's worth the price of admission, so to speak.

So what is the prerequisite to becoming a good filmmaker?

You need a strong sense of confidence to start this process as films are very demanding emotionally, financially, and creatively. Documentaries demand all you have and usually docs can be shot over a course of years. You must be in love with the process. It is a benefit to choose the right people to work with because you can foster life-long relationships and it can be rewarding. You want to find a great editor who you can create with and who is a good listener.

The editor/director relationship in a film is so very important. I prefer to work with an editor, rather than edit myself because editors can take your material in directions you never considered. A good editor will listen to your ideas and come up with a direction you may have missed. What a treat this is. Getting the right editor is as important as raising money. Don't look just for talent, look for someone you can communicate with and like. Remember, the editor is your first audience. You don't want to let them down. You need to get the material they need to make your film.

Do you have any parting words of encouragement to fellow filmmakers out there in the trenches?

Be easy on yourself. Shooting and editing can be difficult and draining. You may miss things each day and make mistakes. You will be under the gun constantly. This is all part of the process. We all experience this. Just keep forging ahead and you will find a way to tell your story in the process. Take it easy on yourself and have the faith to know your film will be finished one way or the other.

Xackery Irving's film *American Chain Gang* has aired in five countries and is now available on DVD on Amazon.com, Netflix and Blockbuster.com. The start of his first narrative project, entitled *Nothing Without You*, represents his next challenge in the world of fundraising — raising a larger budget by convincing actors and financiers of the commercial viability and dramatic qualities of his story. For more information on prior winners of the Roy W. Dean film and writing grants, see *www.fromtheheartproductions.com/grant-pastwinners.shtml*

CHAPTER 2

THE PERFECT PITCH

I don't know how the word pitch first became synonymous with the art of describing a film but it seems appropriate. The film pitch is like the baseball pitch in that it is critical to the outcome of the game. While it is the pitcher's job to get the ball over the plate, it is actually the catcher's job to tell the pitcher what kind of ball to throw.

Your catcher is your investor or your funder. If you pay attention to your catcher you will have a better chance of winning the game. You know that you might have to adjust the speed and the trajectory a little here and a little there, depending upon to whom you're pitching, but the goal will remain the same: you've got to connect the ball with the glove. To do this you will need to create a pitch that will sell and you need to work on it until it is perfect. This is one of the most important steps in the "Art of Film Funding."

In the Appendix you will find a list of funders. Don't even think about getting up there on the mound and going after these funders until you have perfected your pitch.

Go back to the questions in Chapter One that every potential filmmaker should answer and expound upon your answers to the first four questions:

1. List three compelling reasons why this film should be made.

2. Describe your connection to the story and explain why you are the only one who should make this film.

3. Who will benefit from this film?

4. What is the urgency?

Next, write about the concept of your film. Keep writing until you run out of steam, then walk away and let it sit for at least two days.

Sometimes when you start writing you open up a floodgate of creativity. Keep a little notebook in your pocket during the day and on your nightstand when you go to bed so you can jot down ideas as they come. Remember, an unwritten idea is an unfinished idea.

Now go back to your notes and edit everything down to two paragraphs or less. This becomes the first part of your proposal and the beginning of your pitch. The pitch must convey the meaning of your film while capturing all the passion, intrigue, drama, or humor of your story. It must move the audience and leave them wanting more. That's why they fund you; they want to see the film finished.

Writing a pitch is like writing poetry or the lyrics to a song. Use words that give the utmost compression, force, and economy. As you work on your pitch, read it out loud. How does it sound? Does it roll off your tongue or does it sound clumsy? Rewrite it, read it out loud, then rewrite it again. Keep working on it until the words have just the right rhythm and pace.

VISUALLY DESCRIBE YOUR FILM

A pitch must visually describe your film. This is the first mistake most people make. They leave out adjectives. When you tell me that your hero is tall, dark and handsome, I have a visual. Add creative or nerdy and I have an even better visual, plus I have some "feeling" for him. The words you choose are paramount to creating the image for your potential funder. Your words must conjure up a vision of your film so as you speak them, your catcher can imagine your completed film. Visually describing your film is the most important part of the pitch.

We don't talk the way we write. I learned that from the first production I made. I wrote a script about my unique process of evaluating used tape. My company bought 1" tape from TV stations and we processed it on evaluating machines, repackaged it and sold it to other TV stations! We had lots of fun doing this and we made a very nice profit. So when my friend, IATSE Director of Photography Geno Talvin, promised to shoot this "little video" for me as a gift, I sat down and wrote a script that was the same as the copy I wrote to sell my evaluated tape.

He looked at it and said, "This won't work." Just as simple as that he summed up my two weeks of writing. He knew from shooting thousands of pages of dialogue that my script was the written word and not the spoken word. Well, I was adamant that it was perfect and I stood my ground. Geno just smiled that knowing smile and said, "We'll use a lot of your short ends on this production!" And right he was, after 17 rewrites we finally had a decent script.

Please don't make the mistake I made. Write your pitch, then speak it and rewrite it until it sounds natural. Actually if you can catch yourself on tape talking about your film, that is the best way to create your pitch. Use words that you normally use in conversation and you will see the difference between the written and the spoken words.

THE WINNING PITCH BY JOHN MCKEEL

Just the thought of standing in front of an audience scared Jim. He wasn't alone. A recent survey showed more people are afraid of public speaking than dying, so Jim worked very hard to memorize what he thought was a great speech. He wrote and re-wrote it until every word was perfect. Unfortunately, when it came time to deliver his talk, Jim was so nervous he forgot what he was going to say. He stumbled over his words. Jim stopped frequently and his eyes naturally rolled to the top of his head as he tried to remember those perfect phrases he had so meticulously constructed. He lost contact with his audience and the speech was a total bomb.

You've written a great proposal, but now you have to pitch it. Never confuse the written word with the spoken word. They are two completely different forms of communication. Beautiful writing can sound stilted and pretentious when read aloud. Great literature doesn't guarantee great performance, so prepare an oral presentation orally. This is so important I'm going to repeat it. Prepare an oral presentation orally.

How is that possible? You know your material. You've lived and breathed your project for a long time. You've talked about it with friends, family and probably perfect strangers so your first exercise in the preparation of a great oral pitch is to sit down in a room by yourself and just start talking. Let the words come as you describe your passion. As you talk about it, certain sentences will stand out. Quickly jot it down and then keep talking. Again, remember this is an oral presentation, not a written proposal. Don't write down any more words than it will take to remind you of the thought. The key is to get back to talking as soon as possible. It's an oral presentation, so we are preparing orally for it.

If you are having trouble getting started with your talk, answer these questions out loud. Imagine that I am right there with you. Now let's talk:

1. Your film is a jewel with many facets. Can you describe some of these facets and some of the other themes I will see in your final project?

2. Now, if you had to choose only one theme, what is the most important facet? Why?

3. Who are you making this film for?

4. You seem very passionate about your project. Why?

5. Tell me about some of the characters I will meet in your film.

6. What do you hope people will take away from watching your documentary?

7. The three most important topics to address in your pitch are:
   ◈ What is this film about?
   ◈ Why make it now?
   ◈ You have to convince us our money won't be wasted. Tell us why you will see this film through to completion.

After an hour you should have pages of great sentences that will trigger great thoughts. Now it's time to find your theme.

Look over those pages of sentences you just wrote down. Do you see any themes? It's time to take out more paper and write a different theme on the top of each page. Now copy all of the sentences that relate to that theme onto that page.

Take a break. Have a cup of coffee. Play with the kids and then come back to your notebook. Look through all the pages. One will stand out. You've done it! That's your theme for this pitch but how will you organize those random sentences into an organized pitch?

Try giving a four-minute talk from just the notes on that particular page. A couple of things will happen. First, a natural rhythm will develop. You'll discover you need to say this before that. A rough outline will develop. You will also find that some of the sentences aren't as powerful as the others. Discard them and you will be left with pure gold.

(John McKeel wrote this for my monthly newsletter to filmmakers. If you want to be on the mailing list for information like this, please sign up on the first page under newsletter at *www.fromtheheartproductions.com*.

KNOW WHO'S WHO

At a seminar one of my students asked me how I pitched my grants to get my donations. I was stunned. It took me a minute to realize and explain to him that I was the grant. It was part of me and my pitch changed with each potential funder. First I analyze their needs. Usually this may be a matter of minutes; since I know the benefits of the grant, I only need to assess their needs.

But I do not always close someone at the first meeting. Why? Because if they don't know me or know the incredible films we have supported with the grant, then I would waste a potential funder by pitching too hard too soon. In an instance like this, at the first meeting, you need to make a good impression. Please, don't over pitch. Remember, **funders don't fund films, they fund you**. Make an excellent impression; find a way to get their card by saying you may want to ask them for advice in the future.

I know for any donor to give goods and services or money to my foundation, they want to know who I am. They need to know my passion or your passion for your film and you need to know who they are so your first meeting will always be to make an excellent impression and to learn all you can about them. Who are they? What do they do? What is their passion?

During this "interview" you can access so much information. People like to talk about their companies, their potential future and where the company will be in five years. In America many people *are* their business; when they talk about their business, you get to know who they are. This is important. You must know their needs before you can get a donation or a discount or advice.

Usually when I first meet someone whose company could become a donor to my grant, I take mental notes to outline who they are but I do not pitch them. Not yet. When asked what I do, I tell them about my grant for filmmakers and keep the conversation focused on them. If you have found someone with tons of money then you want to know all about that person before you make an "ask." We will cover this more in another section.

BECOME THE FILM

Your pitch may be the only chance you get to tell someone about your film. You may find yourself standing next to the head of Sundance acquisitions at a crowded cocktail party, or you may find out that the grumpy little old lady sitting next to you on the plane is a wealthy entrepreneur who got bumped to coach. You may be up against some heavy hitters, so make sure you are always ready with your perfect pitch.

I know a documentary filmmaker who raised $5,000 while standing in line at the grocery store. How? Because she created a short pitch under two minutes that truly engaged people and she learned how to take advantage of situations. When someone asks you what you do, you must respond that you are a filmmaker.

Forget that you are a computer guru in your day job; if you really want to make that film, then let everyone know you are a filmmaker. That's what she did. While waiting in line, the man ahead of her began to chat and when he asked what she did, she immediately responded that she was a filmmaker and pitched him. Her film was about Greece and he said, "I'm Greek and my family came from Greece." She took his card and followed up with a phone call to discuss her film and his benefits by donating to the film and she got a check for $5,000.

The biggest mistake filmmakers make with their pitch is not focusing on the story. They often give you the history, why it needs to be made or, heaven forbid, the technical information. They will even tell you how they are shooting on the latest XYZ tape-less camera. This can be distracting. You want them to listen to your story.

Most funders don't know anything about cameras and they don't really care what type of editing system you have, so stay away from technical information in the pitch. Only mention it if someone asks you.

Please don't say you are making a film because you need to get a message to people. As Mr. Warner said, "If you want to send a message, go to Western Union, if you want to make a film tell me a story."

What is paramount to funding is funders fund stories.

Morrie Warshawski came to L.A. and taught a seminar with me. One of the most profound things he said was, "I can tell in 30 seconds if your film will be funded." Can you imagine? Morrie is right: You have 30 seconds to grab your potential funder or investor, and you can only do that with a brilliant, engaging story, passionately told.

I believe you must become the story. Remember the film *Fahrenheit 451*? This film is set in the future and books are not allowed. It's a time when people must live only by the controlled information on their television sets, which is a horrid thought, right?

The hero of this film is actually a fireman who is in charge of burning books and he becomes curious and decides he must understand what is so evil that he has to burn books so he steals one to read. Naturally he becomes an avid reader and soon realizes the importance of preserving books as works of art. Eventually he is forced to flee the city and live in the woods with people who become their books. The only way this band of book lovers can legally live in this society and not own books is to memorize them, every word, every comma, and every paragraph.

That's what you need to do. You must become the film. When you can see the film, when you know every scene, when you know every point you want to make in your story and when you and your film are inseparable, then your pitch moves from your *head* to your *heart*. Now you are communicating with people because we communicate through our heart chakra. You need to touch people's hearts to reach them, especially when you want to be funded.

Originally they said that the heart pumped blood to the body. Now the scientists say, "Whoops, we made a mistake. The heart would have to be the size of a Mac truck to do that, it pumps blood to the lungs and other systems take over for the rest of the body." I believe some day they will say that our creativity lives in the heart. Think of what you do when you are touched; your hand immediately goes to your heart. Don't tell me that great works of art did not originate from the heart, not when you can see the Pietà and gasp at its beauty. Clint Eastwood won the Academy Award with *Million Dollar Baby* because he touched our hearts with the love the three main characters had for each other.

We communicate to each other through heart-felt feelings. If you want to make a point in your film or connect with your audience, then use words that touch people's hearts. This is what people want to hear, heart-felt stories. That's what they want to fund. This is how we communicate, through our hearts and you don't have to use the word love. It's all about nurturing, caring, and supporting each other.

THE WIND-UP AND DELIVERY

You need to have the same level of confidence when you pitch to Sheila Nevins at HBO that you have when you pitch to your best friend. This confidence will come with practice and from knowing with complete certainty that you are presenting a great story that people will be interested in.

You and your pitch need to become inseparable. Write it down and carry it with you. Stick it in your purse or backpack. Sew a special little pocket for it in your swimsuit; just don't leave home without it. I want you to whip it out wherever you are and practice. Practice it on the bus driver. Practice it on your doctor's receptionist. Practice it on your imaginary friend while you are stuck in traffic.

When you go to Starbucks and they say "how are you today?" I want you to pitch them your film. Pitch your film to the checker at your local grocery store, your cleaners, your pizza shop and your mailman. Let everyone in your life know you are making a film. It's another way for you to practice your pitch, and they will be so impressed to know you are a filmmaker. To them you are in a glamorous business. These people will be the first ones you invite to your funding parties and they will be a good support group for you.

PERFECTING YOUR PITCH

◈ Give individual one-on-one pitch sessions to everyone in your family and be sure to write down their comments and questions. As you pitch your story pay close attention to how they respond and listen to what they say.

◈ Are they excited about the story?

◈ Do they act like they want to know more?

◈ Does your pitch stir up interest and stimulate questions?

◈ Remember, potential donors are likely to ask some of the same questions that your family and friends ask. Don't forget to research and follow up on all of their questions so you can be ready with good answers. If a question is asked repeatedly, consider addressing the issue in your pitch.

No matter how hard you prepare you will come up against some questions that you don't have the answer for. Just be honest. Explain that you are still in preproduction and that you have not worked out all the details yet. Try to anticipate challenging questions and don't be afraid to memorize your answers.

Your project is still in its infancy. This is the critical stage when everything will start to jell, so pay attention. Sometimes pitching your project will bring you some great ideas. That's what Xackery Irving discovered when he pitched his idea for *American Chain Gang*. The more he pitched the more feedback he got. He listened and ended up using several ideas that evolved out of discussions from his pitch that improved the film and saved him money.

Practice your pitch and practice your answers until your delivery is smooth and convincing. Become one with your pitch. Memorize it until its part of your DNA. This is the beginning of funding your film.

It is important to create several pitches. First is the elevator pitch. You want to literally be able to tell someone the outline of your story from the first to the eighth floor and be able to hand them your card and leave them wanting more.

The second pitch is under two minutes. This is your visual description of your film passionately delivered. You may have to disappear and jump up and down several times to rev yourself up, but the passion you have for your film can be contagious and it must be part of the pitch.

Once you finish, say nothing... absolutely nothing. That's paramount to the funding process. Give them some time to process what you have just said. Remember, you have been carrying this film for years and this is the first time they have heard about it.

Don't continue on because they must have time to gather their thoughts. Wait for them to say something. Usually they will ask you a question about the film. Wonderful, this is what you want, you have engaged them. They are interested. Now what do you say? Well, if it is a good question to answer, answer it and let them have time to respond.

If it is not a good question to answer, then beg the issue just like the politicians do. Answer the question with a follow-up to your pitch. This follow-up has more details on the story and may even include why you are making the film and why you are the only one to make it.

I have so many wonderful filmmakers who call me to pitch their films. Usually during the first two minutes I have questions for them and I wait until they finish to ask my question. If they understand how much we can handle at one time, they will stop talking, those who don't keep going for five to sometimes fifteen minutes. By the time they are finished I have forgotten whatever it was I wanted to ask and definitely forgotten any comments I wanted to make.

I have a beautiful garden of flowers all growing in the sand at my beach house in Oxnard Shores because of these long pitches. I just go outside and work on my garden knowing nothing will stop them until they run out of steam or pause for another espresso. Please don't do this. Realize that your job is to engage people with your pitch, not overwhelm them.

After several weeks of pitching your project to friends, patient family members, and complete strangers, your pitch should feel as comfortable as your favorite pair of blue jeans. Your pitch will be on a much higher level and will contain the elements that will capture the interest of anyone you speak to.

Remember, it is a good pitch if:

It is entertaining.

It tells an engaging story.

You enjoy it.

You are passionate about your film.

You touch people with your story.

It makes your project exciting and desirable.

It communicates how your film will make a difference.

It creates a sense of urgency.

It works, and you get funded!

CHAPTER 3

THE PROPOSAL

Your vision will become clear only when you can look into your own heart... Who looks outside, dreams; who looks inside, awakes.

— Carl Jung

Reading proposals is a passion of mine, which is a good thing since I read over five hundred proposals and view over a thousand corresponding DVDs a year for my Roy W. Dean film grants. Filmmakers frequently ask me how they can improve their applications.

First, remember, grantors or investors are usually under a deadline to read and make a decision on something that should never be judged: your art. Your potential funder is probably reviewing hundreds of proposals, one right after the other, so find a way to make your proposal unique.

I consider the introduction or synopsis to be the most critical element in the proposal. It is the first thing I read when I pick up a new film proposal because it tells me how compelling the project is and reveals how passionate the filmmaker is. Sponsors use the synopsis during the selection process as a way of categorizing and separating one type of film from another. If your synopsis is dynamic and is strategically placed on your application, it will remain active in the sponsor's mind.

This is a visual industry, yet only 10% of the applications I receive include pictures, which always amazes me. Since the person reading your proposal is probably very visual, consider dropping a few pictures or graphics into your proposal.

How about submitting a picture of yourself with your application? Include a photograph taken during your last film shoot — something that shows you in action, behind the camera or giving direction. Even if it's just your student ID, put that shining smile on the page and let us see who you are! Passion, perseverance, and personalization are what you need to win grants, so don't be afraid to put your heart on your sleeve to win that grant!

How many grants have you entered? Tell us about them so we can see how determined you are to make this film. Do you really want this grant? Are you willing to dedicate the next three years of your life to produce this film? Find a way to communicate your dedication in your proposal. Include a personal film statement. Tell us what is driving you.

Remember:

Grantors want compelling films.

The first two paragraphs must be dynamite, knock me off my seat!

Be impeccable with the truth.

Do not commit to things you cannot do. Sponsors can tell when you are overstating.

Sponsors know if your budget is unreasonable.

A guaranteed audience, such as a commitment from PBS, puts you on top.

Demonstrate solid marketing, distribution plans, and outreach distribution.

Have you secured a distributor or another grantor?

Bringing a scholar or expert on board as a mentor will shift the scales to your advantage.

Show how your film relates to the goals of your potential sponsor or distributor.

Is your project one of a kind? If so explain and include information to back it up.

If there are projects in the market place with a similar message or subject matter to yours, make sure you demonstrate how yours is unique.

Give specific information about your audience and include the full demographics.

Please, don't put hand-written information on the proposal or the cover pages.

Attach letters from donors to your application as a form of support.

Music and picture rights must go in the budget; they are expensive and donors look for this.

Put your name and the name of your film on submitted tapes and on the outside of the DVD case. When donors are reviewing scores of tapes they often get interrupted and it's easy to confuse DVDs.

Please don't use insulated bags that are lined with that horrid, gray, fluffy stuff. We all hate them. Some donors won't even open these types of packages because the filaments can damage their players. Plastic boxes and bubble wrap are a much better choice.

MORE SUGGESTIONS

Mention any creative fundraising ideas you are using in your application. For example, filmmakers often barter with other filmmakers to get their projects completed. Donors like to see filmmakers who use creative funding techniques, so tell us about them.

I usually call my finalists and discuss their film application. When possible I give them guidance and suggestions on how they can improve their proposal. The most important thing I tell them is to submit again next year!

The producers for the wonderful film, *The Flute Player,* applied three times before they won my Roy W. Dean NYC Grant, but once they won they were on their way, subsequently winning a $50,000 Sundance grant and a PBS airing.

Winning one grant leads to success with future grants, so mention prior grants that you have won in your cover letter and any awards anyone on the crew has won.

Use a PR person to promote your accomplishments and you can easily pave the way for even more funding and distribution.

Avoid using technical jargon in your application unless your proposal is to a grantor who has specifically asked for technical information. The people reading it will not know what a 20 to 1 zoom is nor will they recognize the latest digital camera you want to use. This can be confusing and divert them from the real issue of your film.

A funder who was speaking at a conference I attended told the audience about an applicant who entered her grant seven times! Each time the filmmaker asked the funder how he could improve his application and he incorporated their ideas in his proposal when he applied the next year. The filmmaker finally won on his seventh try. Many times the information given to filmmakers by grantors can improve the film so entering ITVS, for example, can benefit you with advice.

Once you start on your journey you are committed. Never give up. You may have to apply several times but don't despair. I tell filmmakers to stand by the suffragettes' motto, "Never Give Up!"

If you have made mistakes there is always another chance for you... you may have a fresh start any moment you choose, for this thing we call "failure" is not the falling down, but the staying down.

— Mary Pickford

A Conversation with Writer/Filmmaker JanEva Hornbaker

When I came across JanEva Hornbaker's proposal during our Roy W. Dean New York Film Grant competition, I was struck by how well she managed to capture the heart of her story. I found her proposal to be exemplary and asked her if she would share her secrets for dynamic proposal writing.

Eva, what is the number one rule of proposal writing?

The number one rule of writing anything is to understand who your readers are and what you are trying to accomplish. This sounds like two rules but actually they are very integrated.

The film proposal is a tool designed to sell two things: your idea for a film, and your ability as a filmmaker to successfully produce, market, and distribute your film. You need to know everything you can about the organization you are applying to, and more specifically, the person who is going to read your proposal, if you are going to convince them to invest in you, which is what it always boils down to.

The funder's deadline is three weeks away. What are the first steps toward creating a perfect proposal?

The first step is to make sure your project fits the sponsor's funding guidelines. Once you have determined this you need to dig in and start researching the organization and the people behind the organization.

Read their mission statement and jot down key words and phrases used to describe the goals and objectives of the organization, then go to your proposal and use these same key words to describe your project. It's absolutely essential that you make a connection between the funder's goals and the goals of your project. This shouldn't be a stretch if your project is a good match with the funder.

Funders support interests that are closely tied to the source of their funds, so find out who is funding your funder. You can get this information right off their website or from their tax return.

How did you organize your proposal?

My education background is in library and information technology so I studied grant writing in college; however, when I went to write my first film proposal I found very little information that was geared specifically toward putting together an effective film proposal. I read everything I could find and researched a lot of different funders on the Internet and made a list of what each of these funders wanted, then I made my outline based on this list.

Did you find a lot of variation in what different funders wanted?

Oh yes. Some organizations will only want a one-page synopsis while others want something that resembles a doctoral dissertation. I put together a general outline based on my research. That way I had all the information in one computer file. You are going to need all of this stuff anyway for distribution and marketing so my advice is get it together early on and customize it to each funder.

Customizing it is the key, isn't it?

Definitely. It's essential that you follow each funder's guidelines to the letter. If the funder doesn't ask to see a budget, don't include it. If they want a two-page synopsis, make sure you only send two pages. And make sure you address each individual funder's goals and objectives.

Funders want to be able to scan a proposal and immediately come away with information — what the film is about, the filmmaker's approach, style, goals, and objectives. They can do this if the proposal is organized into clearly defined headings.

You did not sacrifice style. Your proposal was not a dry analytical treatment. What can you share on how to achieve style in the proposal?

You have to give your reader all the information they need to make an informed decision, but how you say it is as important as what you say.

You are describing your ideas for a motion picture so it is essential that you show your reader instead of tell your reader what you intend to do. Ezra Pound said, "The image is more than an idea. It is a vortex or cluster of fused ideas and is endowed with energy." If you are going to energize a reader with your ideas then you have to do more than just describe your project; you need to actually transport your reader into your film.

Your opening paragraph does just that. Can you take us through the process of how you wrote this?

Sometimes when you're writing about something that you're passionate about it just flows, but this can be dangerous. It's critical not to miss any key ideas, so I start by writing down exactly what it is that I need to communicate. Then I rewrite it adding descriptive words.

Could you take your opening paragraph here and break down the process?

Sure. I write the information I need to convey, which is:

World War II ended over five decades ago, yet thousands of Americans are still missing.

As you can see this sentence provides information, but it does nothing to help the readers conjure up a visual picture. Like most filmmakers I think in pictures, so I go back and rewrite the scene as I see it. One of my favorite writing teachers used to say, "Walk your reader through the corridors and hallways of your story." I think the best way to do this is to remove yourself from your story and approach it completely fresh, as though you've never been there.

You're so familiar with your story that it's easy to forget that the scenes are only in your head. You can't just say, "This story is about explorers who look for lost Americans," and expect your reader to see that fantastic scene that is in your head.

Close your eyes and picture the scene, then put it down on paper. Sometimes it helps to take the concept you want to describe and reduce it to one scene, then work from there. You have to add physical detail, because physical detail is going to pull your reader into the story.

So using this opening paragraph as an example, I worked in some descriptive words and ended up with: *The battlefields of World War II fell silent over five decades ago, yet more than 78,000 young Americans still lie in shallow makeshift graves, rusting wrecks, and abandoned battlefields thousands of miles from home.*

Shallow makeshift graves and rusting wrecks give the reader some very vivid pictures. Young Americans — who could read that and not be moved? You have to describe your locations, describe your subject, and describe your subject's actions so the reader is transported into the scene. What if I write: *This film will be shot in Europe and Asia as we follow searchers on different expeditions to find missing Americans.*

Again, I've given the reader the information, but that's not my only objective here. I want to show the reader. So I add description to give it energy: *We will follow unique explorers across dramatic backdrops of Europe and into the deepest jungles of Asia as they search for the scattered bones and the rusted dog tags of young soldiers.*

The trick to effective writing is to layer descriptive language with specific language so you don't end up with something that is too vague. You want to create mood but you don't want to overdo it.

How do you know when it's too much?

When you sacrifice clarity for style you've gone too far. Funders don't want to read through tons of adjectives to get to the point. Make sure your proposal clearly demonstrates what your film is about and what you are trying to do. Save descriptive words to illustrate your subject, your location, if you have a dramatic location, your subject's motivation. Good writers control their style to match their purpose.

What is your biggest proposal writing challenge?

Usually if I'm writing my own proposal the biggest challenge is to know when to stop. When you're writing passionately about your subject it's tempting to keep going. Pretty soon you end up with something that resembles the Los Angeles phonebook.

Once you've mastered the art of creating these wonderful paragraphs that draw the reader into the story, your next step is to chop it down to the minimum pages allowed. It's the hardest thing but it's a necessary part of the writing process. You just have to do this, knowing that your best work is going to be what is left after you have eliminated all of the fluff and repetition.

William Strunk was really big on omitting needless words. He said, "Vigorous writing is concise," and he said that "a sentence should contain no unnecessary words, a paragraph no unnecessary sentences." I think a lot of people think that omitting needless words means they need to cut down their sentences and paragraphs to the point where they sacrifice style, but this is not what he meant.

Strunk went on to explain that you do not include unnecessary words and sentences, "for the same reason that a drawing should have no unnecessary lines and a machine no unnecessary parts." You're not going to leave out an integral part of a drawing to make the drawing smaller. You're not going to leave off an essential bolt to make the machine lighter. Strunk said, "Make every word tell." That's a very powerful statement. I think most filmmakers can relate to this because this is the essence of good filmmaking. Make every scene count.

Eva, how do you stay on track?

The best way to stay on track is to work from a design. That way you're not going to veer off in a direction and write about things that are not essential. Know exactly what you are trying to accomplish, then develop an outline so you achieve all of your points.

FUNDING OUTLINE

The following outline works well for funders. Use this guide as your standard outline and add additional elements according to each sponsor's requirements:

Log Line
One sentence that describes your film, the genre, and the length of your film.

Introduction/Synopsis (*from Carole's point of view*)
Your introduction is the most important part of the film proposal (after your log line). Potential funders want to see two or three dynamite paragraphs that visually describe the film you want to make. If your project is a documentary, chances are you don't know what the final product is until you've finished your final edit. That's okay; just tell the story. People fund engaging stories. Don't let them get lost in paragraph after paragraph about the history. Tell the story.

Creating this visual description of the film is an excellent exercise to help you, as the filmmaker, visualize what your story really is about and how you plan to tell the story. It is an exercise that will take your film to a new dimension. Focus on these three paragraphs because they are what make us stop, sit up straight, and visualize the film with you. Once you've got our attention, we will read every single word. Follow Eva's outline below. If your film is engaging, and you've put it into a concise outline, we will want to fund it.

Background and Need
Acquaint the reader with essential information about the background of

your story and your main characters. Don't bombard the reader with information. Give them just enough detail to capture their attention and motivate them to keep reading.

Next, explain why you want to do this film and why it will be of interest to others. What specific concerns will be addressed and why? Who will benefit and how? What will your film accomplish?

This is where you will insert the hook! You have already determined that your film fits the sponsor's guidelines for funding. Now carefully study the sponsor's mission statement and use it to create an original statement that demonstrates how your film relates to the sponsor's specific goals and priorities. This is a critical part of your proposal and it is something that most of your competitors will overlook.

Approach, Structure & Style

This is where you will describe how to approach your story as a filmmaker. Structure is the framework that holds up each element of your story. Describe how your story will unfold and how the subjects will move through each of these elements from beginning to end. Is your story an intimate personal journey or an exposé? Are you going to use narration? Is there a connective thread that will tie all of the elements of the story together?

Sponsors want strong stories that have strong characters. How will your subjects relate to each other and how will they impact the story? Will your subjects experience personal growth? Will they help others grow? How will they carry the story forward through the conflict, the climax, and the final outcome? How will your audience react to the dramatic tension and what will they learn by the end of the story? Describe how your film will stir viewers to action and inspire them to make a difference.

Documentaries can be character driven or concept driven. In America we love films that are character driven, whereas Europeans like concept-driven films more than we do. If your film is concept driven, I suggest that you take some of the characters and wrap your proposal around them for the American audiences.

We want to know who these people are. Are they fathers, religious, caring, giving people? Tell us the essence of the person and give us some visual description if you can't put a picture in the proposal, let us see and feel your characters.

If you are shooting life as it unfolds you may not know the final outcome. Explain this, then describe several possible outcomes and describe how you will approach each of these scenarios. Remember, a story does not have to have a clear-cut solution to have resolution. An open-ended film that leaves unresolved issues can be even more compelling than a story that reveals how the lives of the characters or events turn out.

Style includes all of the techniques that will give your film its own unique quality or tone. This might include camera work, lighting techniques, or your interview style. Include everything that will project your personal imprint onto the story. Avoid getting lost in a lot of technical detail. Instead, explain (show) how a certain technique or style will be used to carry the story forward or illuminate a specific character.

Avoid describing one specific approach unless you have completed all of your research and are convinced there is only one way you can tell the story. Research can reveal twists and turns that can dramatically alter your approach and changing approaches once a sponsor has already funded you can be sticky. If you are not sure which way you will approach your story, describe several approaches that you are exploring and explain how your subjects might respond to each of these approaches.

Coming up with an idea for a film is easy; nailing down the best approach is the hard part. If you have not decided on an approach, exploring and writing about different methods and ideas will draw you closer to your project.

Theme

The theme is what your story is about. If it is difficult to pinpoint an exact theme then your story is probably underdeveloped. Don't worry, dig deeper and do more research. Your theme will emerge as you continue to research and write.

When I first started researching the idea for *Searcher for Souls* I concentrated on how the ongoing consequence of war affects a family for generations. It was an important theme but I knew something was missing. It was only after I went to Europe and spent two months researching my subject that another theme began to unfold.

Philippe Castellano is a French explorer who has spent over 20 years searching for lost American flyers who fell from the sky during the Second World War. As I followed and observed my subject I began to notice remarkable similarities between Philippe and the young American flyers he was looking for.

As you research your story, don't forget to stand back and observe. Look for hidden themes that connect the elements of your story.

Audience, Marketing, and Distribution

Your sponsors will want to know about your intended audience. Is your film about a subject that has worldwide appeal? Do you plan to target a specific community? Is it educational or commercial? How will the market support your audience and how do you intend to distribute your film to this audience? Give statistics that support the size of your audience and explain how your film will appeal to these audiences. Never say "everyone" will love this film. You need to know the demographics based on age, location, income, etc.

How have you approached distribution? Are you pursuing a specific network or cable television market? Does your film have a rental market? Will it be featured in public libraries, museums, or university collections? Will you enter your film in festivals? Sponsors want to see that you have a distribution plan and that you are exploring several options. Provide copies of letters of support from key individuals, networks, and anyone that can help support the fact that your film will be seen.

Budget

Your budget must be a reasonable projection of how much it will cost to produce, distribute, and market your film. Make sure your budget is consistent with the production ideas you have described. Explain where you plan to come up with the rest of the funds to meet your budget. This is also where you will describe how you will use the award if you should win.

Make sure you include a brief statement acknowledging the goals and objectives of the foundation and make it clear that you will use the award accordingly. Let the sponsor know how much you need this grant and that it will be used to create a film that will help advance their cause.

A film budget can have many hidden elements that can come back to bite you. If your budget is too big you might scare off a potential sponsor. On the other hand, if your budget is not in line with your production ideas a potential sponsor may feel you are too inexperienced or unrealistic. There are budget templates and budget software programs out there to help you create a budget, but most beginning filmmakers need to consult with a professional who knows the ins and outs of breaking down a script.

FILMMAKER'S STATEMENT AND BIOGRAPHY

Include a short biographical sketch of each of the principal filmmakers. Describe any film grants that you have won and sponsors that you have secured. Be sure you attach the appropriate documents in an appendix. Include past awards and notable achievements as well. Attach letters of recommendation from industry professionals, letters from key officials supporting your project, and letters of support from industry mentors and advisors.

If you need to brush up on your writing skills Eva suggests William Strunk's *The Elements of Style*, now available online at *http://www.bartleby.com/*, and Purdue University's online writing lab located at *http://owl.english.purdue.edu/*.

Both of these resources feature search engines that allow you to easily find answers to your writing and grammar questions. Just remember, if you hire a professional writer to help you with your proposal you need to make sure your passion is projected in the final proposal.

The most important thing is never give up! Keep applying for those grants and keep your project in front of potential funders.

For a list of experienced grant writers, see *www.fromtheheartproductions.com*.

CHAPTER 4

LOADING THE BASES

Even if you're on the right track, you'll get run over if you just sit there.
— Will Rogers

RULES OF THE GAME

You've polished your proposal and perfected your pitch. Before you step out of the bullpen, make sure you understand the rules of the game.

Rule #1: Know the Catcher Before You Pitch

The number one complaint from funders is that too many applications do not fit the foundation's guidelines. Don't try to throw a fastball past a seasoned funder. Carefully read the guidelines and criteria of each potential funding source. If your project doesn't fit, don't apply.

Before you pitch anyone, know who they are and how they can help. Filmmakers need more than money, you need mentors, people who know wealthy people who want to be an associate producer while they sit in their paneled offices and you make the films.

Rule #2: Develop a Strategy

You can't invite a bunch of friends over, order pizza and beer and send off a mass mailing of your proposal. It just doesn't work that way. You must have a specific strategy based on each individual funder. To develop this strategy you need to know where each individual funder is coming from. You must know what makes them tick. You must understand their objectives. Your proposal has to fulfill their needs, which means each proposal has to be specifically written for that funder.

My criteria are that a project must be unique and make a contribution to society. I know filmmakers have read my website when they write, "this film is unique and will make a contribution to society because..." You need to hang your hat on their requirements.

Rule #3: Play the Field

Don't make the mistake of focusing all of your efforts on one funder or on one specific type of funding. Keep your options open. Learn everything you can about different financing opportunities that are available to independent filmmakers and romance every appropriate funding source you can find.

One of my grant-winning filmmakers told me she applied for five grants and won four. How did she do that? She spent her time reading the requirements, the number of people who apply, what type of films the organization had funded in the past and then she decided which ones to put her time in. She chose grants that she felt she had the best chance to win and she wrote a special proposal to each one of them. It worked with me, I loved Rebecca Dreyfus' film *Stolen* from the two-page proposal she sent. She had me wanting to know more about the story and she became one of the top five finalists in the NYC film grant.

The judges looked at this concept of her investigation of the Vermeer stolen from the Gardner Museum in Boston and decided she would not win many grants. Her story was so engaging, they awarded her the grant. In addition to our grant, Rebecca sold the idea to Court TV and created a brilliant film.

Funders want to fund films that will be completed and distributed. This means they want to know that you are out there focusing on additional funding. I love it when I get an application that says "here is the list of organizations where we are applying." That tells me that they are not depending on my grant, they are investigating the field and they know where they have the most potential for funding. All funders and donors like to see you are diligently applying for grants and personal donations.

Rule #4: There's No Crying in Baseball

Don't view a rejection as failure, rather see it as an opportunity to learn and improve. Follow up with each funder. Thank them for their consideration and ask for feedback. If the funder still shows interest in your project, ask if you can reapply in the future. If the funder is not interested in supporting this particular project, thank them for their time and keep the lines of communication open; they may be interested in funding future projects.

I give everyone a free consultation when they apply for the Roy W. Dean grants. Most filmmakers take advantage and set up appointments with me to discuss funding opportunities and what they can do to improve their proposal. Most state and federal funding organizations will give you feedback, you just have to be persistent to make an appointment, because it is worth it.

If you are not accumulating several rejections a month, you are not doing your job. Remember, even the best grant writers end up with far more rejections than they do grants.

SCOUTING THE MAJORS: RESEARCHING FUNDERS

You know your funder is out there floating around somewhere in cyberspace but somehow you just keep missing each other. When you get tired of knocking on the front door maybe it's time to try something different.

Try searching for films that are similar to yours. Find out who funded these films and research these funders. Research documentary film sites, online film and video magazines, and online video distributors. Netflix has a wonderful collection of documentaries and often you can find funding names on the filmmaker's website.

Watch films and videos that are similar to yours and check out the list of funders in the credits. What businesses, individuals, and corporations do the producers thank? You've just found a list of sponsors who fund film projects like yours! Put these sponsors high on your list of potential funders and start researching their websites.

Is your film about a specific cause? Find nonprofit agencies that advance this cause and find out who their sponsors are. You've just found a list of funders who fund your subject! Research these sponsors and see if they fund media or film projects. These are people who might be willing to act as your sponsors or mentors, and may lead you to additional funding opportunities.

You've been surfing the net for years, but are you up on the latest search tools? Do you really know Boolean logic? Do you know how to access information that normal search engines can't reach? Do you know the difference between a spider, a crawler, and a MetaSearcher? If not, take an afternoon and brush up on your surfing skills. UC Berkeley offers an award-winning Internet tutorial located at *http://www.lib.berkeley.edu/TeachingLib/Guides*.

The Internet has revolutionized the way we access information, but please don't forget about your local library. Your library has an entire collection devoted to foundations and grants, including some of those expensive databases. Take the time to pay a personal visit to your library and meet the grants and foundations librarian. She can show you valuable trade secrets on how to search different databases and give you pointers on how to find other possible donors for your film. Your local librarian may turn out to be one of the most helpful people on your film crew!

In fact I recommend finding a librarian who loves your film and giving her/him a researcher credit on the film in exchange for helping you. Believe me, they can find things in a matter of minutes that might take you hours.

ORGANIZING YOUR SEARCH

Some people are good at finding information — they're so good they accumulate file cabinets and desk drawers full of computer printouts, newspaper articles, and magazine clippings. You know how it is: You can't get to it today, but you may want to read it someday, so it's added to the stack of papers precariously perched on the corner of your desk.

This is not information, it's clutter. Anything unfinished, unused, unresolved, or disorganized bogs us down and can keep us from moving forward. You will need to keep a list of potential funders and the type of films they fund so you can keep track of your contacts. Please don't let the list get away from you. It's tempting to start compiling a pie-in-the-sky list of potential funders for future projects, but try to keep your eyes on your current goal.

The key to being a successful researcher is not to accumulate piles of information that you may need someday, but to know how to find the information you need when you need it.

There are all kinds of complicated databases and fancy tracking systems designed to organize your business contacts; however, your objective is to get your film made, not learn how to use some complicated color-coded database. A simple list is all you need. It should include the funder's name, address, their web and email address; your contact person; and a place for notes.

We always keep links to hot funding sites on our *www.fromtheheartproductions.com* first page.

Bobby Mardis, Carole Dean, Carey Feldman,
Barbara Trent. L.A. Dean Grant Awards

Barbara Trent, (Academy Award winner Panama Deception*),*
Carole Dean, Robert Townsend. Roy W. Dean Awards, L.A.

CHAPTER 5

FOUNDATIONS AND GRANTS

A foundation is a nonprofit organization that donates (or grants) money, equipment or other supplies to organizations and individuals. Foundations are also called charitable trusts, endowments, and public charities.

Private foundations are usually funded from one source, typically an individual, a family, or a corporation. Public foundations are built from multiple sources, including grants from private foundations, government agencies, and donations from private individuals. Foundations have a responsibility to uphold the principles of the foundation and make sure their funders' donations are being used for the intended purpose.

If you've searched for funding in the past you already know that many foundations will not grant money to individuals. Will these foundations make an exception? Sometimes, but it's rare. Donating funds to individuals is more complicated because the IRS requires nonprofits to obtain advance approval before distributing funds to individuals.

So, what's a starving artist to do? One option is to find a fiscal sponsor.

FISCAL SPONSORSHIP

Fiscal Sponsors receive and administer funds and provide various levels of organizational support to individuals.

Another important step in the "Art of Film Funding" is to investigate the possibility of using a fiscal agent for your project. Fiscal sponsorship can give you access to funding opportunities and other resources available to 501(c) (3) nonprofit organizations. Private individuals will also be more likely to donate their hard-earned money if you have fiscal sponsorship because they can use the donation as a tax write-off.

A fiscal sponsorship is a relationship and like all relationships it is important to find a good match. Each fiscal sponsor has different guidelines and goals. Some fiscal agents charge a fee or commission; others are simply altruistic spirits who are dedicated to your cause. Just make sure you and your fiscal sponsor have a clear agreement regarding the management and disbursement of funds, what fees, if any, the fiscal agent will charge, and who will retain legal identity and control over your project.

Read their website and then talk to them with any unanswered questions. Don't be afraid to ask how long it takes from the time you give them a donation until you get your check back in the mail.

Schools, arts organizations, or other local community groups often sponsor individual filmmakers. New York Foundation for the Arts (*www.nyfa. org*) posts a list of fiscal sponsors that are located all over the country. Women Make Movies (an excellent place for women's films), Film Arts Foundation in San Francisco and Film Video Arts in NYC are all excellent companies that will help and support you through the funding and filmmaking process.

FINDING THE GRANTOR TO MATCH YOUR FILM

The money to make your film is out there. Foundations have money and resources already set aside to give away to the right individual or organization. It's their job to give these resources away. Your job is to make sure your project matches their criteria and guidelines.

Choose a potential funder from the list in the Appendix and visit their website. Start with their mission statement, then go directly to their funding guidelines. When you find a funder that looks promising, dig in and explore their website from top to bottom. Learn everything you can about this funding source. When was the foundation established? Who established it and why? Find out who funds the foundation. As you research, jot down questions that come to mind.

If you've gotten this far and the foundation still feels like a good match, dig a little deeper. What causes have they funded in the past? You're probably not going to want to pitch your documentary about endangered marmots of the San

Juan Wilderness to an organization that is an ardent supporter of the Independent Taxidermists of America. Knowing what type of organizations or individuals a particular funding source has embraced in the past will give you additional insight into the types of projects they fund.

IRS 501(c) (3) defines nonprofit, charitable, tax-exempt organizations. IRS Form 990 is used by tax-exempt organizations, nonexempt charitable trusts, and political organizations to provide the IRS with information required by section 6033. Why should you care? Because you can find out a lot about an organization by accessing their tax forms.

I know, it sounds positively sneaky, doesn't it? Don't worry, I'm not asking you to put on a cat suit and slip into their business office at night with a flashlight. These records are available to the public. If you're into snooping (and what great filmmaker isn't?) then you'll want to stay awake for this next part.

Form 990 discloses all kinds of juicy tidbits about an organization's finances, board members, and you guessed it, their philanthropic activities. Accessing this one form will tell you what kind of programs the organization supports and the names of all grant recipients for that fiscal year. It will also give you the name, address, and phone number of the operations officer (the person in charge of the grant you are applying for), and whether or not they accept unsolicited proposals.

You can access information on over 100,000 U.S. private and community foundations for free through the Foundation Center's Foundation Finder, located at *www.fdncenter.org*. If you don't have the name of a foundation, GrantSmart (*www.grantsmart.org*) offers a database of U.S. grant makers and foundations you can search using keywords.

Give it a try! Access the Foundation Finder and type in "Internet Science Education Project," and you will be given direct access to a PDF link containing this foundation's most current individual tax records. Here you will learn that the Internet Science Education Project supports the advancement of time travel to the past. Cool!

Part I, 25 on Page 1 of their Form 990 tells you they donated $321,215 in contributions, gifts and grants during the 2001 fiscal year. Zip on over to Part VIII, 1, and you will find the name of their president and discover that he was paid $108,210 for this dubious distinction. Part IX-(A) gives you a summary of their four largest direct charitable activities, which included donations for the research and development of "nanotechnology and the advanced propulsion of space craft."

Beam on over to Part XV, 3, and you will find a list of all of the grants and contributions ISEP paid during the fiscal year as well as a list of grants and contributions they have approved for future funding.

You may not be the least bit interested in a foundation that funds nano-technology or space travel, but it doesn't take a rocket scientist (sorry) to see how this one little tax form can provide a wealth of information about a foundation that you are interested in. The Foundation Center has a very slick diagram of a 990-PF that shows you exactly where the most important funding information is located. You can download it for free at *http://foundationcenter.org*.

Find a potential funding source for your film project and check out the operations officer. Who's on the Board? Who won last year's grant competition? How about the year before? Try to find websites of past winners and learn every-thing you can about their projects. Email them and congratulate them on their award and say something positive about their film. Tell them you are applying for the same grant and ask them if they have any suggestions, tips, or advice.

Remember to keep jotting down questions. You will need them later.

A grant can be a stepping-stone for a first time filmmaker who is breaking into the industry. Barbara Leibovitz had never made a film before when she won her Roy W. Dean Grant and she has since gone on to make documentaries for major cable companies with her husband under Leibovitz-Hellman Productions, Inc.

There are other foundations out there that will take a chance on an emerging filmmaker if the project and the filmmaker match the foundation's philosophy. If you are a first-time filmmaker, make sure the grant you are applying for sup-ports emerging filmmakers. Perhaps you can increase your chances if you attach an experienced crew to your project. You would also increase your chances of winning a grant if you take a prior grant winner from the organization your film matches on board your crew. I know from giving grants that when I see a prior winner of my grants on the crew of a project it immediately instills confidence.

The next step in the "Art of Film Funding" is to find a foundation that looks promising. Now comes the part you've been waiting for! Take out your list of questions and choose the best one. You are going to call to the person who funds the grant. Place your call in "prime time" between 10 a.m. and 12 p.m., or between 2 and 4 p.m. and ask to speak directly with the operations officer in charge of the grant. If they don't answer, try again later. If you must, leave your name and number and the best time you can be reached, then make sure you're ready when they call back.

If you leave your cell phone number, keep your cell phone turned on and be ready with pen and paper handy. Don't worry, they will call you; it's their job. You did your homework. You know what the foundation is about and you know they support projects like yours, so they will be interested in what you have to say.

Individuals who work for nonprofits are passionate about their cause. They are overworked and underpaid. They believe the world needs more films on important issues and they want to help you get your film made.

Remember, this call is to connect with the decision maker for the grant you want to win. Your job is to touch them, remembering that we communicate through the heart chakra. This connection puts energy to your application; it is the voice behind the film. It's you and the film you want to convey to the funder through your passion so that later during the selection process, when they see your name on the application, they feel they know you.

Now what are you going to say when you get them on the phone? Remember that pitch you've been working on? You are going to tell them who you are and give them the concept of your film using that stunning under-two-minute pitch that you have worked so hard on. Write down key points in case you get nervous and keep it with you so you are ready when the phone rings.

You know your pitch by heart. I know this and you know this, but you just might be a tad nervous so believe me, have your notes near. Your initial approach is critical so let's go over the steps:

You have the name of the person, the correct spelling and pronunciation.

You have read this person's bio and you know about their past contributions. Compliment them and thank them for their continuing efforts to independent filmmakers.

You have read the website thoroughly and you know what type of projects they fund.

You have an important question to ask that is not answered on the website.

You have your pitch in front of you.

You're organized.

You will not keep them on the phone long.

You will not take another call with them on the line.

You have researched prior winners and you know that your film fits within the scope of previously funded projects.

Get ready to take some notes!

Be relaxed and make the impression of a dedicated, passionate filmmaker who is determined to fund this film with or without them.

I love it when filmmakers ask questions. Sometimes they ask how many applications we receive, or how many grants we fund per year. These are important questions and they are not answered on my website. I can hear them doing the math in their heads as they try to determine what their chances are.

Most filmmakers will pitch their project, then pause and wait for my response. This is good because it allows me time to process what they have just said. I usually reply with a question. They will typically have a quick answer that will lead to another question. This is what you want to achieve with this first call. You want to spark interest and draw the funder into the heart of your project.

Do not keep the funder on the phone too long, and do not over-pitch your film. Take a breath between sentences and allow the funder adequate time to respond. We know you are passionate about your film, but learn to listen to feedback and remember to come up for air!

Once in a while I'll get some eager filmmaker on the line who sounds like he's flying on his third or fourth Starbucks. Information is coming in so fast and furious that I don't know what's hit me! I don't have time to ask questions because he never stops. When he finally pauses long enough to take a breath, I find that I've lost most of my questions, and just when I start to regain my balance he'll start up again. All I can do is wait until he runs out of steam.

I would have talked less and listened more if I had my life to live over.
— Erma Bombeck

Listening is an art. My father, Roy W. Dean, was a wonderful listener. When dad retired I asked him to move to Southern California and help me run Studio Film and Tape. I opened shop in 1968, and started selling short-ends. I noticed that there was always a lot of leftover film at the end of each feature film production and thought if I could get access to all this unused film I could sell it. I ignored all the skeptics, put on my mini-skirt and boots, marched over to Universal Studios and asked them for "those little ol' short ends that you really don't want." Before long I was buying up short-ends all over Hollywood, testing them and selling them for a profit.

I was thrilled when dad sold his house in Dallas and moved to California in mid-life to start over again with me. He could have had any job in the office, but he chose to work at the front counter because he wanted to meet the filmmakers when they came in to buy film and sound stock. Dad never grew tired of listening to filmmakers describe their latest projects. He would literally end up spending hours with one filmmaker because he would ask the magic question that every filmmaker loves to hear: "So tell me, what you are shooting these days?"

Renee Ross and I got pretty good at anticipating the magic question. Dad would be up there at his post chatting away with some new filmmaker while Renee and I were busy working behind the scenes. Suddenly we could sense it. He was going to ask! Renee and I would stop, look at each other then we would start waving our arms, trying to get dad's attention. We'd shake our heads and mouth, "No! No!"

But it never did any good. Every time a new filmmaker came through the front door Renee and I knew that dad was going to ask that magic question. We could be scrambling around, waiting on customers, pulling our hair out, and dad would be up there at the counter listening intently as some filmmaker described his latest masterpiece.

I always try to remember dad's patience when I have a "Starbucker" on the phone. Sometimes I will go outside, water my plants, prune my roses, come back in and fix a cup of hot tea while the filmmaker goes on like an Animaniac on crack.

Often when people go on like this it is because they are nervous. Calm yourself. Don't feel as though you need to fill every moment of silence with some profound statement. Develop the art of listening. When you let funders participate in the conversation they will be able to process what you are saying. They will formulate questions and will ultimately remember more about you and your project.

Back to your phone call: After you have delivered your perfect pitch, ask the funder if your project fits their criteria then listen. Remember, your phone call serves two purposes: you are trying to find out if the funder will accept a proposal for the film you want to make, and you want to create a connection with this person. This is probably the first person that will read your application; it may be the only person who reads your application, so leave a good impression.

Funders will often ask questions to determine whether or not a particular project fits their foundation's criteria. Don't worry if you can't answer every question.

If you are still in preproduction and have not made a decision regarding a particular question, just explain this to them. Above all, listen to what they have to say. Stay awake, take notes, and pick up all the clues you can.

If you find out that you have made a production decision that will disqualify your project consider changing directions. When you play the funding game you must understand that you may have to include or exclude specific criteria in order to get funding from a particular organization. Believe me, there are worse things in life, so consider it. What you want to do is maintain control of the film and most of these grants can help you do that.

What do you say if the funder tells you that your film does not fit the foundation's criteria? Thank her for her time. Offer some sincere words of gratitude for the job she is doing and let her know you will contact her again when you have something that fits their criteria. Then go out and buy a nice Hallmark card and write a personal note thanking her once again for listening to your pitch. Remind her of the title of your film, and send along your best wishes for the future success of the foundation.

If she gives you the thumbs up, thank her for her time and confirm her address (oh, and please wait until you hang up to let out that scream). Go out and pick up a nice Hallmark card and write a brief note inside thanking her for the time she spent discussing your film about the endangered marmots of the San Juan Wilderness. Include a condensed version of your pitch and let her know that you will be applying for the grant. Sign your name and post it with a colorful endangered-species postage stamp.

Why send her a card? Because these film funders talk to each other. If you become a grant finalist with another foundation she will probably either hear about it or read about it. She will remember your card and think about you and your project in a good light.

You have now made two connections with the woman who will be handling your first application. Make a note on your list of potential funders and call her back in six to eight weeks with another important question that is not answered on the website. Send her a card for every occasion from Independence Day to National Marmot Day. Include a brief note about your film along with your condensed pitch and wish her a happy holiday.

Keep each potential funder close to your project by keeping them up to date on your progress and achievements. Let potential funders know if you win another grant, or if you have found an award-winning director for your project.

When Albert Maysles agrees to be your mentor send your potential funder an update. Remember to keep track of each contact that you make. When you keep your funders involved in your progress they will be drawn deeper and deeper into your project. When your application crosses their desk they will remember you and your film. I know this from experience.

JanEva Hornbaker was a finalist for my Roy W. Dean L.A. Film Grant, and was applying for our New York grant for her documentary, *Searcher for Souls*. Eva's film follows modern-day explorers who search for the remains of more than 78,000 Americans still missing from the Second World War. Eva had the most fantastic adventures while she was in Europe researching her film, and she took the time to share each dramatic event with me.

I felt as though I was right there with her through it all as I received email after email from exotic locations in the south of France and southern Italy. She told me about her special press conference with the mayor of Cannes; the rainy afternoon in southern France when she discovered the whereabouts of a lost American flyer; and her phone call from the Pentagon. With each email I grew closer to Eva and her project.

There is something special that happens when a funder picks up an application from a filmmaker who has kept her close to the project. Once a funder has been swept into your passion she is inwardly cheering for you. She is already connected to you and your film.

Keep all of your notes on each foundation organized and continue to look for questions that you can ask. When the next month rolls around, pick up the phone and make your second call.

Reintroduce yourself and your project and ask another question that is not already answered on the website. Get the answer, take notes, thank her, and let her get back to work. In six weeks, call back and introduce yourself and your project once again, ask another important, unanswered question. Take notes, thank her, and let her get back to work. As you work on your proposal you will generate more questions and so it is natural to keep in touch this way.

Filmmaker Jilann Spitzmiller told me that she keeps a file of granting organizations by the deadline of their grants. This way she knows when she has to have the application ready. Jilann always called me to ask questions about the grant and she has won two of our grants, so it works!

Decide how many organizations you will research each day, then make a commitment to sit down and put in your quota every day. Give up those CSI reruns and use that time to search the Web. Filmmakers often go back and use the same funders for subsequent projects. Just know that while your initial search may be time consuming, it can also lead to future funding.

Work your way through the list of funders included in this book. As you work, add funders you find along the way. Look on my website, *www.fromtheheart-productions.com/interviews.shtml*, for interviews with winners of the grants to find where and how they funded their films. You will have to kiss a lot of frogs to find a prince (or princess), but once you've found one it's worth it.

CHAPTER 6

RAISING FUNDS FROM INDIVIDUALS AND BUSINESSES

I have a confession to make. When I was running Studio Film I used to hide in a corner office so filmmakers couldn't find me. Of course my wonderful dad (who was defenseless against a filmmaker's passionate pitch) would give me up every single time!

Small businesses and corporations are tiny untapped goldmines for independent filmmakers. Local businesses and corporations always have managers (or dads) who are very accessible and easy to talk to. Be it my dad, or one of my employees, someone was always knocking on my door in the middle of the day with some filmmaker's proposal. It was usually only a one-page proposal, which was a blessing since business seemed to grind to a halt whenever this occurred. Customers could be lined up at the counter but it didn't matter.

Everyone in the office got wrapped up in the drama that was unfolding. You could practically hear the drum roll in the background. Would she say yes or no? Looking back now I realize this was probably a conspiracy since everyone knew the buck stopped with me. People everywhere (yes, even people in Hollywood) want to be involved in a film.

When I scanned these proposals I would look for the following things:

- ◈ The story synopsis (hopefully brief and to the point).
- ◈ Why the filmmaker was making the film.
- ◈ Exactly what the filmmaker needed and why.
- ◈ Who would benefit from the film.
- ◈ What the filmmaker was willing to do for me (an end-credit, product placement, etc.).
- ◈ How much the donation would mean to the filmmaker.

If you have a fiscal sponsor, make sure to note this on all of your proposals. Your tax-deductible status will go a long way when looking for donations. Customize your proposal for each individual business you approach. When you make it personal the recipient feels special.

Start by making a list of all the stores and restaurants near your location. Visit the managers of these businesses with your one-page customized proposal in your hand and the best smile you can muster. Don't forget to dress the part. Wear a Kodak Film cap and have a Sony bag slung around your shoulder. Make sure they see you and think Spielberg.

Sometimes you have to leave your proposal with an employee. Pitch the employee the same way you would the manager. Be considerate to all of the employees. If they are anything like the wonderful people who worked with me at Studio Film, once they get caught up in your enthusiasm they are going to beg their manager to become involved in your film. Think of the employees as your support team.

Mention how much your crew enjoys their pizza, or how impressed you were the last time they did some copy work for you. Talk about your film and give your pitch as though you are asking for a $10,000 grant.

Most managers can make the decision right there on the spot without going to a corporate supervisor. I did business at Kinko's for years before I asked who I could see about getting a discount. When the woman at the counter told me she could help me I was flabbergasted. I thought I would need to fill out reams of forms that would be sent off through the chain of command. All I had to do was explain that I represented a nonprofit organization that helped filmmakers and ask for a discount. It was that easy!

Most independents forget that all of the little miscellaneous budget items add up. You are going to be into Kinko's for about $800 and Office Depot for another $1,200. The caterer is going to hit you up for about $2,500 for lunches, and you are probably going to have to fork over about $800 a week for equipment rental. All of these little extras can easily add another $6,000–$10,000 to your bottom line.

Go through your shooting script and your budget and make a list of all the things that might be donated through local businesses and corporations. Are you going to need a rental car? What about office supplies? You know you're going to have to feed your crew and your new cameraman can put away three pizzas in one sitting!

Your list might include car rental agencies, cell phones, grocery stores, bagel shops, the local pizza parlor. List any business that advertises. Target small businesses like the little mom and pop coffee shop around the corner because it is often more productive than going to a large corporate business like Starbucks. Local business people want to support their community and they will be receptive to your needs.

A business in a bustling neighborhood may have a lot of healthy competition. If this is the case, then mention the discount offered by their competitor and ask if they can beat it.

The most popular labor-saving device is still money.
— Phyllis George

If you can't get it for free, do your homework and know what you can get it for. Dov S-S Simons of the Hollywood Film Institute says you can get a discount on everything in your production budget. According to Dov, "No one who knows anything in the industry pays the rate card price." Know what the going rate is and ask for a discount.

Studio Film's three-tier price index was installed on every employee's computer. Businesses do this. Every salesperson knows the lowest price they can quote. This is the rate you want, even if you just buy ten items. Once your name is linked in the computer with a special rate you will get that rate every time you make a purchase. I have made special arrangements with David Cohen of Edgewise. Filmmakers who enter my Roy W. Dean grants will receive a discount for all of Edgewise's products, including film, tape, and digital supplies. If you apply for my grant or if you are an emerging filmmaker and you would like to receive this discount, call my sweetheart, Phillip Loving at (800) 824-3130 and he will get you in the computer as a Roy W. Dean grant applicant or a student from this book.

Bobby Mardis (one of my favorite producers) once told me that he never takes anything personal when he is producing a film. He gets the local production book, goes down it from A to Z, and starts asking. He explains how much he can spend and what he needs. If a business manager can't accommodate him he thanks her, tells her he will try her again on a future production and he moves down the list and calls the next vendor. He keeps at it until he finds someone who will give him what he needs at the price he has budgeted.

When you contact Kinko's, Jim's Car Rentals, or the local bagel shop, begin by asking for a donation in exchange for a mention in your film's credits, a copy of the completed film on DVD or for product placement. If they can't accommodate you and they are the only game in town, ask them if they would be willing to give you a 25% discount if you promote their business on your website. Always ask for a donation first and save the request for a discounted price as your last resort.

Remember, most companies work on a 25-40% profit margin so when you ask for a 25% discount you are asking the company to donate most of their profits to the film. Let them put a sign in the lobby that mentions they are donating to your film. Tell them you will pose for pictures, or let them shoot pictures of the cast and crew during production to use in an ad for the local paper.

Turn it into a great PR opportunity for them. Sometimes just offering to give a local businessperson a copy of the finished videotape is all it takes to get a smile and a donation.

I suggest you go to Abel Cine and get their prices for camera rentals and while you are there ask if you can take a picture with their latest camera. Of course you want to have your camera person with you so you can be pointing to the shot. Once you have this picture you can scan it into your computer and now you have a production shot to use as a public relations trade for services. Just put the name of the targeted company like "Nextel Supports Filmmakers" for the heading on the page, then your production picture and below that put in the details. "Nextel phones are being used in the National Marmots documentary."

You can create several of these for your intended donors and when you go to pitch Nextel, show them this donation advertisement and give it to them for display in their lobby. Don't forget to mention the credit at the end of the film. Visuals work every time.

Once you go over your budget carefully and list all the printing, copying, beverages, food, bottled water, coffee and bagels, cell phones, cars, airline tickets, restaurant charges, and so on, you will be amazed at how much you can save by finding resources through local businesses. Be sure to read Patti Ganguzza's chapter on branding for more information on free goods.

You can also negotiate with your crew. Many producers look for a production assistant who has a truck or an SUV and they arrange a flat weekly salary that includes the use of their vehicle.

Your P.A. should be one of your first employees as they can free you from time-consuming jobs, like local pickup and deliveries. They can even do your shopping, get the cleaning, or walk the dog. Your P.A. can do those time-consuming jobs that take you away from the focus of your film, while you work on the art of funding your film!

After producing 140 shows, working with countless filmmakers over the last 35 years, and raising close to $2 million in goods and services for my Roy W. Dean film grants, I have learned some valuable lessons. Never forget that the film business is a business. Before you approach a business or an individual, make a list of all of the benefits they will receive from your proposed venture. If their benefits do not equal or outweigh your benefits, then you need to rethink your proposal.

Your contacts will be more responsive when they know you are concerned with their image and their profits. This is how you create long-term friends in our industry. Remember, this is just one of many films you will make and people stay in our industry.

RAISING FUNDS FROM INDIVIDUALS

You will get 60% of your money from individuals. That's what the statistics show. So learning how to approach individuals is paramount to the art of funding.

When filmmakers approach individuals, they are looking for either an investor or a donor. It is essential that you disclose exactly what you are looking for and that you are completely honest when you discuss your film's investment potential.

Have a good attorney on board before you approach an individual investor. Do not take one dime from an investor until you have presented the investor with an investment memorandum. Mark Litwak discusses the legal side of the producer/investor relationship later on in the chapter on financing independent films. It is essential that you heed Mark's words. There are laws that protect investors and these laws are very clear.

Contributions do not require paperwork. Just send your donor a letter of thanks and the information they need for their taxes and you're on your way to the bank! Of course approaching an individual donor will require a serious investment of your time. Please do not approach your family and friends and immediately ask them to donate toward your film. Remember, when you ask someone to donate or invest in your film they are essentially investing in you. Give them time to see your tenacity and they will be there when you need that extra bit to tide you over.

Romancing individual funders requires as much skill as creating a great pitch or writing a strong proposal. You must sharpen your people skills and be prepared to spend some serious time dodging the moths that fly out of their purses. "Doing time" sound like a line from *The Sopranos*, but that's exactly what it takes. You need to put time into building a relationship with any potential donor.

If you met someone at a party and proposed marriage over cocktails they would think you were crazy! You have to win their interest, their trust, and their confidence first. Potential donors need to know you and they need to know your film. They need to know why this film has to be made and why you are the only one who can make it. They need to see how dedicated you are to the project. Get them interested in your film before you ever ask them for a thing. Invite them to production meetings, script sessions, and fundraising parties.

A filmmaker told me a wonderful story about a wealthy donor he was courting. The donor told the filmmaker that her husband had taken a small business and turned it into a multimillion-dollar corporation. She told the story with great pride, and it was obvious that she loved and admired her husband very much, so the filmmaker asked her if he could film an interview with her husband. He taped the interview, did a little editing, and presented her with an hour of her husband's life story.

She immediately attached herself to the filmmaker because the filmmaker knew what was important to her. Do you think he got his donation? Of course he did! But he built a relationship with her before he even thought about asking.

So, where do you find these wealthy philanthropists? The society section of the paper is a good start for rich, grant-giving philanthropists in your area.

Remember those old address books you stored in your closet after you bought your palm pilot? Dust them off and start looking for names. Find people in there who could easily part with five grand or more and not miss it. You might be surprised at how many names you come up with. As the years go by people move up the ladder, so don't discount someone who was a sales manager back in 1993. She might be the head of the company today. I don't care if you haven't talked to her in years. Pull out that name, make that phone call and tell her about the film you're making.

Reestablish your relationship. Tell her you are producing a film about a very important issue and you thought she would enjoy hearing about it. Perhaps she has good business sense. Ask her for some advice, but don't mention money. People will donate time to help you when they see that you are on an important quest. Get her involved then send her a one or two-page proposal. Call her up and invite her to a production meeting or a fundraising party.

She may suspect that you are going to pop the money question and she may turn you down. That's okay; you just saved yourself some time. Other contacts will take you up on your offer, especially if you have asked for advice in their area of expertise. The key is you must get to know these people. You must understand who they are and what their needs are before you can ask for money. Remember, you need a lot more than money; you need support, especially from people who know people with money. You need people to give you house parties to fund your film; you want people to open their phone books to you to invite their friends to parties to support you. You need legal advice and you need accounting advice, and getting that free can be a great bonus to you and the film.

Take some time and brainstorm. Think about people you have worked for over the past ten years. What about your spouse's affiliations? Do you know someone who donates time to a public official? If so, ask if you can get an introduction. It may take weeks for you to come up with a list but that's okay. Fundraising is an important part of the art of funding your film. Most of the producers you meet in Hollywood will tell you that they "have several projects in various stages of production," which is a dead giveaway that they are out there looking for money.

If you are doing a film about a woman who has survived cancer, seek funding from cancer survivors, from family members of cancer victims, and from nonprofit cancer organizations. If you are doing a film about the plight of our oceans, whose name comes to mind? How about Ted Danson and the American Oceans Campaign?

Contact Mr. Danson, tell him about your project and ask him for some advice. Go to the American Oceans Campaign website and research their sponsors. Remember Form 990 from the chapter on foundations and grants? This form also lists individuals who have donated to the foundation.

How do you get to know potential donors once you have found them? It may be as simple as picking up the phone and calling them. Give them your two-paragraph pitch but don't ask for money. Tell them that you are researching your subject and ask them about their organization. Look for people who can help you with information on your subject matter.

Concerned citizens who have money usually know other concerned citizens who have money. Take the time to get to know each individual and listen to what they have to say about your subject. Once you have established a relationship, find a role for this person somewhere on your project.

Perhaps they could help throw a fundraising party, be the expert advisor on your subject, or act as your mentor. Investors and donors will pay special attention to your proposal if you have people like this on board.

You must be persistent. When I first started out in the film business skeptics told me that no one in their right mind would buy short ends. I had to overcome some heavy opposition to get going, but I was determined. Capturing a market is like fishing with a net. If you work one market at a time it is much easier to capture the entire market when you land your first sale within that market.

I started out by making cold calls to film schools. I had to keep at it for over a month before I got my first order, but as soon as I took that order I hung up and called the film school down the road and told them their competitor just placed an order. Suddenly they were interested. My cold call sales ratio went from a 5% return to a 30% return because I was working within a tight industry where people know each other. I stayed with my idea of selling to one market (film schools) until I captured one fish in that market. Businesses and corporations are more open to a new idea when they discover their peers are interested in the idea.

Consider doing the same thing when you look for individuals to fund your film. If Mary Smith from Americans for Cleaner Oceans has agreed to act as your mentor, go to similar organizations within the community and make a list of their board members. Call each person and develop a relationship. Let them know that Mary Smith from Americans for Cleaner Oceans is working with you. These methods will provide you with advisors, mentors, and donors.

The rule of the industry is:

If you ask for money you get advice. If you ask for advice you get money.

What if you can't get them on the phone? What if your potential donor is as reclusive as Howard Hughes? Get to know his secretary or his personal assistant. This is how good sales people become successful sales people. Secretaries and personal assistants can get you through to the people you want to know, so take some time and create a rapport with these people. Get on a first name basis with a potential donor's secretary. Chat with her about her vacation. Ask her about her children.

If you are professional and personable, and if you have a good pitch, you will get through to the person you want. A secretary's job is to protect her boss. If she believes that you will not embarrass her, and that you have something important to present, she will put your call through.

It's all in your approach. Sherrie Findhorn was one of my top sales people. Before Sherrie came to Studio Film she worked for the Yellow Pages. This is where she learned to smile on the phone. That's right, Sherrie told me that sales shot up when some executive put mirrors on every sales person's desk and asked them to smile when they made their cold calls. Try it! Especially on a day when you feel like biting the heads off nails. You will be treated better and it will lift your spirits.

Don't be afraid to go to the top of the ladder. I know these people are often hard to get to but that just makes success that much sweeter! Who do you think wrote my first ad for Studio Film and Tape NYC back in 1970? The late Ira Eaker, co-founder of Back Stage! The first time I went to see Ira he asked to see my copy. I was so green back in those days I didn't even know what a copy was, but Ira took the time to work out a great ad for me. I ran that ad for years. Ira and I remained good friends right up to his recent death. Sometimes the nicest people are at the top. They may be hidden away by a protective secretary but if you believe in your project you can find a way in.

"Okay, Carole, so when do I get to ask the sixty-four thousand dollar question?" Be patient, grasshopper. Don't even think about asking for money until you have all your preproduction ducks in a row. Form your production company and put together a solid preproduction package while you're getting close to these potential donors and investors.

POPPING THE BIG QUESTION

You have put together a strong preproduction package and you have taken the time to establish a good relationship with your potential donor. You know who they are and what their values are, what is important to them. This "ask" has to have their interest at heart, it has to benefit them in some way, which could be a tax deduction or you may want to dedicate the film to their deceased mother or offer them an associate producer credit for a generous donation.

Now you are ready to ask! It's a good idea to take them out for dinner at a nice restaurant, look them right in the eye, and ask them if they will donate to your project. Say something like, "Would you be willing to donate $10,000 to my film?"

They have heard your pitch so many times they know it by heart so don't pitch them again. Instead, give them a production update. Tell them about some of the grants you have applied for and talk about where you expect to get the rest of your financing. Be 100% honest in every statement that you make.

They know all about the paperwork inside that preproduction package lying next to you on the table. You have discussed many of these things with them over the past year and they have given you advice along the way. Perhaps they even helped you with some of the paperwork inside that package. Don't remind them that you have a nonprofit fiscal sponsor and that their donation will be tax deductible. They know that. This is not a why don't you look it over and let me know later meeting, this is a look me in the eye and give me an answer meeting.

Remember, you are asking this person to invest in you. You already know they trust and respect you. You know they want to help you complete your film. You have invested a great deal of time to bring this person into your film and you would not be sitting across from them now if they did not have the same passion for your project that you have. Your chances of walking away with a check are going to be ten thousand times better than if you had just sent them a package in the mail and followed up with a phone call.

How much are you going to ask for? If you ask for too much you will probably walk away empty handed. Most donors do not like to admit that they can't afford to donate $70,000, but they might be able to swing $10,000. Do your homework and know how much they have donated in the past to causes like yours and make sure you approach them with a figure they can afford. Don't embarrass them by asking for too little — that's even worse than asking for too much!

Every one of us has a comfort zone and when we give donations we usually write checks for that same amount, from the Red Cross to saving the oceans. Find out what that person usually donates and ask for that amount. Sometimes the richest people will always go back to the same amount. One wealthy socialite always wrote $4,000 checks. By getting to know her, the filmmaker knew that was her comfort level, so that's what she asked for and that's what she got. Had she asked for $10,000 she would have been turned down, if she asked for $2,000 then she would have lost $2,000. Know the magic number.

The person who gives you this $4,000 will often give it to you again. They just need to be kept current on the film and when you are coming down the home stretch they will be there with you for another donation.

Every person who donates to your film must be considered equal. It's like my dad who put in the same time with the $100 sale as he did with the $10,000 sale. Your many $50 donations can become $5000 when they know you are serious and determined to make that film. Keep every name of all the donors and put them on your email list.

If you want to make that film, set a deadline and start working. I know that you work on your grant application right up to the deadline, then FedEx it overnight, because I'm the one that gets bombarded with a ton of applications the day before the deadline! Filmmakers always work best under pressure.

Barbara Trent told me that she always used to get her grant applications in just under the wire. One of the grants Barbara applied for finally eliminated their deadline policy and opened the door for submissions anytime during the calendar year. Barbara said she never applied for the grant again. We need deadlines, so set one and start getting results.

I want you to open your mind to all of the creative ways to raise money. The money is out there and it is mostly in the hands of individuals. You just have to approach fundraising with the same level of creativity that you use throughout the entire filmmaking process. Think of fundraising as another art form.

FUNDING PARTIES, INSTANT CASH

Pasta Party

Mindy Pomper entered my grant for her film *Save a Man to Fight*. It is a great story of the women in the Second World War who took over men's jobs so the men could go to the front lines. Her film includes women pilots who flew planes towing targets for the men to practice their shooting skills. Can you imagine? Yes, women were expendable and Mindy's film is cut with government propaganda films where women were told they had to wear rubber girdles to hold in that little tummy. Marching in the hot Texas sun with a rubber girdle; it's hard to believe what these women did for their country.

Mindy won my grant from her heart-felt pitch where she along with four other finalists pitched their films at Raleigh Studios to a packed house of filmmakers eager to learn how to win grants.

While Mindy was making her film she would get out her phone book, call all her friends and say, "I need some cash for production so I'm giving a dinner party. Please come and hear all about my film, many new things are happening and I have some footage you will really enjoy seeing." She would also say, "Bring a friend, it's a $40 donation for dinner."

She always had a full house and averaged $60 per guest. Mindy did this twice a year and took in a nice piece of change to keep her petty cash full. Plus she kept her friends up to date on the status of her film and she enlisted their ideas for funding.

Mindy was smart to fill the room with filmmakers and non-filmmakers. This way the filmmakers could entertain single guests so no one felt left out. I recommend you always have filmmakers as "shills" at your parties. Their specific job is to latch on to some potential funders and keep them meeting people and learning about the film so they are more prone to feel comfortable. Having someone answer questions gets them closer to the film.

I believe that your initial $50 or $100 donation can turn into $300 or $500 or even more once your donors see you moving forward and this only works when your stay close to them and they know how hard you work to make this film happen. Just tell them the good stuff; if they knew all the pitfalls of a filmmaker it would freak them out.

Staying in touch with every donor is paramount to the art of funding. Get everyone's email and be sure to create a special mailing list of these names. You want to keep in touch at least every two months with a Rah! Rah! email telling them the progress you have made. Give them the results of funding parties, grants you applied for, comments from anyone important in the filmmaking industry and let them know what has happened since the last email.

You don't make "the ask" from this email list until you need something. Keep them up to date and then when your coffers are running low, ask for what you need in the email telling them where you are and what process is next and let them know how much you need for this process. Seldom do you want to tell your potential funders your short will cost $30,000 or you doc $300,000. They can't imagine where you will get all that funding. Handle it like you are feeding them an elephant, one bite at a time.

If you haven't already promised to put their names in the credits, do this when you need funds. The amounts you choose are up to you but many film-makers say $100 is a rolling credit, $500 is three names on a screen and $3,000 gives you a full screen credit. For larger donations you want to talk to them in person.

Faun Kime's Successful Party

Faun spent time and effort on this party and it paid off with great PR and a net donation of $10,000 for her film, *The Tomato Effect*.

Faun hired an assistant immediately because there is lots of work involved and your assistant's salary will pay off with donors, potential donors and perhaps a second or third party.

My list of 44 things to do for a funding party is really built around this type of party. Creating your website so it will hold lots of logos is important. This is the quid pro quo that you trade for that weekend from Hilton or the organic winery for that free case of last year's award winner.

The donor's logos will be on your first page so you want to hold logos on both sides to maximize the number of donors.

FUNDING EXTRAVAGANZA OUTLINE

1. You need to plan a date at least 60 to 75 days in advance.

2. Hire an assistant for $10 an hour plus a bonus based on how much you bring in, perhaps 10% of the income as their bonus; they will earn it, believe me.

3. Get your website up first. Contact my donors, *silkem@gmail.com* and *graphics@skullco.com* — they love to work with filmmakers.

4. Your website has to have your film's pitch and the first two paragraphs must fully explain the story of your film. Make them dynamite.

5. Design the site for logos on the left and right sides to accommodate lots of ads.

6. Your site has to give the meaning of the film quickly and succinctly.

7. You need a place for people to send donations with an address for mailing and Pay Pal for impulse money. People who surf the web don't want to call you, they want to click on buttons to send you money, so make this possible.

8. You need to know who in politics or the sports world or the entertainment field will like your project. Then make a target list of these people because you need a local "star."

9. Start with your search for a local "star." Someone whose name is well known.

10. Set your date for the event based on their calendar so it is locked in.

11. Create personal invitation letters to other people who would know your "star" with an outline and pictures of your film. Follow up with phone calls to their offices.

12. If you have to reach athletes, see if you can find their managers and you can send packages either directly to them or to the managers. Each letter has to appeal to them for their personal support of your subject matter. You can offer then a thank you credit at the event and on the film. You want their support for the project (not money) first and you want them to come to the event second. Once they see your passion and get to know you then make the "ask."

13. Find a caterer who will give you a major discount using your website as your repayment for their reduction in price. Let them know you will feature them boldly on your website as "catered by" and you will put them in your program and give them credit on the film and mention them in any PR opportunities. This will work!

14. Give a down payment on your Visa card to seal the deal.

15. Look for more people of the same ilk as your known guest. For example, if this is the mayor's wife, like Faun had for her party, read the papers for socialites and contact them with your package and a personal letter inviting them to the party stating the mayor's wife is coming.

16. If this is an athlete, use the same practice: find any other athlete in the city who may be less known. Remember, athletes follow athletes, politicians follow politicians, etc. Now you are 100 times more likely to get any of these people to come to your event because you have a name they want to meet. Send them your proposal; call back with a personal invitation.

17. Faun charged $75 and she said she would never charge an entrance fee again because she made most of her money on the silent auction so your job is to get them there.

18. Now the fun begins: You are inviting everyone in your phone book, your mother's phone book, your father's phone book, the kids you went to school with and the man you worked for ten years ago who is now the manager.

19. You need a great invitation. You might want to use a photo that represents your film. This way you have branded your film and people can see your vision. Using postcards with an invitation on one side can work.

20. Creating an invitation just for this event is another way.

21. You need to send out four times the amount of invitations to get your core amount. If you want 100 people, send out 400 invitations and you can expect to get about 150 or so RSVPs and you may have 100 people show up (these are Hollywood statistics).

22. At the same time you want to find donors who will give you things you can auction off. Faun said that people sometimes ran the auction up to the full price because they wanted to get something for their donation.

23. Guide your donations toward women. Men say "Honey, I think we should donate" and the women say, "Okay, but what can I get for it?" (Sorry, gals, but that's true.)

24. Call hotels for rooms on the weekend when they are slow. You want to auction off two nights at the Hyatt or one night at the Hilton.

25. Each hotel has a PR person just for this reason, to give rooms away when you have something in return to offer them.

26. What's that? Demographics, demographics, demographics! My film audience, my party audience fits your demographics.

27. You have to do your demographics and know what your film fits; age 18 to 38 and median income of $80,000 is a good one. Hyatt and Hilton both want that group of people.

28. You call up the PR department and ask them to go on your website while you have them on the phone. You show them where you will put

their logo and then begin to tell them what you want. You pitch them the two minute short pitch that has everything in it.

29. They like the concept of the film, they say can't do two nights but can do one night, you say "Wonderful!"

30. It has to be an open-ended gift to be used in whatever time limit they give you.

31. Go after yoga lessons.

32. Wine by the case or six bottles at least.

33. Tango lessons. Who takes them? No one, but it sounds so romantic.

34. Bouquet of flowers.

35. Potted plants from a nursery.

36. Three hours in a limo, what woman would not like that?

37. A free tour of the opera house, etc. Be creative.

38. Go through the yellow pages and use your imagination. People love to be part of a movie and you're making a movie! You are a producer and they will be part of the funding for the film.

39. They will get a DVD of the finished film and be on your website as a donor.

40. Now you have a room and food, go after some free booze. That should be easy. Many liquor companies want to be in films or around film people.

41. What about entertainment? You are in the entertainment industry so who do you know that might be able to perform for 10 to 15 minutes for you? You might want some Latin dancers or some interesting musicians to play while people talk.

42. As the time draws closer, call your main person and tell them how things are progressing. Let them know that you have all these wonderful donors for silent auctions so people will go home with certificates for donating to your film, and "ask" them if they have any friends that you could invite? This is a big ASK. They should give you a few.

43. Send them packages first then call them and say "the mayor's wife suggested I invite you to this event as she/he is coming." Pitch it succinctly and focus on how much you need their support to make this film. When they say, "Okay", ask them if they can give you the name of any of their friends that might enjoy a great event like this because "Yolanda" is dancing or the local TV star is the host and it should be a fun evening.

44. When these people RSVP, ask for their friends names and invite them too. The same with the names from your mother and father's phone books call to see if they are coming and ask them for more names.

I know this is a lot of work but look what will you have at the end of the event:
- ◈ Tons of people who love you and your film
- ◈ A list of supporters for your emails
- ◈ Names for advice that may eventually bring you money
- ◈ A core group of donors for more parties and other films

YOUR FUNDRAISING TOOLBOX

The Ten-Minute Promo

A ten-minute promotional tape is one of the most valuable resources you can have in your fundraising toolbox. Barbara Leibovitz won the Roy W. Dean film grant with her promo for her film, Salvaged Lives. She was so confident she would win that she had her camera ordered and had me open the office at seven o'clock the next morning to get her raw stock! Less than a month later Barbara presented her uncut footage to the East Coast IFP where she secured more financing. This is what it takes to make a film. Visualizing is paramount to funding.

Film is a visual medium and it's hard to sell this kind of product on paper. Creating a five to ten-minute promo tape is one of your most important goals in the art of funding your film. Be sure to read my interview with Fernanda Rossi on creating your promo tape.

Win a Grant

Barbara knew winning the Roy W. Dean Film Grant would provide her with the needed equipment and professional services. Look for grants like this to support you in the beginning so you can get out there and start shooting. Winning a grant is like priming the pump; it will empower you as a filmmaker and start the ball rolling for more funds and donations. Potential investors and donors are more likely to fund a filmmaker who has already won a grant. Use the name of the donor on all of your grant applications and hire (or trade with) a public relations person to get the most you can from this first win.

P-a-r-t-y!

In *The Fundraising Houseparty*, author Morrie Warshawski tells filmmakers to find a wealthy supporter who shares their cause, and ask them if they would be willing to throw a fundraising party. If you find someone who is well connected, they will have an amazing house and an amazing guest list. Think about it. They will invite friends and associates who can write a $500 or $5,000 check without batting an eye! Pick up a copy of Morrie's book; he has perfected the fundraising houseparty down to the last detail, even the invitations (*www.warshawski.com*).

Try the "Mindy Pomper pasta party" or the "Faun Kime extravaganza." Full interviews with both filmmakers can be found on *www.fromtheheartproductions. com/interviews.shtml.*

Shoot Your Donors!

During your fundraising party have several experienced camera people with digital cameras roam the room and conduct short interviews with possible donors. Edit it on your home computer and produce a short video that addresses your film's cause while highlighting these featured interviews. Offer a copy to guests for a $100 donation. Follow up with everyone who purchased a copy and ask them if they would like to do a more formal interview in exchange for a tax-deductible donation.

I interviewed my dad using an old mini-VHS camera. He told wonderful stories about playing in watermelon patches in Dallas and how the boys would drop a ripe melon on the ground then dig their hands into it enjoying ever last bite. These tapes are priceless and I wouldn't trade them for the world. Think of ways to sell the concept of creating a family interview. It is a marvelous way to leave something for the grandchildren. You can set your own prices. You might charge $3,000 for an hour, $2,000 for 30 minutes. You are a professional film producer and you will be using the latest Hollywood equipment and techniques. Always sell the sizzle.

Give 'em Credit!

Have you ever noticed that some films seem to have more producers than cast? Producer credits are like money in the bank. An executive producer credit can be worth $50,000 or 50% of your budget while an associate producer might bring in $20,000. The numbers are based on your budget and the sky's the limit. Be creative and make up a title!

The next time you watch a film sit through the credits. When you come to the part that says, "The Producers wish to thank...", read the names and start adding. Each one of those names can be worth $1,000 or more. A full screen credit could be worth $3,000. A dedication to the memory of a sponsor's loved one could bring in $10,000 or more.

Finding and developing relationships with funders is hard work but take heart. The hardest part is going after your first funder. Once you get that out of the way you will build your portfolio of funders and other funders will follow. Before long you will create your own network of funding sources. Remember, if you are honest and professional it will be a positive experience and your funders will be there for future projects.

Mindy Pomper, Carole Dean.
Roy W. Dean Awards.

Carole Dean. Barbara Leibovitz.

CHAPTER 7

TENACITY PAYS OFF:

INTERVIEW WITH JILANN SPITZMILLER OF PHILOMATH FILMS

Philomath Films is headed by Jilann Spitzmiller and Hank Rogerson and is a film company that embraces characters and narratives on the fringe that have relevance for us all. In taking us outside of our normal assumptions and experiences, Philomath offers up projects that stretch the mind, entertain the spirit and reach straight for the heart. Their latest documentary feature, *Shakespeare Behind Bars*, embraces the cinema vérité narrative style that the company is known for; giving us a unflinching gaze into the dark areas of the human psyche and showing us that there is always the possibility of change. Philomath Films productions have won numerous awards including Audience Award at AFI Fest, Best of Show at Bend Film, and many Best Documentary Awards. Their work has debuted at festivals such as Sundance, SXSW, and Edinburgh, and has been broadcast around the world. They are three-time recipients of ITVS funding and two-time recipients of Sundance Institute funding. They were finalists and recipients of the Roy W. Dean Grant in 1999 and 2003, respectively. For more information, visit *www.philomathfilms.com*.

As producers who have completed three ITVS projects, what advice can you give producers who want their film on PBS?

We've been extremely fortunate to have been funded by ITVS three times — twice for the documentaries *Homeland* and *Shakespeare Behind Bars* — and once for a multimedia website, Circle of Stories, which plays at *pbs.org*. My husband and filmmaking partner, Hank Rogerson, and I have done all of the grant writing and producing together.

I think it's important to first understand the connection between ITVS and PBS. ITVS is funded by the Corporation for Public Broadcasting and is the largest funding service for independent programming on U.S. public television. If you are funded by ITVS, there is a very good chance your film will air on public television, but it is not guaranteed. It may run on national PBS or may be offered by ITVS to PBS affiliates if national PBS doesn't pick it up. It is best to check out their website for yourself, which is *www.itvs.org*.

I think we have been successful with ITVS funding for a few reasons. Number one, we keep in mind the ITVS mission, which is to serve underserved audiences — particularly minorities and children. ITVS provides broadcasting for American audiences, so we also keep that in mind. ITVS funds all genres of projects, including drama, documentary, docudrama, animation, experimental works or innovative combinations.

We have worked very hard on how we present our materials for the application. We've really developed concise and descriptive writing skills. You must be able to communicate your vision and story with detail and vitality. You've also got to have a dynamite work-in-progress tape that keeps people wanting to see more.

We are also very tenacious. We applied for funding five times on our last project, *Shakespeare Behind Bars*, until it was finally funded. Each time we were rejected, we got feedback on our proposal and reworked it according to ITVS readers' advice. After the third time applying, our proposal did not change much. What changed were the different reader groups that saw our proposal and finally we hit pay dirt with the right reader group. They liked the film and recommended it for funding.

Sometimes your proposal might be strong but you are unlucky with the composition of the reader group. Funding by committee is very subjective. After you have the writing down and are communicating your project clearly it becomes subjective *and this is an important part of the process, finding the funders who will be subjectively compelled to fund your film.*

What is the proposal process for ITVS?

The three-phase application process is pretty arduous and can take up to five months. The first phase you submit a fairly summarized proposal and work-in-progress tape. The second phase is just submitting more copies of your work-in-progress. The third phase is more involved, where you submit a longer proposal and more detailed budget information. There is also an unspoken fourth phase, which is if you are considered for funding, then you may need to negotiate the final funding amount and submit even further documentation supporting your ability to finish the film with that amount of funding.

What tips can you give us on creating the proposal for ITVS?

It is important to be able to describe how the film will look — the visual description, the style, who the characters are, what's interesting about them. How do the characters relate or contrast to each other and generally, what's the overall content or theme of the film.

Also, speak directly to the question of "why are you the right person to make this film." Convince them that you know this subject intimately and that you have the insight to make a compelling, outstanding film.

Your work-in-progress video tape is also essential and must quickly and effectively showcase your story, characters and your filmmaking ability. Sometimes we've spent several weeks or months just editing a sample tape until it strikes the right balance. It's helpful to screen it for a variety of people to see what they are getting from it before you submit it for funding.

From reading hundreds of applications I want to see the film from the written word and very few submissions are visual.

You might assume when writing an application you need to write about the themes, but you also need to write about what the film will look like, what the story structure is, what style you will use in your camera work, what type of sound, etc. All of these things need to be in this proposal. People are sitting in a room, perhaps at a desk reading piles of applications and if you don't make your film come alive immediately in language on the page, you will not make an impact on these readers who have the power to fund your film.

You aim for a visual description of the film, even if you are doing a documentary and you don't know how the film will play out?

Exactly. Even though documentaries are unpredictable in terms of what they will eventually look like or what story they will tell, you still need to consult your own personal crystal ball and predict what you think the outcomes will be. That also makes you a better filmmaker because it makes you question your idea and your characters and your content and it helps you see where there may be weak or boring spots.

How did you win the two Sundance grants?

Sundance was our first funder with *Shakespeare Behind Bars*. They came in with $15,000 seed money for R&D before the film had any footage, which is unusual these days. We then applied for a second round of money and we received $60,000, so we got their maximum grant of $75,000.

After we received the initial $15,000 for our idea, we submitted a second proposal for the production money. By then we knew more about our characters, what their story arcs might be and we had more teeth to put into the proposal. Once you start shooting you can add some details of scenes. I always do this; I even add direct quotes from characters to make it emotionally compelling. You might as well be writing a short story. *You have to put an immense amount of stock into the craft of writing your proposal.*

What did BBC ask for when they funded you?

After the award of Sundance's grants, BBC gave us 25% of our budget in return for a licensing period of 18 months for exclusive TV broadcasting in the UK. We actually cut a slightly different version for them according to their particular needs. After we finished the film to our liking, we then tailored it for them with their guidance.

ITVS was the last major funder to come into the project. We were actually weighing an offer between ITVS and HBO. The ITVS offer was more money so we went with them. They are a last-money-in funder; usually they will come in at the end of the film. If you have no funder and are going to ITVS you have to know if the maximum grant they give will cover your budget. ITVS wants to know you will definitely finish the film and that they can offer it to PBS and try to get a national broadcast.

We also won the Roy W. Dean Film Grant for *Shakespeare*, which helped us with a lot of in-kind services during production, post and distribution. The grant offers some interesting services like marketing help and a free screening in a beautiful screening room in L.A. We used this for an important press screening prior to our theatrical release of the film. We also applied to this one three or four times before we got it! Don't take no for an answer!

ITVS contracts for domestic TV only so do you also negotiate when you can sell to domestic DVD, schools and other markets?

Yes they license for domestic broadcast for four to six years and allow you to sell the other distribution avenues of your film. ITVS asks for approval of any sale agreements so they can verify that the ITVS name is on the product. They need to keep their name in front of audiences and they want to check your agreement to be sure the sale does not infringe on ITVS's rights. You can negotiate with them for a theatrical window and the street date of your DVD and a date for your educational sales. Many films made for ITVS do very well in educational markets, churches and libraries. You have a lot of opportunities for income through distribution.

Each time you make a sale arrangement; do you also return money to ITVS for the initial investment?

Yes, ITVS is our only funder that is getting a return on their money. They basically share your net profits in proportion to the amount of their funding.

It is important to know that ITVS puts a lot more into the film besides money. They devote a lot of staff time to getting your film out to the viewing audience. They put a lot into your outreach. They may build a website for the film and they have an in-house publicity person. There are many benefits to their funding beyond the financial assistance.

What is your next film?

We are currently co-producing a documentary with Roger Weisberg and Public Policy Productions about the health insurance crisis in American, "Money and Medicine" (working title), which will air on PBS in 2008 during the presidential campaign.

We're also developing a film about an unconventional school for juvenile delinquents.

Will you take this to a cable station?

We probably won't apply to ITVS initially because of the language, but I am not ruling them out entirely. You always want to keep all your options open.

Another great thing about ITVS is that you keep your copyright and you have editorial control. As filmmakers know, if you are working for a cable channel or a network you often will not have the final editorial control or the final cut.

ITVS WINNING DOCUMENTARY PROPOSAL

Shakespeare Behind Bars — a documentary film

Synopsis

Shakespeare Behind Bars is a documentary in postproduction about a diverse all-male Shakespeare company working within the confines of the U.S. prison system. The film follows 20 inmates for one year as they rehearse and perform a full production of a Shakespeare play at the Luther Luckett Correctional Complex in LaGrange, Kentucky. Five of these men are followed in-depth. In this prison atmosphere, theater is changing their lives, as the words of Shakespeare act as a catalyst for these inmates to examine their past with remarkable candor. They are all individuals who have committed the most heinous crimes, and are now confronting and performing those crimes on stage. In this process, we see these unlikely men testing the power of truth, change, and forgiveness.

Treatment

The film *Shakespeare Behind Bars* opens on two men in a wide, golden field learning a speech from Shakespeare's The Tempest. The camera begins in close as they work on the piece, bringing passion to the famous line, "We are such stuff as dreams are made on..." As their energy builds, the camera pulls further and further back to reveal the larger picture — these men are behind many barriers of barbed wire and metal. An armed guard watches them through binoculars from a tower nearby. But for a moment in time, these two inmates are transported from the bars of prison to the place where creativity and dreams reside (*see WIP tape, start*).

Shakespeare Behind Bars, the film, is about this journey — how the words of Shakespeare act as a vehicle to transport this group of incarcerated men to a potentially better place in their hearts and minds. In this unusual prison theatre program, they have the support and encouragement needed in order to examine their darkest selves, and to shed light on how they might find healing and redemption.

The film will be structured around the creative journey of one year in the life of this group that calls themselves "Shakespeare Behind Bars." This is their seventh year, and the troupe will be performing *The Tempest*, Shakespeare's last play. Combining several genres, *The Tempest* has elements of romance, tragedy and comedy. The play focuses on Forgiveness as the main theme, and also explores the ideas of Isolation, Nature vs. Nurture, and the Father-Daughter relationship. The inmates will cast themselves according to their own crimes, backgrounds and what they are willing to take on emotionally. They will work intensely with volunteer director, Curt Tofteland. Curt is part director, part therapist, part mentor, part father to these men. Whenever they can, the inmates rehearse on their own during Curt's absence. And just as in Shakespeare's day, men play all the female roles.

The film begins in the fall at the start of rehearsals as the men cast themselves and progresses as they rehearse and develop their characters throughout the year. The viewer is a fly on the wall at cast read-through where the men grapple with the text, and have intense one-on-one discussions with Curt who constantly pushes them to find their personal experience within each part. The film will focus on certain key, pivotal scenes of *The Tempest* and revisit them in both rehearsal and performance footage. Through the actors' journeys, viewers will vicariously examine and understand the timeless language, characters and themes of Shakespeare, which can sometimes seem daunting to audiences.

At the heart of the film are the conflicts that the men struggle with inside themselves. As the year progresses, the parallels between themselves and their characters is enlightening and sometimes uncanny. Our audience will first be introduced to these men simply as actors. Their past acts will be revealed gradually over the course of the film to build dramatic tension. Each interview will go deeper into the reasons why they committed their crime, their feelings about their actions, where they are emotionally in the current moment, and how the words of Shakespeare are helping them to process these complicated issues. (See character descriptions below.)

Shakespeare Behind Bars will not glorify these men or excuse their crimes, but rather attempt to take a more humane look at them. The objective of *Shakespeare Behind Bars* is to give audiences a close-up, visceral experience — a unique look at prisons and the incarcerated. To go beyond political rhetoric about crime and the need for more prisons. To shed light on a program that costs the taxpayer nothing, and to profile dedicated individuals who are tackling the shortcomings of the American prison system.

By following these men through this creative process, the film explores the universal themes of redemption, transformation and forgiveness. It will raise questions for the viewer such as: Should we rehabilitate criminals? How does art transform the human conscience? Who deserves forgiveness? The inmates' interviews address these probing questions and provide revealing answers. Because of the unlikely setting of prison, these themes and issues are given a fresh, new angle, and will provide a broad and varied appeal for many communities across the U.S.

The Context

The statistics on the U.S. prison system are jarring, and title cards interspersed throughout the film will help put this particular prison program in context. Since 1980, the prison population in America has quadrupled, while the violent crime rate has stayed about the same. Today more than 60% of those in prison are there for non-violent crimes, and in the past twenty years social programs for education, drug rehabilitation, job training, Head Start, affordable housing, and legal aid have been cut to help fund 700 new prisons nationwide. At the current rate, by 2020, approximately 60% of black males between the ages of 18-34 will be behind bars; 12 million people will be incarcerated nationwide.

Also adding insight will be the prison's progressive and genial warden, **Larry Chandler** (*see WIP, 04:30*). He personally believes in trying to rehabilitate prisoners in a political climate that is largely about throwing away the key. He talks about how politics dictate the way in which the prison system is run, and how this interferes with effective reform. "I guess I'm just a warden who hates prisons," he laughs. "More than anything, the day they come in, you ought to start preparing them for the day they leave." Statistics support his view, as 97% of the Luther Luckett population will be released to walk the streets again. Warden Chandler runs a reform minded institution, which concentrates on education in hopes of making the inmates better members of society. The Shakespeare Behind Bars Program is a part of the overall attempt by Luther Luckett to reform its population through education, therapy and job training, and new members of the Shakespeare Program must have a clean prison record, and be sponsored into the group by a veteran member. Since the program began in 1995, of the 20 inmates who have participated in the Shakespeare company and then been released, only two have returned to jail. This 10% recidivism is far below the national average of 41%. This information will be presented on title cards.

The Characters

The characters in *Shakespeare Behind Bars* are not your ordinary, stereotypical prisoners. These guys are "the best of the best," or so they say at Luther Luckett. Luther Luckett is the most rehabilitatively focused prison in the Kentucky system. It has the most educational and therapeutic programs, and prisoners here are expected to partake, or they get transferred to a prison with less to offer. And within this general population at Luther Luckett, one has to have a clean record to join the Shakespeare group. As a result, at first glance, most of the men in this program do not seem to be hardened criminals. But their past actions all have a deep darkness that haunts them.

Leonard Ford (Caucasian) says that he and the group are "ready to go" with the new season after their summer hiatus. "We're all people trying to achieve something unique for ourselves and take advantage of this process," he says as we see him and the others playing theater games (*see WIP, 10:00*). He underscores that this is no ordinary acting troupe — that they will likely have to deal with someone getting sent to solitary confinement or getting transferred, and will have to recast roles midstream. Leonard is the intellectual of the group, and his work in rehearsals and his interviews provide the film with thought provoking moments from a philosophical mind confined behind bars with plenty of time to contemplate. Leonard believes that Shakespeare Behind Bars is subversive — "It subverts society's desire to separate me from humanity." In 1995, Leonard was married with four kids and working as a computer programmer. He was highly respected within his church community and even ran for the office of mayor. Today, he is serving a 50-year sentence for sexual abuse of minors. At the start of the film, after seven years in prison, he evades questions about his crime. But Leonard says he looks forward to working on *The Tempest* and its theme of isolation — it takes place on a deserted island — and playing the role of the villain, Antonio. "He's a villain who does not get what he deserves, and that's unique." In years past, Leonard has always played the villain, and although he tried to avoid doing so this year, he ended up with the role when another cast member got transferred in the first week of rehearsals.

Over the course of the film, Leonard's role of villain takes on literal meaning within the walls of Luther Luckett. "I pray to God it doesn't get much lower than this," says Leonard in January, dressed in a green jump suit, his hands shackled (*see WIP, 33:50*). "Antonio is fun to play, but not one to mimic in real life." In an ironic self-fulfilling prophecy, Leonard has become the cast member sent to "the Hole," or solitary confinement. "A prison within a prison." On day 21 of a 90 day stint in the Hole (for allegedly messing with the prison's computer system), he is a stark example of the effectiveness of isolation. He appears shell-shocked and his interview is raw. For the first time, Leonard admits to his crime of sexually abusing seven girls. He has spent a lot of time in the hole rehearsing his lines to blank walls, and thinking about mercy. As he makes his bed, washes his hands, eats his lunch alone, we hear a cacophony of delirious inmates shouting obscenities at each other from their solitary cells. "It seems that those who need mercy the most are those who deserve it the least." Even though he has been rehearsing in solitary, Leonard will never get the chance to play the role of Antonio. Two weeks later he is shipped to another prison in Kentucky. "Antonio" has to be recast, and ultimately, this new actor, Rick Sherroan, also gets thrown in the Hole just days before the performances. The group must recruit a new inmate who has no acting experience but who admirably learns blocking and lines in only four days.

Sammie Byron (African American/Hispanic) is a leader and mentor in the group, and has been in the Shakespeare program for seven years. This year, as he prepares for possible parole in August, he will take a smaller role in the play and will help coach less experienced members of the troupe. At the beginning of the rehearsal process, he performs the famous St. Crispian's speech from *Henry V* to inspire the new guys (*see WIP, 13:00*). Sammie is a survivor of physical and sexual abuse who had created a seemingly stable adult life with a wife and a successful business. He threw it all away, however, when he strangled his mistress almost 20 years ago. He is now serving his 20th year of a life sentence. As one of the original members of the program, Sammie feels Shakespeare has been a vehicle for him and the guys. "In rehearsals we deal with our own personal pains and what it is we need to change our behavior...it changes lives. It's changed me." Sammie tells us that while playing Othello two years ago, he experienced a breakthrough when forced to strangle Desdemona, his wife, on stage. (Stills from that production will be used to help illustrate this event.) In reliving his crime, he was able to examine the reasons it occurred and then began taking steps to change himself through therapy and job training at the prison. *The Tempest* provides Sammie with an opportunity to further explore forgiving himself, as he works towards his parole hearing a few months after the performance of the play.

Over the course of the film, we see Sammie preparing to be set free after 20 years in prison, while at the same time coping with the fact that he may never get out. "My emotional state — that's what worries me the most about getting out," he says. "Cause I don't want to make the same mistakes I made in the past." Although Sammie is nervous about leaving prison, everyone else in the group is confident that he will make parole and do well in the transition to life on the outside. They look to him as a mentor, not only regarding Shakespeare, but also as someone who has truly grown and changed in prison.

Hal Cobb (Caucasian, homosexual) is hoping for insight and forgiveness regarding his crime, and he lobbied hard to play the lead role. "There is a part of me that wants to play Prospero, and there is a part of me that wants to run" (*see WIP, 06:45*). He knows too well that he will have to confront his demons by playing a controlling and plotting vengeful type, who in the end chooses forgiveness. He speaks about only knowing numbness while growing up, and never being allowed to communicate his real feelings. Hal grew up in a fundamentalist family, went to Bible college, became a preacher, got married and had a daughter. But he felt he was living a lie and going to hell because he was a closeted homosexual. One morning he electrocuted his pregnant wife in the bathtub by knocking a hair dryer into the water (*see WIP, 55:15*). After passing his wife's death off as an accident, he moved to Los Angeles with their small daughter and began studying acting. Ten years later he confessed his crime in a 12-step program, and his roommate turned him in. In the eight years he has been in prison, he has not seen his daughter because she requested they not communicate. She is now 19. Hal will play Prospero in *The Tempest*, who, along with his daughter, has been banished to an island for 12 years. He hopes that playing Prospero will bring him closer to his own daughter and closer to gaining her forgiveness. "Resolution can't come without communication, and not talking is what got me here... my hope is for one day to find forgiveness, and I hope this play will help me do that."

Throughout the year, Hal dedicates an enormous amount of time and energy to the play. He researches his role and the theme of Forgiveness in the prison library, and constantly coaches others on their parts. Eventually, as the months pass, he realizes that this is all just a distraction from "the true work" he needs to do. "It's difficult to reverse 46 years of suppressing," he says as we see him receiving his daily medication of Zoloft. "I feel like if I really allow myself to feel all my shame and anger, I may never surface." By performance time, Hal realizes the only forgiveness he can ever expect is his own.

"Red" Herriford (African American/Caucasian) will play Prospero's naïve and virginal daughter. Red is currently at Luther Luckett for armed robbery, and has severe learning disabilities. As a consequence, he has always played smaller roles in the Shakespeare group, but this year, he is stepping up to play the much larger part of Miranda, the 15-year-old female ingénue. But it is not a role he chose willingly. He feels that Hal and others "put the role on him" because of his size and looks. Then, despite himself, one day in rehearsal he connects deeply with his character when he realizes that, like Miranda, he was told at age 15 of his true lineage — that the father he had never known was white. The parallel with his chosen character shocks him, and opens him to exploring his own pain, confusion and anger regarding his past. "It's hard to explain. This part here is just perfectly, truly for me... these virtues, and these feelings I'm having." Red struggles to articulate in front of the other men who at once support him and tease him for identifying with a young woman's pain (see WIP, 18:00).

Over the course of rehearsals, Red is constantly irritated by others and what he takes as their criticism. As he exits rehearsal one day, he says to Sammie that he is frustrated with Hal because he is so controlling, "just like my own father. Always in power." This father-child dynamic continues to play itself out for the rest of the film, and is another example in the film of the striking parallels between the characters in the play and the inmates.

Richard Hughes (Native American/Hispanic) believes that he "will never be redeemed by his Creator." A former Marine scout sniper, he killed 48 people in Lebanon, and another 12 in Desert Storm. But he is not proud of this since he feels it "sucked all the humanness out of me," as he became "a robot performing someone else's mission." One night five years ago he killed another man, execution style, who had threatened his fiancé. Brought up in a climate of violence by his father who was also in the military, Richard sees incarceration as his vision quest. Reconnecting with his Native American heritage, he regularly holds Cherokee ceremonies on the prison yard, and he is learning the Cherokee language, both of which we filmed. Richard is a "newbie" in the theater group, being sponsored by one of the group's old-timers. He sees Shakespeare Behind Bars as a possible tool to help him regain a sense of the humanity within himself. It's also a way to keep the boredom of prison life at bay.

In the early spring, Richard reaches a major personal milestone with his character, Sebastian, when he realizes that he has always been a "Sebastian" — a follower who did everything to please others (see WIP, 43:45). "My character is me — I've been a Sebastian all my life." He has the epiphany as he realizes for the first time that he did not have to kill his victim, that he did have a choice. An in-depth discussion in rehearsal occurs concerning this. Another member named Gene Vaughn offers that when one begins to take responsibility for their own actions, it is then that they start to heal and change. "I've been trying to rationalize what I did," Richard responds. "But each time I tried to justify the murder, a little voice said maybe it ain't quite right." He continues to work through this revelation until the performances.

Curt Tofteland is a lifetime Shakespearean actor and director who has been coming to Luther Luckett to work with adult male inmates in the "Shakespeare Behind Bars" program since 1995. The film will touch upon Curt's journey, as a person coming in from the outside, trying to help repair lives devastated by acts of self-destruction. Although he works with professional actors most of the year, he says that working with this group of inmates is far more rewarding because of their courage and dedication. Curt also thinks Shakespeare would have appreciated this motley acting company of convicts. "People in the theater back in Elizabethan times were thought of as pickpockets, thieves, rapists and murderers." Curt believes in seeing these men for who they are today, not for who they were, and not as defined solely by the crime they have committed. For Curt, his key direction for these guys is: "Tell the truth."

Dramatic Structure

The film will follow a three-act structure and will largely play out like a character piece. What supplies much of the dramatic tension will be the pace at which information is revealed about each of our characters. We will learn about each main character's crime at different points in the film, beginning with Sammie in Act One, followed by Leonard, Richard and Red in Act Two, and finally Hal in Act Three. As the viewer gets to know them as actors, they will begin to wonder what these seemingly charming and interesting men could possibly have done. Then, as the viewer learns about each dark past, they will have to wrestle with the conflicts presented by appearance versus truth, character versus action, past versus present, vengeance versus forgiveness. As Prospero learns to forgive those who wronged him in the play, the viewer will go on the same journey, deciding whether or not to forgive these felons in the film.

Act One of the film will set up our main characters and their inner conflicts, as well as the external conflicts they are dealing with, such as going up for parole after 20 years in prison, in Sammie Byron's case, or trying to reconcile with family, as with Hal Cobb. It will lay out the main themes of *The Tempest*, and give a clear idea of how the Shakespeare program is run and directed by Curt. For the viewer, the text of Shakespeare becomes more accessible, as we see Curt breaking it down, and the guys beginning to learn and understand it. We'll get a solid sense of place at Luther Luckett, as the film crew was allowed unfettered access to daily life in the prison. And as rehearsals begin to take off, we will see how the words and characters of Shakespeare are beginning to open the men up, exposing emotions and issues that need to be resolved.

Act Two will provide for further character development as rehearsals progress, and as interviews deepen. In this act, more of prison life is shown as a backdrop to these interview sequences — such as inmates receiving their daily meds, doing laundry, in the cafeteria chow line, or seeing their families during weekly visiting hours. In rehearsals, a general sense of ennui has taken hold as the guys are at different levels of commitment with the play, and the performances seem like a long way off. Key events of this act will be Leonard getting thrown in the Hole and Richard's epiphany.

Act Two continues to build toward the performances and the tension and nerves in the group are starting to rise, as evident in vérité scenes in rehearsal. Sammie steps back as the group's leader in order to let some one else take charge, but at this point they are a "ship without a captain." Both in rehearsals and on the yard, guys are critical of each other, and arguing as their egos clash. Some of these men are learning to use communication skills for the first time, and understanding how to take and give criticism, as well as how to work in a group. As Red says, "This is what happens when you put together a cast of convicts. It ain't Mary Poppins theatre." This is illustrated perfectly when the cast loses their Antonio once again, as Rick gets thrown in the Hole for selling drugs. In a humorous scene that breaks some of the tension, we see the men, about 20 this time, rehearsing on the recreation yard without Curt's supervision. They choreograph the play's banquet scene into a free-form break dancing sequence, and create a rap song from Shakespeare's text.

Act Three. Finally, May arrives and it's performance time (*see WIP, 1 hr.*). With two cameras catching all the action, we see Sammie speaking his lines to the wall, Hal and Red holding hands, Richard checking entrances and exits with the "new" Antonio, Ray, and Curt shouting orders to anyone who will listen. The men huddle up and with a "1-2-3 Shakespeare!" the play begins. The first performance is for the prison population and will briefly cover parts of some scenes from the first half of *The Tempest*. These will be scenes that are already familiar to the viewer, since we can recognize them from the rehearsal process (such as the scene where Red connected with his character, Miranda, for the first time.) This performance footage will be intercut with audience cutaways and backstage footage, such as the guys coming backstage to apologize to each other for missing lines, or high-fiving another cast member for a job well done.

The rest of *The Tempest* will be briefly covered in footage from the second performance, which is done for friends and family. Once again, key scenes and lines will be highlighted, such as Prospero's line "The rarer act is in virtue/than in vengeance" (*see WIP, 1 hr. 9 min.*). These moments will also be intercut with backstage shots — Hal adjusting Red's costumes, Sammie looking out at his family. The play comes to a close and the men have an opportunity to speak to their families. For Hal, none of his family comes, but a former member of his church shows up to support him. Sammie is overcome with grief, unsure whether this is his last play at Luther Luckett. The energy is high, the emotions are deep, but the moment is brief, as the men must get back to their dorms to be counted. In a slow dissolve sequence, we see the men exit the visiting room for a final time as the lights go out.

Epilogue: It is the fall of 2003, and Sammie Byron did not get parole in August. He was given six more years. But in a bizarre turn of events, he will be getting out of Luther Luckett for a short period of time, as he and the inmates are going "on tour" with The Tempest (see WIP, 1 hr. 10 min.). Transporting prisoners is an enormous security risk, so the men will be shackled and wearing orange jumpsuits as they are given the opportunity to see the outside. A familiar face rejoins the cast as Leonard Ford has come back to Luther Luckett, and for the first time he will not play a villain. He will replace one of the fairies.

The second prison they visit is a woman's prison where the reception is electric. The women get charged up by the performance, and it's Gospel meets Shakespeare. It's a high note after a year of soul searching and hard work. The Epilogue will be used to tie up story arcs with title cards over footage. Over the course of the year and the film, we will see men changed — enriched, challenged, awakened, and fulfilled. In a time of ever-shrinking funding for the arts, this documentary demonstrates to general public television audiences the universal idea that a creative process offers everyone the opportunity to change.

Shakespeare Behind Bars on **Public Television**

Public television and this program will be a perfect match up for several reasons. This film will raise vital issues regarding the role of rehabilitation in the criminal justice and U.S. prison system — issues that deserve more public discourse and consideration as we continue as a society to put more and more people behind bars as a "solution" to crime. As prisons become severely overcrowded and more privatized into commercial corporations, the questions regarding how much rehabilitation should exist and what works deserve further examination. In addition, the film raises the larger question of the relevance of art in society, and whether or not the arts can be a path to growth and a source of healing.

Public television, and specifically the participation of ITVS, affords a project such as this an important element of public outreach, which will result in viable public dialogue on these issues. This film would not have the same impact on a commercial cable channel. A public television broadcast offers far greater opportunities to promote follow-up discussion groups, both in communities and on the World Wide Web. For these reasons, the filmmakers would like this film to be accessible to the widest possible audience, not just those who are able to subscribe to pay TV.

Communities Who Will Benefit From This Program

This film will appeal to and serve citizens in a wide range of disciplines, such as those interested in public policy; the criminal justice system; the arts; theatre; education; and psychology. These categories touch people in all geographical and cultural corners of the U.S. In addition, prison issues are relevant in any community, due to the prevalence of prisons nationwide. In terms of racial and social communities, the cast of characters in the film is quite diverse, but their stories are universal in nature. In addition, anyone who is interested in the psychological healing process — whether to address grief, anger, or abuse, among other issues — can draw inspiration from this film. This film also has a valuable educational aspect, potentially demystifying Shakespeare for viewers.

Most specifically, this film can inspire dialog for the incarcerated, as well as those working with or who are touched by the criminal justice system, including victims and law enforcement. This Shakespeare program can serve as a model to others who would like to explore healing through the arts. And the focus on incarcerated men gives voice to people who have been largely forgotten by society.

Convicts are often stereotyped, stigmatized and disenfranchised even though they may be striving to change, or have successfully put their past behind them.

Filmmaker's Relationship to Subject/Community

Director Hank Rogerson has been an actor for over ten years and has been involved in Shakespeare and other theatre programs throughout his career. While directing the film, he was able to understand the inmate's journeys as actors, and could bring to light those internal processes of discovery that happen when studying a part. For example, Hank asked Red about playing the role of 15-year-old Miranda, and how he would physicalize the part. He asked Red "How would a 15-year-old girl stand?" It's something that Red hasn't thought of yet, and the moment is poignant and revealing as Red envisions the delicateness and innocence of the body language of his character (*see WIP, 18:00*).

Shooting Format, Style, Approach

Shakespeare Behind Bars is shot in 16x9 on DV cam, in a cinema vérité style — straightforward and intimate, revealing the emotional journeys that the inmates are taking. Complete access within the prison itself has yielded a variety of footage of life inside the wire and will provide for textured montages of prison life. We filmed our main characters in a wide variety of activities, in order to avoid too many "talking heads," and this vérité footage will be woven together with interview clips.

Transitions between scenes will consist of anonymous, close-up shots of prison life, which convey the tedium and repetition of daily life. And the film will use the visual theme of reflection — in mirrors, windows or puddles — to underscore the inmates' own process of self-reflection in the Shakespeare program. The film will have some titles to give background on the inmates, the prison, and the prison system in the U.S. The film's opening theme song will be a polished version of a rap called "Honor" that the inmates created using text from *The Tempest* (*see WIP, 1 hr. 08 min.*). The soundtrack will have ensemble instrumental music, as well as rap and hip-hop themes, echoing the music created by the inmates for the play. The sound design will incorporate the natural sounds of prison — steel doors, P.A. calls for count, crickets mixing with the electric buzz of floodlights.

The editing will reflect the moods of the scenes themselves, whether it is heated scene in rehearsal, or a slow scene of a man praying in his cell. We will also experiment with the convention of time, using slow motion, freeze frame and time-lapse.

Length Considerations

In cutting this film to 56:40 for public television, we may find that five characters are too many to follow. At this point, however, we cannot say which of the five we would be eliminating. This will be revealed through the editing process.

CHAPTER 8

FINANCING INDEPENDENT FILMS:

A CONVERSATION WITH
ENTERTAINMENT ATTORNEY MARK LITWAK

Mark Litwak has been a donor for my Roy W. Dean Film and Video Grants for over ten years, and is a great patron of the art of filmmaking. Top filmmakers quote Mark on a daily basis. I sincerely believe Mark's books are a good investment, whether you are new at filmmaking or a seasoned veteran. You will save problems and avoid giving away the store if you have a solid grasp of the legalities of the film industry. Visit Mark's website at www.marklitwak.com, where you can find more about his books and read many helpful articles that he has written and posted for filmmakers like you.

Mark, in your article you talk about several ways to finance films. Which would you say is the most common and why?

There are several ways to finance films including by territory pre-sales, investors, studio funds or some combination. Many documentaries are funded with grants and donations.

The popularity of each financing method varies over time. At one time, a lot of pre-sales were being used to finance production but right now it is very hard to do presales because there is a glut of completed films on the market, and buyers often prefer to license a completed film than take a chance on a project to be produced. Most first-time filmmakers do not have the track record and ability to attract the name actors necessary to make pre-sales.

Nowadays filmmakers mostly rely upon equity investments for financing and production incentives such as tax breaks and refunds from various states and countries that help subsidize the making of a film. A new federal law — the 2004 tax act — provided new IRC Section 181, which permits a 100% write-off for the cost of certain motion pictures. Under the new law, independent producers may write off a movie in a single year if 75% of that budget is spent in the United States. The limit goes up to $20 million if the movie is made in a low-income area of the U.S. Under this legislation, the cost of producing qualifying films can be fully deducted from income for tax purposes in the year the expenditures occur. Principal photography must commence after October 22, 2004, but before January 1, 2009. This federal incentive can be combined with state incentives. Puerto Rico offers a 40% rebate. Hawaii and Louisiana also have very generous incentives for investors. A listing of state, federal and international incentives can be found at *www.marklitwak.com/resources/domestic_programs.html*.

Is Canada still subsidizing productions?

Yes, Canada provides incentives and so do many other countries. In addition to the incentives offered, at times there is a favorable exchange rate when converting U.S. dollars to Canadian dollars, which can be an added attraction. Likewise, in some countries in Eastern Europe production expenses are so low that the net effect is similar to shooting in a country offering a generous incentive.

Have you heard that the New Zealand Film Commission will match up to $2.5 million in funds if your film has "strong New Zealand" content and uses New Zealand people on the crew and for post?

I know that both New Zealand and Australia have very popular programs to encourage production. We have an extensive listing of production incentives available in various countries including New Zealand and Australia, and also have a listing of the incentives various states offer. Both are posted on my website: Entertainment Legal Resources at *www.marklitwak.com*.

Mark, how early in production do you believe filmmakers should see an attorney?

It depends on the experience of the filmmaker and whether there are legal issues that need to be resolved. For a first timer pretty early, for an experienced filmmaker, he or she may not need help for a while. There are some filmmakers who may have a legal education and lots of practical experience, who may never need help from an attorney.

I know of cases where filmmakers did not get the appropriate releases and paperwork and ended up spending more on attorneys later in the production than they would have if they had consulted with one early in production.

That's often the case. Sometimes filmmakers produce a film and cannot obtain distribution for it because they did not properly secure their copyright. I know of a producer who did not get a release from an actor, and then lost touch with that actor, and could not locate him. This caused problems when it came time to demonstrate to the distributor that the filmmaker had rights to the actor's work.

In some instances if you are raising money from third parties, you need to see an attorney before you accept funds to make sure you are complying with the law. If the person giving you the money is doing so because they are making an investment, their interest is considered a security, unless the investor is actively involved in producing the film. And if securities are involved, then you need to comply with state and federal securities laws. You may need to make certain disclosures, which is usually done via a private placement memorandum (PPM). This document discloses all the risks of the investment to potential investors before you accept their money.

If someone wants to give you money as a gift, that is, with no expectations or obligations attached, mazel tov! Take the gift and thank them — you don't have to comply with the laws that govern investments, although gifts are sometimes taxable, and the gift giver may want to obtain a tax deduction.

In documentaries there are often donations of money or in-kind services. There may be gifts from family or friends or charitable contributions. In order for the person making the gift to receive a tax deduction they may want to give the money to a 501(c)3 corporation, a type of nonprofit entity. If you don't have your own 501(c)3 corporation, you can arrange with an existing one to serve as an umbrella organization for you. The International Documentary Association offers this service. They will accept the money, take a small administrative fee, and then pass the funds on to the filmmaker. This enables the gift giver to receive a tax deduction and allows the filmmaker to make their film.

How should you handle gifts?

If someone is making a gift, that should be clear to both parties up front. It is a good idea to have the donor confirm in writing that a gift is intended. If they are giving you money and they expect to share in any kind of revenues from the film, then it is not a gift, but an investment. If the film does not generate revenue, then the investment may be a write-off, and the investor may be able to take it as a loss on their income tax return. Remember, films are risky investments.

When someone is making a gift there are usually few legal issues involved, for example a large gift might be subject to gift tax. But investments are governed by complex security laws at the state and federal level that try to protect investors from being defrauded and taken advantage of.

When filmmakers bring their film ideas to you, do you help them with the investment package?

Yes, we can prepare a private placement memorandum (PPM) and related documents.

Does the filmmaker give you the creative side?

Yes, in preparing the PPM the client supplies a synopsis of the story, a budget summary, and bios of the people involved. We take care of all of the legal disclosures, and all of the descriptions of how the movie business works, all the risk factors, and all the required legal notices.

What about ancillary rights of books or music? Does this go into the original package?

If you are making a feature, then ancillary rights and other sources of revenue can include home video, TV, book novelizations, soundtrack albums, merchandising, etc. The filmmaker can include these sources of revenue in the film's gross receipts and share them with investors. They can also be excluded from the revenues shared with investors, but this may discourage investors from participation in the project. At any rate, revenue from ancillary sources needs to be clearly addressed when dealing with investors.

Have you been successful in helping filmmakers find funding once you have created the package?

We are lawyers, not investment bankers or fundraisers. The task of raising financing is usually borne by the producer. The attorney makes sure the producer is complying with the law. However, on some occasions we have assisted our clients by introducing them to sources of financing or making suggestions how to structure a deal attractive to investors or distributors.

What is gap financing? Is it still popular?

Gap financing has to do with financing based on presales. Presales are when a filmmaker or a distributor approaches a distributor for a country, before the film is produced, and persuades this distributor to sign a contract to pay a license fee for the distribution rights to the film when it is completed. If the contracts are with reputable and solvent distributors, the filmmaker can use these contracts as collateral for a production loan. The filmmaker borrows money from a bank, which may lend 80 to 90% of the licensee fees in the contracts.

The filmmaker produces the film and delivers it to the distributors who have licensed it. The distributors pay their license fee to the bank that lent the funds to the producer. The filmmaker can make additional sales and earn profits from licenses to unsold territories.

Gap financing is when the bank is lending you more money than the value of the presale contracts. Let's say you make distribution deals for Germany, Spain and Italy. The total face value of all these distribution deals is $500,000. But you need to borrow $600,000 to produce your film. The difference between the amount covered by licensee fees in the contracts, and the amount borrowed, is the gap. Banks charge additional interest for covering this gap because they are taking greater risk. If the film is made and you don't enter into any other licensing agreements, then the bank may suffer a loss. Gap financing is therefore more expensive to the filmmaker.

I noticed that most producers create a Limited Liability Company instead of a C or S Corporation. Why is this?

An LLC is a relatively new vehicle, and has some advantages over a corporate form of organization in that it allows the profits and losses to be passed through to the members without being taxed at the company level. This avoids the problem of double taxation that you might have with a C corporation where the income for the corporation is taxed, and then the same money is taxed again when paid out in the form of dividends to investors. This reduces the flow of money back to the investors.

Another way to avoid double taxation is to set up a partnership, which passes profits and losses through to the partners. Here there is no taxation at the company level. But the problem with partnerships is that there is no limited liability for the general partners, only for the limited partners. So the general partners may be concerned that they may lose their houses or other assets if they are sued because the company has defaulted on its contractual obligations.

By setting up an LLC you have all of the advantages of the partnership form of business without the liability exposure imposed on the general partners. In an LLC you have managing members of the LLC, who are typically the producers, and the non-managing members, who are the investors. They both receive limited liability and there's no double taxation because the LLC can elect to have the IRS treat it like a partnership for tax purposes, that is, all the profits and losses pass through to the members. That's why the LLC form of business has become so popular. But LLCs are not always appropriate. In some instances it may be wiser to set up a corporation or a partnership, or use some other business entity.

Do you see theatres moving to digital cinema in the future?

Yes, increasing numbers of theatres will be exhibiting pictures digitally. Ultimately, movies will also be distributed digitally, which will result in much more efficient and cost-effective means of distribution than the present system of shipping prints. Digital distribution could be accomplished by beaming the picture by satellite from the studio directly to the theatres where it will be captured on a computer hard disk and then exhibited. Information such as how many times the movie was shown could be beamed back to the distributor. The studios will be able to avoid the expense of having to ship thousands of 35mm celluloid prints to theaters and back, and they won't have to pay for environmentally sound disposal of old prints. The major studios could save close to a billion dollars a year in print and distribution expenses if films were digitally distributed.

One could also distribute digitally over an Internet or broadband connection, or by shipping packaged media, such as a DVD, to a theater. That would be less expensive than shipping a 35mm print, which is quite heavy and bulky.

The big obstacle to digital cinema is that most of the savings of changing to a digital distribution system inures to the benefit of the distributors — the studios — but the cost for buying digital projection equipment and servers, which are fairly expensive, is an expense that has traditionally been borne by theatre owners — the exhibitors.

Exhibitors already have 35mm projectors, which last many years, and they are not anxious to spend more money to install digital technology in their theatres if most of the savings go to the studios. Recently studios and exhibitors have agreed on some formulas for sharing the cost of the transformation to digital.

The theatre owners wouldn't see a return on their investment from new digital equipment?

If someone comes to your theatre and sees the movie on a digital screen instead of from a traditional screen, they pay the same price for a ticket and some popcorn. So from the point of view of the local theatre owner, why pay $50,000 to install a digital projection system if it doesn't generate any additional revenue?

Would you say we are going to experience an explosion of low-budget films on the market due to the new digital technology?

It has happened already. There are an enormous number of low-budget films being made on digital media. Some of the digital media is better than others. The 24P high definition cameras have very good quality. The lower level stuff is not quite as good, but people are able to make their movies for much less money. than shooting on film. By shooting digitally, you don't have to pay for developing and processing. Plus digital cameras are inexpensive. If you buy a Mac computer, for $100 extra you get a version of Final Cut Pro that allows you to edit a movie on your computer.

What legal advice would you give to a first-time filmmaker?

I think it really depends on the filmmaker and their level of industry expertise. Filmmakers need to spend a lot of time perfecting their craft as a filmmaker, and also gain an understanding of the business side of the industry, including what they can and cannot do legally. They need to know what sort of rights they need to secure in order to make a film, and how to protect themselves from liability. They can do this by consulting an attorney or by reading and educating themselves.

Filmmakers also need to be aware of the marketplace for films, and whether there will be a market for their film once finished. It can be educational to visit film markets like AFM to learn which types of films attract distributors around the world.

I have written a book called *Deal Making in the Film and Television Industry*, which is a primer for filmmakers to learn about many of the legal issues involved in production.

Is this available on your website at *www.marklitwak.com*?

Yes, and at *Amazon.com* and most bookstores. It is widely available. The publisher is Silman-James Press.

Would you call this book Filmmaking Legalities 101?

Yes, it definitely is.

Independent Film Financing

The following was written and edited by Mark Litwak. (Author's note: These materials are offered for use as a teaching tool only. They are designed to help you understand some of the legal issues you may encounter in the entertainment business and enable you to better communicate with your lawyer. They are not offered as legal advice, nor should they be construed as such. They are not a substitute for consulting with an attorney and receiving advice based on your facts and circumstances. Moreover, the cases and laws cited are subject to change and they may not apply in all jurisdictions.)

Independent films can be financed in a variety of ways. In addition to filmmakers using their own funds to make a movie, the most common methods are: 1) loans; 2) investor financing; 3) borrowing against pre-sales (a loan against distribution contracts); and 4) distributor-supplied financing.

Loans

Loans can be secured or unsecured. A secured loan is supported or backed by security or collateral. When one takes out a car or home loan, the loan is secured by that property. If the person who borrows money fails to repay the loan, the creditor may take legal action to have the collateral sold and the proceeds applied to pay off the debt.

An unsecured loan has no particular property backing it. Credit card debt and loans from family or friends may be unsecured. If a debtor defaults on an unsecured loan, the creditor can sue for repayment and force the sale of the debtor's assets to repay the loan. If the debtor has many debts, however, the sale of his property may not be sufficient to satisfy all creditors. In such a case, creditors may end up receiving only a small portion of the money owed them.

A secured creditor is in a stronger position to receive repayment. In the event of a default, designated property (the secured property) will be sold and all the proceeds will be applied first to repay the secured creditor's debt. Unsecured creditors will share in whatever is left, if anything.

The advantage of a loan, from a legal point of view, is that the transaction can often be structured in a fairly simple and inexpensive manner. A short promissory note can be used and the transaction often is not subject to the complex security laws that govern many investments. Thus, there is usually no need to prepare a private placement memorandum (PPM). Keep in mind that if the agreement between the parties is labeled a "loan," but in reality it is an investment, the courts will likely view the transaction as an investment. Giving a creditor a "piece of the back-end," or otherwise giving the creditor equity in the project, makes the transaction look like an investment.

The difference between a loan and an investment has to do with risk. With a loan, the entity that borrows funds, the debtor, is obligated to repay the loan and whatever interest is charged, regardless of whether the film is a flop or a hit. The creditor earns interest but does not share in the upside potential (profits) of a hit. Since the creditor is entitled to repayment even if the film is a flop, the creditor does not share in the risk of the endeavor. Of course, there is some risk with a loan because loans are not always repaid, especially unsecured loans that don't have any collateral backing them. That risk is minimal, however, compared to the risk of an equity investment.

In a pre-sale agreement, a buyer licenses or pre-buys movie distribution rights for a territory before the film has been produced. The deal works something like this: Filmmaker Henry approaches Distributor Juan to sign a contract to buy the right to distribute Henry's next film. Henry gives Juan a copy of the script and tells him the names of the principal cast members. Juan has distributed several of Henry's films in the past. He paid $50,000 for the right to distribute Henry's last film in Spain.

The film did reasonably well and Juan feels confident, based on Henry's track record, the script, and the proposed cast, that his next film should also do well in Spain. Juan is willing to license Henry's next film sight unseen before it has been produced. By buying distribution rights to the film now, Juan is obtaining an advantage over competitors who might bid for it. Moreover, Juan may be able to negotiate a lower license fee than what he would pay if the film were sold on the open market. So Juan signs a contract agreeing to buy Spanish distribution rights to the film. Juan does not have to pay (except if a deposit is required) until completion and delivery of the film to him.

Henry now takes this contract and a dozen similar contracts with buyers to the bank. Henry asks the bank to lend him money to make the movie with the distribution contracts as collateral. Henry is "banking the paper." The bank will not lend Henry the full face value of the contracts, but instead will discount the paper and lend a smaller sum. So if the contracts provide for a cumulative total of $1,000,000 in license fees, the bank might lend Henry $800,000. In some circumstances banks are willing lend more than the face value of the contracts (so-called gap financing) and charge higher fees.

Henry uses this money to produce his film. When the movie is completed, he delivers it to the companies that have already licensed it. They in turn pay their license fees to Henry's bank to retire Henry's loan. The bank receives repayment of its loan plus interest. The buyers receive the right to distribute the film in their territory. Henry can now license the film in territories that remain unsold. From these revenues Henry makes his profit.

Juan's commitment to purchase the film must be unequivocal, and his company financially secure, so that a bank is willing to lend Henry money on the strength of Juan's promise and ability to pay. If the contract merely states that the buyer will review and consider purchasing the film, this commitment is not strong enough to borrow against. Banks want to be assured that the buyer will accept delivery of the film as long as it meets certain technical standards, even if artistically the film is a disappointment. The bank will also want to know that Juan's company is fiscally solid and likely to be in business when it comes time for it to pay the license fee. If Juan's company has been in business for many years, and if the company has substantial assets on its balance sheet, the bank will usually lend against the contract.

The bank often insists on a completion bond to ensure that the filmmaker has sufficient funds to finish the film. Banks are not willing to take much risk. They know that Juan's commitment to buy Henry's film is contingent on delivery of a completed film. But what if Henry goes over budget and cannot finish the film? If Henry doesn't deliver the film, Juan is not obligated to pay for it, and the bank is not repaid its loan.

To avoid this risk, the bank wants an insurance company, the completion guarantor, to agree to put up any money needed to complete the film should it go over budget. Before issuing a policy, a completion guarantor will carefully review the proposed budget and the track record of key production personnel. Unless the completion guarantor is confident that the film can be brought in on budget, no policy will issue. These policies are called completion bonds.

First-time filmmakers may find it difficult to finance their films through pre-sales. With no track record of successful films to their credit, they may not be able to persuade a distributor to pre-buy their work. How does the distributor know that the filmmaker can produce something their audiences will want to see? Of course, if the other elements are strong, the distributor may be persuaded to take that risk. For example, even though the filmmaker may be a first-timer, if the script is from an acclaimed writer, and several big-name actors will participate, the overall package may be attractive.

The terms of an agreement between the territory buyer (licensor) and the international distributor can be quite complex. Parties may disagree about the meaning of terms used in their agreements. The following terms are standard AFMA definitions, which are generally accepted in the industry. They are used to interpret whatever document they are attached to.

Equity Investments

An equity investment can be structured in a number of ways. For example, an investor could be a stockholder in a corporation, a non-managing member of a Limited Liability Company (LLC), or a limited partner in a partnership.

An investor shares in potential rewards as well as the risks of failure. If a movie is a hit, the investor is entitled to receive his investment back and share in proceeds as well. Of course, if the movie is a flop, the investor may lose his entire investment. The producer is not obligated to repay an investor his loss.

The interests of individuals and companies that do not manage the enterprise they invest in are known as securities. These investors may be described using a variety of terms including silent partners, limited partners, passive investors and stockholders. They are putting money into a business that they are not managing (i.e., not running). State and federal securities laws are designed to protect such investors by ensuring that the people managing the business (e.g., the general partners in a partnership or the officers and directors of a corporation) do not defraud investors by giving them false or misleading information, or by failing to disclose information that a reasonably prudent investor would want to know.

In a limited partnership agreement, for example, investors (limited partners) put up the money needed to produce a film. Investors usually desire limited liability. That is, they don't want to be financially responsible for any cost overruns or liability that might arise if, for instance, a stunt person is injured. They want their potential loss limited to their investment.

Because limited partnership interests are considered securities, they are subject to state and federal securities laws. These laws are complex and have strict requirements. A single technical violation can subject general partners to liability. Therefore, it is important that filmmakers retain an attorney with experience in securities work and familiarity with the entertainment industry. This is one area where filmmakers should not attempt to do it themselves.

Registration and Exemptions

The federal agency charged with protecting investors is the U.S. Securities and Exchange Commission (SEC). Various state and federal laws require that most securities be registered with state and/or federal governments. Registration for a public offering is time consuming and expensive, and not a realistic alternative for most low-budget filmmakers. Filmmakers can avoid the expense of registration if they qualify for one or more statutory exemptions. These exemptions are generally restricted to private placements, which entail approaching people one already knows (i.e., the parties have a pre-existing relationship). Compare a private placement with a public offering where offers can be made to strangers, such as soliciting the public at large through advertising. Generally, a public offering can only be made after the U.S. Securities and Exchange Commission (SEC) has reviewed and approved it.

There are a variety of exemptions to federal registration. For example, there is an exemption for intrastate offerings limited to investors all of whom reside within one state. To qualify for the intrastate offering exemption, a company must be incorporated in the state where it is offering the securities, and it must carry out a significant amount of its business in that state. There is no fixed limit on the size of the offering or the number of purchasers. Relying solely on this exemption can be risky, however, because if an offer is made to a single non-resident the exemption could be lost.

Under SEC Regulation D (Reg D) there are three exemptions from federal registration. These can permit filmmakers to offer and sell their securities without having to register the securities with the SEC. These exemptions are under

Rules 504, 505 and 506 of Regulation D. While companies relying on a Reg D exemption do not have to register their securities and usually do not have to file reports with the SEC, they must file a document known as Form D when they first sell their securities. This document gives notice of the names and addresses of the company's owners and promoters. State laws also apply and the offeror will likely need to file a document with the appropriate state agency for every state in which an investor resides.

Investors considering an investment in an offering under Reg D can contact the SEC's Public Reference Branch at (202) 942-8090 or send an email to publicinfo@sec.gov to determine whether a company has filed Form D, and to obtain a copy. A potential investor may also want to check with his/her state regulator to see if the offering has complied with state regulations. State regulators can be contacted through the North American Securities Administrators Association at (202) 737-0900 or by visiting its website at *www.nasaa. org/nasaa/abtnasaa/find_regulator.html*.

Information about the SEC's registration requirements and exemptions is available at *www.sec.gov/info/smallbus/qasbsec.html*.

An "offering" is usually comprised of several documents including a private placement memorandum (PPM), a proposed limited partnership agreement (or operating agreement for an LLC, or bylaws for a corporation), and an investor questionnaire used to determine if the investor is qualified to invest. A PPM contains the type of information usually found in a business plan, and a whole lot more. It is used to disclose the essential facts that a reasonable investor would want to know before making an investment. The offeror may be liable if there are any misrepresentations in the PPM, or any omissions of material facts.

State registration can be avoided by complying with the requirements for limited offering exemptions under state law. These laws are often referred to as "Blue Sky" laws. They were enacted after the stock market crash that occurred before the Great Depression. They are designed to protect investors from being duped into buying securities that are worthless — backed by nothing more than the blue sky.

The above-mentioned federal and state exemptions may restrict offerors in several ways. Sales are typically limited to 35 non-accredited investors, and the investors may need to have a pre-existing relationship with the issuer (or investment sophistication adequate to understand the transaction), the purchasers cannot purchase for resale, and advertising or general solicitation is generally not permitted. There is usually no numerical limit on the number of accredited investors.

A "pre-existing relationship" is defined as any relationship consisting of personal or business contacts of a nature and duration such as would enable a reasonably prudent purchaser to be aware of the character, business acumen, and general business and financial circumstances of the person with whom the relationship exists.

Other documents may need to be filed with federal and state governments. For example, a Certificate of Limited Partnership may need to be filed with the Secretary of State to establish a partnership. In California, a notice of the transaction and consent to service of process is filed with the Department of Corporations. If the transaction is subject to federal law, Form D will need to be filed with the Securities and Exchange Commission (SEC) soon after the first and last sales. Similar forms may need to be filed in every state in which any investor resides.

In the independent film business, PPMs are usually a Rule 504 offering to raise up to $1,000,000, or a Rule 505 offering which allows the filmmaker to raise up to $5,000,000, or a Rule 506 offering which doesn't have a monetary cap on the amount of funds to be raised. A 506 offering also offers the advantage of preempting state laws under the provisions of the National Securities Markets Improvement Act of 1996 ("NSMIA").

504 Offering

Under Rule 504, offerings may be exempt from registration for companies when they offer and sell up to $1,000,000 of their securities in a 12-month period.

A company can use this exemption so long as it is not a so-called blank check company, which is one that has no specific business plan or purpose. The exemption generally does not allow companies to solicit or advertise to the public, and purchasers receive restricted securities, which they cannot sell to others without registration or an applicable exemption.

Under certain limited circumstances, Rule 504 does permit companies to make a public offering of tradable securities. For example, if a company registers the offering exclusively in states that require a publicly filed registration statement and delivery of a substantive disclosure document to investors; or if the company sells exclusively according to state law exemptions that permit general solicitation, provided the company sells only to accredited investors.

505 Offering

Under a Rule 505 exemption, a company can offer and sell up to $5,000,000 of its securities in any 12-month period. It may sell to an unlimited number of "accredited investors" and up to 35 non-accredited investors who do not need to satisfy the sophistication or wealth standards associated with other exemptions. The company must inform investors that they are receiving restricted securities that cannot be sold for at least a year without registering them. General solicitation and advertising is prohibited.

Rule 505 allows companies to decide what information to give to accredited investors, so long as it does not violate the antifraud prohibitions of federal securities laws. But companies must give non-accredited investors disclosure documents that are comparable to those used in registered offerings. If a company provides information to accredited investors, it must provide the same information to non-accredited investors. The offeror must also be available to answer questions from prospective investors.

506 Offering

Under Rule 506, one can raise an unlimited amount of capital. However, the offeror cannot engage in any public solicitation or advertising. There is no limit as to the number of accredited investors that can participate. However, only 35 non-accredited investors can participate.

Accredited investors include (among others) the following:

a) any natural persons whose individual net worth, or joint net worth with that person's spouse, at the time of the purchase exceeds $1,000,000;

b) any natural person with an individual income in the two prior years and an estimated income in the current year in excess of $200,000 or joint income with spouse of $300,000;

c) any director, executive officer, or general partner of the issuer of the securities being offered or sold, or any director, executive officer or partner of a general partner of the issuer.

Under Rule 506, each purchaser of units must be "sophisticated," as that term is defined under federal law. Note that an "accredited investor" is not the same as a "sophisticated" investor. The term "accredited investor" is specifically defined by the federal securities laws, while the term "sophisticated investor" has no precise legal definition. Both terms generally refer to an investor who has a sufficiently high degree of financial knowledge and expertise such that he/she does not need the protections afforded by the SEC. An investor who is considered "sophisticated," might not meet the precise definition of an accredited investor.

As with Rule 505 offerings, it is up to the offeror to decide what information is given to accredited investors, provided there is no violation of the anti-fraud provisions. Non-accredited investors must be given disclosure documents similar to those used in registered offerings. If the offeror provides information to accredited investors, the same information must be given to non-accredited investors. The offeror must be available to answer questions by prospective purchasers.

Under Rule 506, each purchaser must represent that he or she is purchasing the units for his or her own investment only and not with plans to sell or otherwise distribute the units. The units purchased are "restricted" and may not be resold by the investor except in certain circumstances.

Intrastate Offering Exemption

Section 3(a)(11) of the Securities Act provides for an intrastate offering exemption. This exemption is designed for the financing of local businesses. To qualify for the intrastate offering exemption, a company needs to be incorporated in the state where it is offering the securities; carry out a significant amount of its business in that state; and make offers and sales only to residents of that state.

There is no fixed limit on the size of the offering or the number of purchasers. The company needs to carefully determine the residence of each purchaser. If any of the securities are offered or sold to even one out-of-state person, the exemption may be lost. Moreover, if an investor resells any of the securities to a person who resides out of state within a short period of time after the company's offering is complete (the usual test is nine months), the entire transaction, including the original sales, might violate the Securities Act.

Accredited Investor Exemption

Section 4(6) of the Securities Act exempts from registration offers and sales of securities to accredited investors when the total offering price is less than $5,000,000.

The definition of accredited investors is the same as that used under Regulation D. Like the exemptions in Rule 505 and 506, this exemption does not permit any public solicitation. There are no document delivery requirements, but the anti-fraud provisions mentioned below do apply.

California Limited Offering Exemption

SEC Rule 1001 exempts from registration offers and sales of securities, in amounts of up to $5,000,000, which satisfies the conditions of ¤25102(n) of the California Corporations Code. This California law exempts from California state law registration offerings made by California companies to "qualified purchasers" whose characteristics are similar to, but not the same as, accredited investors under Regulation D. This exemption allows some methods of general solicitation prior to sales.

ANTI-FRAUD PROVISIONS

All security offerings, even those exempt from registration under Reg. D, are subject to the anti-fraud provisions of the federal securities laws, and any applicable state anti-fraud provisions. Consequently, the offeror will be responsible for any false or misleading statements, whether oral or written. Those who violate the law can be pursued both criminally and civilly. Moreover, an investor who has purchased a security on the basis of misleading information, or the omission of relevant information, can rescind the investment agreement and obtain a refund of his/her investment.

Mark Litwak is a veteran entertainment attorney with offices in Beverly Hills, California. Litwak also functions as a producer's rep, assisting filmmakers in the financing, marketing and distribution of their films. Litwak is the author of six books including Risky Business, Financing and Distributing Independent Film. *He is also the author of the popular CD-ROM program* Movie Magic Contracts.

Mark has provided legal services or acted as a producer rep on more than 100 feature films. He has been the executive producer of such feature films as The Proposal *(Miramax/Buena Vista),* Out of Line *(First Look) and* Pressure *(Blockbuster). He is the creator of* Entertainment Law Resources.

CHAPTER 9

BUILDING THE FOUNDATION FOR FUNDRAISING TRAILERS:

A CONVERSATION WITH STORY CONSULTANT FERNANDA ROSSI — THE DOCUMENTARY DOCTOR
(*www.documentarydoctor.com*)

Story consultant Fernanda Rossi helps filmmakers — from first-time filmmakers to Academy Award–winning veterans — craft the story structure of their films. She has doctored over 100 documentaries, fiction scripts and fundraising trailers, most of which have been funded, awarded and distributed. In addition to private consultations, lectures and seminars, she has served as a festival juror and grant panelist. Ms. Rossi is the author of the book *Trailer Mechanics: A Guide to Making your Documentary Fundraising Trailer.*

In your book, Trailer Mechanics — which, by the way, is excellent and I recommend to all my students — you state: "In order to connect with your film in a meaningful way you need to align your values to the theme of the film." Please explain why this is important.

Filmmaking, as a process, has three components. One is the story, the other is the filmmaker and the third is the viewer. In order for the story to work, filmmakers have to know why they are making this particular story and what motivates them. The value is their strongest connection with the film.

The other two are *fascination* and *moral obligation*. The first one is when we come across something that infatuates us: an exhilarating event, or an exotic experience. Moral obligation happens when we witness an event that needs attention; saving the whales or banning child labor in Africa. These elements are very important in getting a filmmaker started, but they are not enough to get him or her through the perils of the long and sometimes exhausting filmmaking process.

The value, on the other hand, is a deep reliable source of motivation. A value is part of our belief system; it is with us every day, all the time. Our values conform to our inner compass and deal with reality and decision making. Therefore if we find what part of our values are represented in the film and understand the film as an extension of our inner world, then our connection and commitment to it is much stronger.

The second function of value is to give coherence to the story. It's an invisible thread that brings all characters and themes together. Very much like the premise works in a fiction piece. Fascination is not a very good thread for a film; it is difficult to fascinate an audience for 90 minutes. Moral obligation makes films very preachy, contrived and even propagandistic. Value is not seeking to convert but to share a point of view in a more subtle way.

To summarize, I believe that the story is not frozen alone in space; there is a filmmaker and an audience. Value is the first organizing principle to bring all these elements to work together in a cohesive manner.

You state that while making a film, filmmakers' abusive behavior and procrastination are often times a display of their creative fears.

I see it every day!

Well, how do we help filmmakers recognize this and get back on track?

In all professions there is a big underestimation on how our emotions play into our professional performance. Athletes are probably an exception. In sports, they appear to be very clear how mismanagement of your anxieties can affect the outcome. They train, concentrate, meditate and visualize, they do whatever it takes to minimize interference. In the corporate world, the emphasis is not in the emotions but at least they address all complementary aspects of a job, from decision making to leadership.

It seems in the film business — this might be very subjective, because I'm immersed in it — everybody is eager to spend the money and time taking every workshop on shooting, editing or writing, and there is very little attention paid to management or emotional issues that diminish a good outcome.

Yes, from my 33 years running three corporations, I know that when someone gets angry easily or is often rude to people, it usually means they are "overwhelmed, don't know how to make a decision or they are ill."

Yes, filmmakers are part artists and part business people. There was a Harvard business book that said a filmmaking project is nothing else but a temporary corporation. A film project and a regular corporation share more characteristics than we want to admit. Filmmakers should take all the same workshops that a CEO takes!

Another factor to take into account is our own endorsement of such misplaced behaviors. We equate abusive behavior with the unmistakable mark of genius. We put up with the most outrageous conduct, convincing ourselves that the pain is worth it because we are in the presence of sheer brilliance. Conversely, we downplay nice people as probably not too talented. But I'm not so sure that anybody's film is worth anybody else's suffering or mistreatment.

There is a romantic vision of the artist as a tortured, troubled person. Beethoven or van Gogh might have been difficult, but that doesn't make every moody person a Beethoven or a van Gogh. Far from that, I believe those type of artists are successful in spite of themselves or most likely they succeed thanks to the legion of tolerant and skilled people around them.

The reason artists have tantrums of various types is because they don't understand the creative process and can't manage the fears that come along with it. The creative process is very anxiety provoking. There are lots of decisions to be made and a lot of judgment to endure. It gets intensified by the financial pressures and amount of money required to make a film.

Understanding the role creative anxieties play in our performance and relationship with others is crucial for the completion and success of a project. I would dare say that fear is the shadow of value. Value is the positive force that moves the project forward and fear is the negative pull that threatens the completion of the film. You can't have one without the other, but we can all learn how to manage them to our advantage.

Very true! So how can a filmmaker understand this?

The first step is to be aware of our creative process and fears, to identify when we are reacting to the very process of creating and wrongly taking it out on our colleagues or ourselves. There are many ways to deal with all the stresses of filmmaking, but just awareness is a great start.

Among the many situations that emerge from mismanagement of fear, there is one that interests me very much because it is particular to filmmaking and collaborative arts in general. I call it "re-owning" and it stems from the fear of losing control or authorship of the film.

Filmmaking is a collaborative art; therefore there is an overlap of creative processes. A filmmaker not only has to deal with the challenges regarding the making of the film, but also must manage everybody's creative input and anxieties. And as I said before, people barely know how to manage their own creative process, let alone the process of a group of others.

"Re-owning" then happens when a director or producer mismanages the input of his or her team. Let's say somebody gets called to participate in the project. This person — whether shooter, editor or a consultant, like you or me — makes a significant creative contribution. Or maybe the director lets someone else take the lead for a while in order to take a break and replenish.

In an ideal scenario this situation will balance itself out, no problem. The filmmaker welcomes and acknowledges their input, thinks about it, evaluates it and takes action without losing his or her vision and center. Unfortunately this is not the case with everybody all the time. Most likely the concurrent creative process of several people creates friction. A filmmaker might feel threatened that he or she is losing control over the project. In order to "re-own" the project, the filmmaker has to "kill" the witnesses and messengers. This killing is metaphorical, of course, but very real in terms of fights, firing or not giving due credit to those who contributed to the film. The filmmaker becomes the worst enemy of the film, trying to hold on to authorship in the most detrimental way, by alienating others.

The Academy Award winners, nominees and other very accomplished people I had the pleasure to work with were for me great examples of how to create healthy collaborations. What I observed in them is that yes, they are dedicated and talented with good stories to tell, like many other people. But above all, they were gracious. They believed in abundance, in sharing and collaborating — as in a real exchange, not as in "you all help me and you only get a pay check, if that." They understood that a filmmaker has to first be a listener, then a doer, first a giver, then a taker and always a skilled manager of everybody's creativity.

Because the team sincerely felt part of the film, they pushed the project forward creating good opportunities for the filmmaker, whether by word of mouth or just general good karma!

Yes, the crew became one unit working together with a unified vision. Actually, this united vision creates the film.

Exactly. The film is important, but the filmmaker's personality and the market circumstances are the determining factors for success.

Now, regarding the making of the trailer, how important is it to identify whether a film is topic or character driven?

Extremely important, it's the first set of questions to ask when getting ready to plan, write, shoot or edit a trailer. It will determine the structure of the trailer and lead you to new questions.

Is this a topic-driven or a character-driven film?
If character-driven: Does this character have a goal, an obstacle or opponent? Or is this just the description of the life of the character?
If a topic-driven film: What's the main issue? Is it a conflictive issue? What are the secondary angles of this topic?

The answers to the above questions can serve as guidelines to start the structuring of the fundraising trailer. From there the trailer can keep growing and finding its own voice.

How do you recommend someone take 50 hours of footage and create a less than ten-minute fundraising promo?

I think I will begin by saying what not to do. Part of our fears and our procrastination get us to do a lot of labor-intensive things that look like work but are not directly involved with telling the story. Sometimes those activities that are always costly and time consuming, like logging or transcribing, are necessary at some point in the film but are not indispensable to develop the trailer or the story.

The other factor that reinforces the idea of doing these activities before cutting a trailer is the fact that we are still working with methods that were right 20 years ago when people shot only 30 hours of footage. For 20 hours, it made sense to log everything and transcribe everything to cut the film. Back then fundraising trailers didn't quite exist. Today the average filmmaker is shooting 120 hours. And they are going by a methodology that worked before Final Cut Pro or Avid entered the market, before there was a DVD or digital cameras. We can't use the same techniques we had for 20 hours when we have this many more hours of footage today and expect the same results.

However, sometimes filmmakers shoot just for the trailer and have less than ten hours of footage. Even then I suggest using more intuitive approaches, which are less labor-intensive and focus on story development. Approaches that make more business sense if the point is to get the fundraising trailer done efficiently so more money and support can be brought to the film.

The more I consult and witness this process, the more I realize it rarely makes sense to log everything, at least not all in one pass. *It seems more efficient to build the story from memory and confirm the impact of those memories by looking at that specific material only.*

Let's say we shot something a month ago and there are a few scenes that still come to mind strongly whenever we think of that time. If it made an impression on the filmmaker, it is going to make an impression on others. Therefore memory is the best selector of material. You can select ten moments you like. Then start logging just that, and apply the questions above to guide you in how to organize that material.

On the other hand, if we go and log everything, everything becomes important again, making it difficult to choose what to include in the promo. Besides, it takes a week to view 50 hours and that is if you work all day. When I used to be an editor, I did not want to be stuck with one project for a year so I was forced to develop techniques that would help me edit faster and have more fun. Even though I would have made more money doing it the long way, for my sanity, I had to come up with ways to shorten my own editing time.

This is a brilliant idea, to list the ten things you remember the most to start the fundraising promo.

Yes, it's more organic and it serves the story better. More importantly, it's working for a lot of the filmmakers I worked with in consultations. And their editors are happier too. But I think I can already hear readers saying, "What if I miss a scene that is really important. What if I forget something?" I know of filmmakers at the premiere of their film wondering if they left something out! If a scene was that good it is very unlikely a filmmaker will forget it. If something was left out and you didn't remember it till the day of the premiere, it probably wasn't worth keeping.

That's once again a manifestation of fear that can sometimes lead to procrastination. When people are about to lock picture for trailers or rough cuts, this fear comes up and they delay locking picture for several weeks. They go back and look for something they may have forgotten. "What if..." becomes their mantra. And rarely, they do come up with something but I doubt that the one scene they found is going to make such an important difference in the outcome of the film overall. This is, of course, different from purposefully looking for scenes when the story presents holes.

Going by memory is an initial step. Eventually we have to go through other footage. But it's a way to make the process manageable so the story can emerge organically.

Do you tell people when they are shooting to make notes of their favorite scenes?

I think it is better for the shooter/filmmaker to be present, alert and sensitive to what's going on in the moment. Sometimes appearances can be deceiving, that's why when working by memory we still have to go to the footage and check. Because when you are on location the situation can be very powerful but when you see the tape later on, that something that moved you may not feel the same. Filmmakers try to convince their editors to use something by saying, "Oh, if you had been there..." and that's the point, we weren't. If it doesn't come through the footage and we can't feel it then it is not going to get a reaction from the audience.

You normally teach filmmakers to use the "Who, What, Where and Why" in the fundraising trailer. Do you consider these part of the main story structure of the trailer?

Yes, they are an intrinsically important part. A fundraising trailer is a seven to ten-minute audio-visual pitch of the film. To use more familiar wording, it is a short without an ending. People tend to think that a trailer or promo is like a music video. Nothing can be farther from the truth. Grant foundations or development departments of a network don't want to see something flashy necessarily. That only proves that you have a skilled editor. It doesn't prove that you have a story or that you have access to a character or that you have a distinct voice and style for this film.

The only way to prove you have a story and an engaging character is by showing some scenes. The scenes need to show who they are, what motivates them, if there is an opponent or something working against them.

In addition, we have to create a final scene that shows there is potential for the story to grow, namely a cliffhanger or hook. It is obligatory to have this element for every trailer. A fundraising trailer or promo with a definite conclusion is doomed to fail because any grantor or broadcaster who sees a wrapped-up story can say, "Oh, thank you for sharing. Nice little story." The story is complete. We have closure. Then what's the point of telling a longer story about the same topic? But if we have a short without an ending, then we want to know more. The cliffhanger gives the promo the sense that there is something else that can be explored in the longer version of the film.

These are just the foundational elements of the structure of a trailer. It gets a bit more complicated after that. There is a way of choosing the "Who", the "What" and the "Why" and a way of a evaluating which one would be the best to show the main story line.

When I watch promo tapes for the grant, I like to see something engaging in the first minute. Would you agree?

The first minute is extremely important. This is where the true artistic craft comes in. The first minute generally sets the tone and style for the piece. We have to convey the "Who" and the "What" of the character or topic right away. It's important not to start with a long explanatory text. For some reason people seem compelled to throw in a long statement saying, "This story started when..." I call it the didactic syndrome. We all want to be understood, and sometimes make great efforts in explaining everything just in case someone doesn't quite get it. Trailer audiences are industry people. They will get it without long small typeface scrolls. This does just the opposite. It kills any expectations the viewer may have had from reading the title.

The same goes for long monologues whether is in voice-over form or talking heads. If somebody is saying something, it better be a shocker, something really meaningful and short. I like to start a trailer with vérité footage if at all possible. Close-ups of engaging, charismatic characters are good too, if they are, once again, saying something that relates to the Who and What.

There are lots of exceptions, of course. These are just some primary guidelines. The main exception to consider is "invested audiences". If a person

— individual donor, grant maker or broadcaster — is very interested in the topic or the filmmaker, then you can have the worst trailer in the world and still get funding. But for the most of filmmakers this is not the case. When competing for a grant among hundreds of projects, a well-crafted trailer can make a difference.

I see lots of promo tapes where the filmmaker uses a card with words to move the film along so you have a bit of information. When do you think it is okay to use cards?

Full screen cards with text from top to bottom with black background in the middle of a trailer tend to stop the flow of the story. It's a risk, structurally speaking. I'd suggest to use text on moving images instead, i.e. vérité footage.

The text should be information that helps move the story along, complementing the images that we are seeing. Text and images are two completely different formats and they have to flow together whether it's simultaneously or consecutively. Integrating them can be a challenge. The sentences have to be thought out very carefully. Each word counts, because each word can become an asset or a distraction. I favor sentences that are simple, direct and not more than two or three lines at a time in the lower third of the screen.

Do you think independent filmmakers should create a promo and just shoot one scene?

My motto is "better something than nothing." Years ago we could get away with just a synopsis, a piece of paper and the promise of shooting something some day. Today it is impossible to do fundraising for an audiovisual medium without... well, audiovisual material, unless you are requesting funds for production development. The technology is there, available, and that's great, but it raised the bar of demands on filmmakers. There is no excuse not to have something to show to potential funders when cameras and desktop editing software is so accessible.

If the only thing the filmmaker can present is just a scene, so be it. They can complement that with some photos and a voice-over narration. This is better than nothing.

There are cases where a trailer is not possible, let's say the story takes place in another country and no development grants came through yet. Then the filmmaker can use visual research material to put together an audiovisual presentation.

It might not be a trailer, but perhaps a PowerPoint program that explains the project. These are extreme cases, desperate measures. But they can work.

A filmmaker got into the finals of our grant with a PowerPoint program and a heart-felt presentation telling us the story of the film.

Yes. Ultimately you want your project to have a chance. Sometimes you just want to put a foot in the door, creating a precedent for your project. Paper and black ink can be compelling. Some filmmakers are very good writers. If you are competing with other people who are presenting the same type of material, great. But in the "scissors, paper, stone" game of fundraising, visuals beats paper!

All this information is very important. Fernanda, how did you become interested in story structure?

I became interested in structure very early on. When I was eleven we had to write an essay on a novel we'd been reading in class. I presented a drawing showing structure of the story and the character's arc. I couldn't name it that, but I knew it represented the spine of the novel. The teacher said, "Not sure if you are lazy or just understood it so well that you don't need words." Fortunately he was working on his PhD in literature, so he said, "Your analysis of story structure is very good." Maybe thanks to that validation early on I'm a story consultant today.

Another pivotal episode happened many years later with another teacher. I had been a prolific writer in my childhood and teens. Writing was fun and liberating. I even made drawings of my short stories and performed slide shows with them. There were no rules, just the joy of telling a story.

I went to film school. I had one of those well-intentioned teachers who used to ask midway of a script, "Now what's the conflict... what's this and what's that?" I got a writer's block that lasted three years. I'm grateful to her because this caused me to become interested in how the creative process works. That's when I realized that story structure and creativity go hand in hand, many things interconnect. I added the creative process as another area for research and my consulting practice.

And last I got interested in business etiquette and how interpersonal relationships affect creativity and filmmaking. I get many emails from all over the world with all types of questions. And behind each question — no matter where it comes from — you can see there is a bigger question that exceeds the issues of the film. Filmmaking is just another path to whatever we are meant to do. It's not just all about getting the money for the film. It is also about growing and learning from the film you are making. To use the process of filmmaking as a mirror to see who we are and what we are contributing to society.

Yes, and to enjoy the process! Fernanda, people praise your work. Everyone I send to you is exceptionally pleased with the outcome. You must love what you do.

Thank you. Yes, I completely love what I do. It's very satisfying to me to research story structure and then have the chance to share it with other filmmakers that put that theory into action. I want to also say here, that you met me early in my consulting career and you were one of the first ones to get what I was trying to do. Since then you have been an invaluable mentor for me. I'm very grateful for that.

Thank you, Fernanda, for the inspiration you bring to us by your story structure theories and teaching.

CHAPTER 10

PRODUCT PLACEMENT AND BRANDING

When someone mentions *E. T.* what immediately comes to mind?

A boy, a bicycle, and a loveable creature silhouetted against a magnificent full moon.

Think of your favorite film and chances are the image that pops into your head comes straight from the film's one-sheet, that coveted poster that once graced the walls of your favorite movie theater.

The silhouette of a lone fireman emerges from a background of searing flames. "Silently behind a door, it waits. One breath of oxygen and it explodes in a deadly rage. In that instant it can create a hero... or cover a secret." (Backdraft)

The hands of a child and adult loosely entwined against a charcoal background which bears a faint typewritten list of names and numbers. The scene is cast in subtle shades of gray with the exception of the child's red sleeve. (Schindler's List)

From the hundreds of applications I read a year, the ones that stay with me are the ones that include a picture, or one-sheet, representing the film's concept. Instant association; this is what you want from the very first day you start to work on your film. You will spend the next two or three years working to develop your ideas into tangible images that will project your message.

Brand these images. Put your message into one identifiable picture that will promote your vision and then go out there and capture your audience. Use some of your seed money to commission an artist and create your very own one-sheet. Quick Print Works of L.A. does this for the winners of my grants. Contact George Benitz at *info@quickprintworks.com* and see what he can do for you.

I have my very own one-sheet, but I must go back a few years to tell you how I got it. I was blessed to have my great-grandmother with me for the first thirteen years of my life. Everyday I would race home from school and beg my

Gigi to tell me stories about my great-great grandfather, Christopher Edward "Tobe" Odem. After Tobe's mother died, his father quickly remarried, but according to Gigi, Tobe and his father's new bride didn't exactly get along. One afternoon after watching a band of cowboys ride through town, Tobe decided it was time to spread his wings. He rode out to join them and never looked back. He was 12 years old.

Tobe Odem was an American cowboy. One of those indomitable Texas spirits, who rounded up longhorn by the hundreds, branded their hides then drove them across Indian Territory forging the Chisholm Trail. As I sat and listened to Gigi's stories I would stare out the window and try to imagine what it was like to cross hundreds of miles of open prairie for months on end without running into one barbed wire fence. It must have been heaven!

I was always full of questions: "How did they find water? How did they find the trail? How did they know which way to go?" Gigi smiled and told me that "Old Tom" showed them the way. Old Tom was not your ordinary steer. Once a fellow cattleman offered to buy Old Tom for $3,000 which was a virtual fortune back in the mid-1800s but Tobe wouldn't think of parting with his prized possession. Why Tobe was so proud of that crazy old steer that he decorated his horns with gold rings!

I listened wide-eyed as Gigi told me about the various outlaws who rode into the Tobe Odem Ranch for some conversation and a bite to eat. According to the law of the Old West, when you had lunch outside visitors were always welcome. Outlaw or lawman, it made no difference. Amnesty always prevailed at lunch, once you hung your gun belt on the fence post. No one judged around the big Odem table as hired hands, bandits, and the Odem family partook of the grub and lively conversation. As soon as lunch was over the outlaws would mount their horses and set off, most likely in the direction of the next train or closest bank.

Gigi's wonderful stories stayed with me long after I left Texas for the bright lights of Hollywood, but as the years flew by I found myself longing for a piece of my past. I decided an oil painting of Tobe Odem would serve to capture the spirit of my roots so I commissioned one of my favorite artists to do the job. Tobe couldn't oblige me by sitting for the portrait but I was confident the artist could capture his spirit if I introduced Tobe through the stories I had heard as a young child. I wrote them all down, then searched through the archives of Dallas newspapers and through volumes of dusty old books to find more. When I had the vision I was looking for I gathered everything together and sent it off to the artist.

I know this is a long story to drive home the importance of a one-sheet but what can I tell you? I'm a Texan and telling tall tales runs in my blood! I could have sent the artist an old photo, but the point is it takes more information if you are going to project the right image. Through my research I learned things I never heard from my dear Gigi. I learned that Tobe lived with a mysterious American Indian woman, that he was a great friend to Chief Quanta Parker, and that his favorite horse was a beautiful Appaloosa. Tobe Odem, 1858-1913. What an amazing life. I sent all this information to the famous authentic painter of Texas history; Bruce Marshall and I waited 18 months for him to create a collage of Tobe's life. And now it's all there in a magnificent portrait of Tobe sitting astride that beautiful horse.

I couldn't help but send the following information to Bruce to enable him to feel the essence of the man.

One of my favorite stories of Tobe is about the night when Tobe and his men had just arrived outside of Dodge after three months on the trail. Yearning for company, they invited some of the town ladies to visit the camp. As the ladies sang and danced, the cowboys gave them all nicknames as was customary.

The ladies stayed for a few days and begged Tobe for a chance to see a stampede. Toward evening on the second day, Tobe took a squint at the sky and said, "Get ready, gals, there's a bad storm coming and they will surely run tonight. I'll give each of you a partner, so the boys can tell you what to do."

The storm came fast, whipping the dust and blackening the sky. When the lightning crackled and sizzled, the steers were on their feet, running with tails over their heads. Latigo Liz, Maud Ketchum, Frog Lips Annie and all the other ladies began to holler and yell. What a sight to see, thirty-five hundred Texas steers racing the wind, horns a-popping and crackling, hoofs churning the Kansas plains. Every time the lightning spit, you could see the steers crowded close and racing along like the devil was after them.

When Tobe Odem made the tally, he was short over 100 steers, a mighty expensive stampede that he might have been able to stop if Tobe hadn't wanted to give the girls a treat.

The point is, please take the time to produce a one-sheet that represents *the spirit of your film.* You might have postcards made with your vision on one side and use the other side for the log line of the film. These PR cards can go on top of your proposals or in the mail as postcards. Use them as greeting cards or calling cards, leave them on desks and counters, and you can pass them around at film festivals. Be creative, don't leave home without them!

People retain information differently. People who are visual tend to store information in pictures, while people who are auditory seem to retain information better through listening. Then there are those who are tactile or kinesthetic. These people seem to absorb information easier through moving, doing and touching. Strive to reach people on each of these levels. I printed my one-sheet on heavy textured paper so family and friends could feel the Old West as well as see it.

You need to create the PR on your film before you even start shooting. I once heard the story of a producer who went through her entire budget before she even stepped foot in the editing suite. However, she managed to scrape together $500 and guess what she did with it? She hired a publicist to do a write-up in the *New York Times*. She sent this article to everyone she knew — friends, donors and associates — to let them know that her project was alive and well. This producer generated so much interest with that one article that she was able to raise the balance she needed to get her film completed. People who had donated to the film wanted her to finish it, so they reinvested in the film with more donations and grants.

Publicists are not just for the rich and famous. Use a publicist to do write-ups in the trades. Do this early in production and use these articles in your proposals and your portfolio. Publicity gets results. Xackery Irving did his own publicity and he used his articles when he asked for discounts and donations. These articles are always prominently placed in his funding packages. It's not always the circulation of the paper, it's *the fact that you are in the paper*. People will read the article and won't always notice it may just be the local Hollywood paper and not the *L.A. Times*.

Never underestimate the power of publicity. Include advertising and promotion in your film's budget and start your campaign from day one, even if production is slated to last five years. The time to start advertising is yesterday.

A Conversation with Entertainment Professional
Patricia Ganguzza, a Pioneer in the Product Placement Field

Patricia Ganguzza started in the TV Spot Sales department of NBC-TV in New York and later moved to the network's Los Angeles affiliate. Today Patricia is the President of AIM Productions, a full-service entertainment marketing company where she oversees the business and development of product placement for over fifty corporate clients including Verizon, The Unilever Corporation, M&M Mars, Kraft Foods, Blackberry, and Cadbury Schweppes. Patricia's branded entertainment success these days includes product integrations on primetime and daytime television. Brands she represents have enjoyed featured roles in shows like *The Apprentice*, *Ellen*, *Megan Mullaly*, *Tyra*, *Crossing Jordan*, *Dancing with the Stars*, *Queer Eye*, and more. She also brings partners to studios with brands for tie-in promotions with their feature films from Universal's *Jurassic Park* to Disney's *Enchanted*.

Patricia's schedule would make the most driven adult beg for mercy, yet she took time out to sit down and talk to me about product placement and branding because she cares about filmmakers like you and she wants you to succeed. So sit back and learn from one of the most knowledgeable, well-respected people in the industry.

What do you say to young filmmakers who are perhaps a bit idealistic about the marriage between corporations and the film industry?

I have spoken and taught classes at NYU Tisch specifically about the business of filmmaking. It certainly is a business. I meet a lot of young filmmakers who think the only business part of filmmaking is the financing. I educate them about the role corporations play in the production and marketing of the majority of films today. Hollywood and corporate America shook hands a long time ago. Although filmmakers come with all of these ideals about not compromising the creativity of their film by having any influence by corporate sponsors, I always tell them it is nice to hold the ideal vision and not have to sacrifice your creativity, but if you remain too rigid in that vein of thinking, your films may never get made. There is a creative way to involve corporations and their products without sacrificing your creative endeavor or compromising the creative vision.

There was a young French girl in one of my classes who said, "I would never compromise by putting some brand name product in my film," and I said,

"Well, enjoy your film career, whatever that is." I am telling you that this is the reality of Hollywood today. Regardless of whether you ever see a brand name in the film or not; there has been one or more companies and brands assisting that film.

How did AIM get into this business?

My background was in advertising, I was an account supervisor and a supervisor of media planning at different ad agencies. I really was able to see how clients spend their money and what they get back in return from the traditional media spending. Commercial advertising was always the halcyon of marketing where corporations spent the bulk of their money. Having been supervisor of media planning, dealing with networks and all the fees associated with it, I was in the perfect space to analyze return on investment and how much it takes to get a brand name and product into the consumer psyche.

One agency I worked with was the first company to produce a mini-series. The mini-series concept was produced as original programming for independent stations in the television markets that had to compete with network programming and found it hard to sell their commercial spots against such strong programming when all they had to offer up were reruns. All of this experience gave me the background I needed to begin to explore a new field that was in its infancy; but offered the opportunity to leap frog over traditional marketing and right into the consumer's line of sight. At one of the ad agencies my accounts included Walt Disney Pictures. Being responsible for new ideas in film marketing, we became immersed in the world of creative content and how best to reach the consumer with it.

Then I met my business partner, Joyce Phillips, who had a young product placement agency. She and I instantly saw the opportunity to merge our experience and expand the company to a full-service entertainment marketing company, specializing in product placement, branded entertainment, and entertainment promotions.

For the last twenty years we have remained a trendsetter and leader in the industry. Of course the pitch to the corporations continually changed because it was an evolving business and there were no textbooks about it and certainly no measurement of what this delivers, which is what corporations want to know, what is the return on the investment?

What is the difference between product placement and branded content?

It is really the same thing. There is an evolution that product placement made over the last twenty years. Products were appearing in films by the natural cause of selection or the creative process and some people were becoming friends with editors and when they saw the product in the films they would think, "Gee, this is a great idea. I should just go tell the corporation that I can get their product in this movie and charge them for doing that!" Actually, the product was placed there by a production person in order to satisfy a set need or a prop need, but people began to see the immediate tie in with corporations. So product placement was really meant to be something that lent authenticity to a set or a scene.

The advantage to getting a product placed by design instead of accident is that it also came with the legal clearance necessary to permit its use. It became a legitimate business when it became a legal practice to authorize the use of a product. With this came the inherent desire by each and every brand to have their product and brand name protected from inappropriate use as well. When you are working on the film the reality is that if you want the viewer to feel like they're immersed in this storytelling, you want the environment to be as familiar to the viewer as possible,

We are a branded nation so the brand names lend authenticity to a character and/or to a set. Product placement agencies actually began popping up to be the intermediary between the studios and the corporations working in the best interests of both; providing the product and also protecting the brand from any placements deemed to be in bad taste or damaging to the brand name. Then it became competitive, because when you've got a placement like Coca-Cola in the hands of a major actor and Pepsi saw it, of course Pepsi wanted to be there and then other soft drinks began vying for the same opportunities. It had the instant ability of making a brand "cool," "hip," and "relevant."

The business sprung up really just to service productions and in the process all of us at young agencies realized it was a money-making proposition. Every agency basically created original models. What we knew we needed to do of course was represent corporations and service productions and during this process make a lot of friends along the way who would facilitate the process: producers, directors, writers, studios, networks, and production people.

A major contribution that we make is that we facilitate the legal clearances for the use of brand name product for the studios, but it is really the producers who benefit from the work we do because through the loan of product we defray their production costs as well. There are a lot of young filmmakers who come to me and ask AIM for funding. A lot of these independent films can be made on a shoestring. Their entire budget may only be from $25,000 to $75,000.

Because product placement has taken a major spotlight roll in feature film marketing, most independent filmmakers who are just coming up see the major films with these large product placements, and they assume those corporations are financing that film.

That is not the case. Generally, they are simply defraying costs by contributing product that would otherwise have to be purchased or rented, and with the fee placements they are securing exclusivity for their brands. With both types of commitments, if it is substantial enough — the value of the loaned goods, or the fee paid — they may receive guarantees from the studio that the product will be featured. The value to the marketer is that their product has the chance of high visibility in a feature film with worldwide distribution.

They are defraying costs.

Yes, take a product placement in a major picture, like a Tom Cruise film, *Minority Report*. Even films of this type do have placement fees for participation that normally can start at $250,000. When you are talking about a film like *Minority Report* and you add all those placements up it comes to one to two million dollars worth of placement and it is only a tiny dent in the budget of that film. So while $250,000 would be a windfall for an independent film, it is a token fee for exclusivity on a film of this size. And on the flip side, a smaller film could not ask for $250,000 for a placement because those fees would only be considered by a company if it is an A-list blockbuster film with a an A-list actor, and a national distribution.

On a smaller scale with a smaller film, these filmmakers will come to me and say, "We have this great opportunity and I can take a product like Snapple and the whole story can be about Snapple and we are only asking for $12,000."

Our clients are spoiled; they are not used to paying for placements when they don't have to. Because I have a soft spot for these young filmmakers I tell them, "I will get you goods and services to keep your costs down and help you with crafts services, which I don't do for large films." However, on a small independent film I will sometimes provide product for craft services because every donation helps.

What do you ask for in return for these donations to independent filmmakers?

If I give beverages and food products, things that you can use for craft services, I will ask them to place the products in the film as well and provide me with a finished copy of the film. I may be able to get them locations for nothing, or I may be able to hook them up with wardrobe or with electronics, or if they need a gym, or exercise equipment. These are all things they would have to put into the budget below the line for sets for props. They always appreciate any assistance I can provide. They must promise me however that they won't forget who was there for them when they started — when they hit it big! I'm always rooting for them.

I can tell you this is a hard sell for me to sell corporations on these independent films because they want to be in the films that have wide distribution and yet I can tell you that more than five of the top ten films at Sundance every year are the films that I helped. In fact some of my clients came back and said "AIM Productions' name was all over the place!" I think that is great. I didn't ask for credits but they gave them freely.

Do people who are looking for product placement need to send you a script first?

Every single project starts with a synopsis so I can take a look and see if the content is something I would consider working on. It is impossible for me to get product into an R-rated film that is full of sex and violence. Remember these are companies that have spent millions of dollars to create a brand image and you can kill it in an instant with a bad placement.

The synopsis is my first glance; then I read the entire script and do my own breakdown scene-by-scene, set-by-set. On a studio property I will provide them with a complete list of what I can provide the production with and which placement opportunities are of keen interest to me for one or more of my brands. From there on it is a negotiating proposition with the studios. Smaller independents, as I said, work differently.

There is a responsibility that we take on and there is a responsibility on the filmmaker to insure that there is not anything damaging or disparaging to a brand. Some films I will give them the product for craft services and I will say, "I can help you with your costs, but please don't place the product in the film anywhere." It is just basically a gift.

On the reverse side if it is a great little film, then I want to see the product used in a manner where I would see the brand name in at least one scene. It doesn't have to be seen more than once to satisfy my placement requirements.

Can independent filmmakers get cash for their films from corporations?

Usually if an independent filmmaker comes to me and they have credentials then I might be able to get a small fee for them, but generally speaking the ones that call me are new directors. For example when Hebrew Hammer came to me they didn't have any credentials for me to sell them, so I basically gave permission and I gave them product to use from my clients because I thought it was a good project.

I didn't get my clients too involved in it because in my primary contract with my client I have the authority to place their product wherever I see fit, so I didn't really enlist them to say, "Oh, you should really do this film and if you like it, maybe give him some money to promote it at Sundance." I didn't do this because they would want to know why I was recommending this film when these producers did not have any credentials. Now, this producer has credentials and that I can talk about to my clients.

Is it easier to get corporations into films with celebrities?

We also worked on *Pieces of April*, which had some celebrities in it. I love the independents. I can certainly say that in some instances I can assist them with funding on a small level but not on a level where a corporation would put up the money to actually produce the film, because my clients are not in the business of film financing, and if they were they would have a better way to measure a film as an investment. Everything in the corporate world is measuring return on their investment. The film business is very risky and it doesn't fit their business model.

Do you find product placement for documentaries?

I have had a lot of discussions with documentary filmmakers and I always tell them to bring the project because this is different. If this is a documentary that will be on a cable network that has a narrow, targeted audience then maybe my corporate clients would be interested in sponsorship. Often we can negotiate a deal with the producer before they partner with a distributor and the partnership adds to the desirability of the property when securing their distribution deals, because there is so much of this out there. It is a tricky proposition though and we have to be careful what we commit to.

Sponsorship money is different than some of the independent films that come to us and ask for finance. Sponsorship money means that we want to associate the brand's name and product with the film property because we think its theme and interest will appeal to some of our consumers.

A documentary comes with credibility about a particular topic that our clients have found out through personality profiles on their consumers that a particular field or topic interests them. For instance, someone who does a documentary on Hollywood legends might be of interest to Revlon, or Max Factor. Then I would help them get some funding from Revlon to put into the film and use it as a sponsorship.

The producers can use this money any way they want. I would negotiate an end-credit with a full screen, "Special thanks for Revlon," and also a lead-in when it airs. It would have to say, "This program is brought to you by Revlon." Sponsorship dollars you can make a case for because it will air on TV and Revlon will get their opening billboard, their closing billboard and the voice over with "Sponsorship brought to you by..." This has immediate value to Revlon if the show appeals to a clearly target consumer segment.

What other ways do corporations use their sponsorship money?

There are many opportunities for sponsorships, integrated product placement, and promotional tie-ins with primetime TV shows, specials, reality series and such. Fox Sports has been very active in this area and has been most creative in their ideas and execution. For example, let's take *The Best Damn Sports Show*. Our clients came in as sponsor of the show and the product placement became part of the deal that we made with them for fully integrated use of the product brand name. There was a commercial commitment as well to secure this.

The structure of these deals usually involves the media commitment. If it is a series for instance, one commercial spot per episode would be the minimum required. In addition to the media dollars, a separate fee is usually charged for the integration of the product within the show. Product is woven into the production through the use of branded segments, product usage, or logo branding somewhere on the set. For *Fear Factor*, for instance, a brand logo can appear on a time clock. For *American Idol*, the branding on set is delivered with the Coke glasses that sit in front of each judge. In all cases the media commitment is predicated on the desire for guaranteed product placement with the series. Not random, but carefully planned.

You do this from looking at the script and knowing where it will be broadcast?

When sponsorship dollars are committed, the sponsor takes a more active role in the creative decisions that will determine how and where their branding, product, and message will be integrated into the show or series. There are no hard and fast rules. Each show will present different opportunities. If we are talking about a skateboarding competition, all we could do would be to show some signage along the skateboarding route. If we follow the model of sports, sponsor branding is seen in some of the most unexpected places.

When you see the players come off the court and they have Gatorade cups in their hands and Nike towels around their necks and the guys are wearing Motorola headphones, it is all branding. No one tells them they have to hold the cup a certain way or turn their head to camera so we can see the logo; it just apprehends us when we least expect it because we are so absorbed in the game. That is what we look for: integration that is organic and placed in a way that doesn't interrupt the viewing pleasure.

I believe branded content is really, from my point of view, a more dedicated integration of the product. Branded content takes on more of the definition of sponsorship vis-à-vis there are dollars committed beyond placing the product in the show.

For instance look at what Revlon did with *All My Children*. The whole storyline evolved around a small business being threatened by a larger company like Revlon. It was all a branded content deal that became a fully integrated sponsorship. There was a physical product on the show. There were verbal mentions that were fully integrated into the story line and this became better branded content than if you just placed the product in someone's hands or on their sets.

Would you say there are two levels of branding?

Absolutely. And yet there is still good value in the passive ones. If I put cereal in someone's kitchen on a primetime TV show, once I've established that this is the cereal that this family eats, for continuity purposes it will always be somewhere on that kitchen set for the life of that season. While it may not be the level of exposure equivalent to branded content visibility, you do get those impressions week-to-week and slowly it builds up an awareness of the brand associated with that character or the show.

Standard product placement in TV is not as accepted by the networks because they feel it might interrupt some bigger deals on the horizon. Networks orchestrate and are now heavily involved in many product integration deals through media commitments mostly with their reality series and in several scripted series as well. These deals help the network sell out their media inventory while giving back (at a price) the desired content integration with their deal. In Europe and abroad, however, product placement in television series is common practice because they don't produce many films over there, so the value of product placement is heavily focused in TV shows.

You mean those product placements we saw in *Seinfeld* weren't paid for?

No, I represented those companies. We placed the Snapple in there, we placed the Post cereals and we placed the Stairmaster in all of those episodes. Every time there was a gym seen in that series we would mobilize $100,000 to $250,000 worth of product and get it over to the set. We would make that gym look as authentic as possible. The scene would be shot and we would ship it right back to our storage. If they had to rent that equipment it would cost them thousands of dollars to do that. I would get it there on our own steam and give it to them for their use at no cost.

We always start by being a production resource for the television productions and feature films we assist. When *Seinfeld* needed East coast seaweed for an episode, we found it. This was the episode where Kramer was practicing his golf swing at the beach.

In terms of goods and services, anything they ever needed I would make sure we found it. I had to call all over the state of Maine to find a company willing to ship over a barrel of East coast seaweed for them to make that beach scene look authentic. I didn't even know there was a difference between East and West coast seaweed at the time! I found a willing partner up in Maine to ship it for me.

On *Seinfeld*, the writers were always writing brand names into the scripts but even though they wrote it into the script, it was my responsibility to get companies to agree to it. Not every company thinks something scripted is funny, especially if they are talking about their brand.

A simple answer to your question is no, they did not pay to be on *Seinfeld*. This is the one show that brought product placement to light because the writers were just so brand friendly. Even though the networks were constantly telling the producers, "You can't do this," every week the producers were like, "Hey, we are your number one show. Are you really going to tell us that we can't do this?"

The producers had all of the power because they had a hit on their hands. Most new, unproven shows don't have that much confidence to defy the networks because doing so might get them kicked off the network. We are all still suffering from *Seinfeld* withdrawal. No show ever organically and consistently promoted brand names the way *Seinfeld* did and it was never offensive.

We do a lot for productions, sometimes on their request, sometimes on our suggestion. For instance, when *Real World* first started, I was the one who negotiated the IKEA deal for their show. I was talking to the producers and I found out that every series is a different house in a different city. One day I was talking to the producer who said, "I have to furnish this house." And I said, "Why don't we just get a furniture sponsor, then you don't have to go buying furniture every time you go to a new house?"

I pitched the idea to IKEA and they loved the association with this show. I negotiated the end-credit with the full logos saying, "Furnishings provided by IKEA." Even though it wasn't an MTV produced show it ended up airing on MTV and if MTV had been the producers I would never have gotten away with that. MTV would have put a big dollar value on that. We did this deal on barter. IKEA completely furnished every house for every Real World from that point forward. The deal has never changed.

How did AIM get compensated for this?

We didn't! IKEA was not a client of mine at the time. I just cold-called them and pitched the idea. Never underestimate the power of the pitch! It was a great way for me to establish our credibility with the producers and strengthened our leverage with them.

I talk to corporations every day about brands and you need to know about how brand marketing works to be able to sell them on an idea. You have to know what excites them and what doesn't. You have to know what they are willing to pay for and what they are not. I read a script a day just for feature films and we work on every primetime television show as well, network and cable.

The film scripts I read are all films in production that were picked up by major studios. Of course in between the studio properties I am reading independents that we regularly help. I am just a big fan of independents. When you watch the Academy Awards, nine out of ten of those awards go to the independents because it is the best work.

We are educating our brands and corporations on getting more involved in the support of film because film entertains and communicates in a way that nothing else can. Each involvement however must be analyzed so they see their return on the investment. We can no longer simply sell the "sizzle," we must deliver the "steak."

Do you have any stories you can tell about documentaries that you have helped with branding?

We worked with this man who is an official explorer for Discovery. He has had many articles written about him in the science section of the *New York Times* about his deep-sea dives. He was the one who was diving for one of Columbus's ships and they did a documentary on it. He called me and told me how much computers are a part of his work. He said they have special software and they map everything out and all of the findings are logged back into the computer. I represented Gateway Computers at the time, so I said I would be interested in giving him a Gateway computer if he can in some part of the documentary show how the computer assists him in this very interesting process of discovery. We would love this and I would encourage Gateway to participate.

We gave him a laptop, which he was so grateful for. In this instance his show was already picked up and financed by Discovery. It is not the distributor's job to take care of your production needs like goods and services that companies like AIM provide.

These kinds of things actually excite my clients because they are great PR stories. They may not get a lot of product placement visibility but they get PR and that is very important to corporations.

Tell us what the corporations want from producers.

We don't ask them to force anything that would not normally occur in their storytelling, because I don't believe that anyone in the product placement world should be forcing creative. I believe that anything that we do for the corporations, which also is at the end of the day what studios want, is to have your product placed in a very organic and relevant way so that the character that is drinking the beverage is relevant to the character and is also relevant to the brand, meaning that this is typically a person who would drink this beverage.

I never force product placement anywhere. I think that the best we can hope for is that we establish the brand as a desirable product. For example in the documentary we had a Gateway computer in the hands of this incredible explorer who relies on his computer to document his findings. That is a great PR story because we want people to take Gateway Computers seriously.

When I place it in TV shows basically I am not looking for the celebrity profile with the lead of the show, but with a documentary, it is another situation. He will give me an end-credit saying, "Computers supplied by Gateway," or, "Special thanks to Gateway Computers." Any time that he is being interviewed he can mention it. I gave him some ideas and brand attributes that will make the client happy to hear.

For instance, someone doing a documentary that ended up on Black History Month for instance, we have a lot of clients who are looking for ethnic consumer marketing. If we were sure that the subject of the documentary was uplifting and complemented the brand strategy, and someone came to me several months before Black History Month, we could potentially find the client who would be willing to sponsor that show.

The way media works in this country is that if you sold your show to the distributor, the distributor needs to make their money back through the commercials they sell. If the producers make a deal upfront prior to closing their distribution deal they usually hold back a few commercial spots for the corporate sponsor they bring in from their end. You can bring the program in as sponsored programming before you hand it over to the networks.

Let's say this documentary gets a company to sponsor their show, in exchange for the sponsorship dollars, the producer gives the corporation a minimum of two or three commercial spots in the show, and usually a voice over, "Brought to you by...," and then they hand it off to the distribution channel hopefully with one sponsor already in place. This will not interrupt the sales initiative of the people at that network who have to sell the commercial spots; but it will lock out competitors in that category. Or a documentary filmmaker can simply get a Letter of Interest from a company and use that for influencing their distribution deal, so the network knows that there are brands already interested in buying media when the distribution deal is in place.

Then of course the sponsor gets the opening billboard and the two or three commercial spots without having to buy them from Discovery Channel, from A&E, from the Learning Channel, etc. This is sponsored programming.

The producers can negotiate these deals and the deal they negotiate with the cable network is, "We will give you this show complete but we want to hold back two of the commercial spots." Generally speaking in a half-hour you have 22 spots so they have 20 more commercials left to sell.

You need to make the deals when you go to the network and expect that you can sell your spots. When you go to the distributor he wants to sell all of the spots so you need to get the spots in the deals you cut at the beginning.

Tell us what types of products you can get for producers.

We represent the entire Unilever Corporation; one of the deodorants, maybe a deodorant for an action show or a personal care product; female product like Ponds or Dove on a show about women. As long as we know there is a distribution in place for the television special or film, we can sell the sponsorship concept on those documentaries.

For instance, *American Idol*: we worked directly with the producer from London in its first season. Verizon was the company that provided the actual phone lines for voting; but they never thought to brand it within the broadcast. Once it became a hit on Fox then every meeting Fox had to be present and the producers had to be present because Fox placed different restrictions on the deal making. The show was a hit, so the network will control everything in the broadcast knowing that the media desirability from corporations is very high. It then becomes a media play first and integration deal second. Although Verizon was first in from a service standpoint, AT&T (now Cingular) reaped the rewards with a huge media commitment the following year and the rest is history.

In many instances on a new show, if the producers can bring the program through a distributor and say, "I have Dove interested in sponsoring part of my program," then the distributor sees a bigger value in the property. The likelihood is that the channel distributor will have an easier time selling the rest of the spots.

Generally speaking I am always asking, "Who are you speaking to? Do you have a distribution deal?" It would be very hard for our clients to put up money for a show that gets produced and never gets aired. There was a show like that called *No Boundaries* that Ford put up half of the money to produce the show and the show never got picked up. They then looked for ways to distribute the show through video and other distribution, so Ford could benefit from the integration and partnership for the money spent.

I heard that there were three levels of branding with Ford. One is where they will come in with a car if they like your script, the second is when they give you all the cars for the film, and the third is when they give you all the cars and some money for the film too. How does this work?

It is based on the project, the deal, and who's selling it. In a feature film they might provide the cars and pay a fee as well if the placement in the film is a featured one. In a show like *No Boundaries* where they feel from a company point of view they can take that whole *No Boundaries* concept into the market place and really use the *No Boundaries* theme and build a consumer campaign off of it; they paid for the rights to do that.

Just giving cars doesn't grant a company the licensing rights. The title "No Boundaries" was perfect; the theme was perfect, so they helped finance the property in exchange for those licensing rights as well. If I place a product in *Will & Grace*, my marketer doesn't have the rights to use *Will & Grace* in the marketplace just because they have a product in the show. I would have to go back to NBC to say, "What would it cost for us to do a *Will & Grace* promotion?"

I went to a studio once to do a tie-in with a hit series they produced and they told me, "This will cost you a million dollars and 16% royalty on everything you sell." I said, "We're not looking for a license. I just want to do an in-store promotion around the show." Because the show had already become a hit series, the studio would not permit a tie-in promotion without a licensing fee.

Although I always tell people there are no rules, you have to keep in mind what will excite the corporation about the project. Because if it makes sense and if there is a distribution and it fits a particular consumer profile, it will have a perceived value.

There are some natural tie-ins. Some people are doing documentaries and let's say they are doing a film on plastic surgery and there is one big face cream that everyone uses after plastic surgery, then this may have a value to this manufacturing company to be in this documentary. What would you charge them? You have to find out what your costs are. What kind of returns would you like? What are you willing to give up for the amount of money you are asking?

I always say that financing is the most creative part of the development of any film or entertainment project. Most people think it's the story. I maintain it's the financing because without financing, no story can be told.

When I started teaching a class at NYU film school, I realized these students come to this school at great expense, with a great time commitment, and it is the only degree at this level that doesn't guarantee you a job upon graduation. Each year they have to produce a student film that will cost them $25,000 to make. It is mind-boggling. You have to have a passion in order to pursue this career. That passion which stems from a "state of mind" must carry through and work in every part of your development. That's why I always tell the students; "Don't think in the total number of $25,000, think of the ways you can chip away at the $25,000."

I tell them to do the math and see how much real dollars you need, and how much can be defrayed with donations. You must go to every resource you can think of because the more people you talk to and the more sources you go to the more you understand how this business works. One of the ways to get people to part with their money is to be able to communicate your vision to them.

Your pitch is very important to your film. I am on the phone every single day. I cold-call everybody. Granted I represent 200 brand name companies but when I am servicing a production I am calling everybody. It is very hard to get corporations to part with their money. You have to give them a reason and you need to understand who you are talking to. My dad used to say, "Remember before whom you are speaking."

You need to understand that the pitch for a corporation may not be the same pitch for someone who wants to get into the film business. You should just use your passion about your film to get them to take their savings and give it to you to be a producer. There are many people who want to be in the film business and they don't have a clue on how to get a return on their money, but they want to be in the film business. Then you just want to be honest and let them know the passion you are communicating is the passion you will deliver in the film. Anyone who invests at this level knows they are investing in you, not the film. There are people who want to get into the film business and they will buy their way in.

There may be people you would never think of asking: a cousin, an uncle, someone you meet at Starbucks. Just never lose the passion for your film. I know two young men who were going to school to become filmmakers who now have a deal for a feature film. Their story is amazing. They are two guys from NYU who wanted to be filmmakers and in order to support themselves through school they started filming weddings — one right after the other — to make the money to produce the school films. By the time they finished school they figured the best story they had was the story they created! They wrote a story about themselves on how they had to film weddings to get through film school and now a studio has picked up this film and thinks that it is a funny script.

Filmmakers and documentary filmmakers have a passion about what they do, but what they don't have is a business head. That is the only thing they are missing. The business head thinks, "How do I manifest the money? Where do I manifest the money?"

When filmmakers call me to ask, "Will Snapple give me $12,000 to make this film?" I say, "No, but let's talk about this film and look for ways to tackle this budget." I tell filmmakers to go to their local stores for help as most of them would love to be part of a film. Go to the businesses you frequent, and the people you know. Go to the places you shop. Get to know the owners of those businesses and talk about what you love to do.

The way you think creatively about your project is the way you have to think creatively about your financing.

Patti, you have so much information to give to filmmakers. I am really glad you are teaching.

I think NYU has such a unique group of young filmmakers it is a joy to teach there. I love to work with the independents. I am the president of the company and I take care of them myself. Just remember, goods will translate into dollars. Every time you have to go out and buy lunch for someone — a bottle of soda, rent a light, rent a cell phone — you may be able to get these things donated and that can save you money on the bottom line.

Again the way you think creatively about your project is the way you have to think creatively about your financing. Remember, *you are in the business of film. It is a business.*

For current updates on product placement see *www.fromtheheartproductions.com.*

CHAPTER 11

THE MONEY MAZE OF PUBLIC FUNDING:
WORKING WITH ITVS & PBS

I always feel like I'm in the middle of a Monty Python movie when I look for information on those public television websites. I can see John Cleese with that comedic expression on his face looking totally baffled by all of it.

There is some money here for you but you need to know how to carefully tread the path and get out of the maze before dark!

When President Johnson signed the Public Broadcasting Act in 1967, he said the creation of public broadcasting would "give a wider... stronger voice to educational radio and television by providing new funds for broadcast facilities."

The Corporation for Public Broadcasting (CPB) provides the largest source of funding for public television. PBS is not a network. It is a private, nonprofit membership organization that funds and distributes programs for more than 340 member stations located throughout the United States. Programs that air on PBS are produced through member stations and the independent film community.

PBS has access to the General Program Fund, which typically funds programming for major mini-series, and the PBS/CPB Challenge Fund, which is designated toward co-producing major mini-series with significant funds allocated for one-hour programming. (These projects must be approved by both PBS and CPB.)

By the mid-1980s, complaints that the CPB had failed to diversify programming and give a voice to unheard minorities were at an all-time high. In 1988 Congress passed a new federal mandate challenging the CPB to negotiate with a national coalition of independent producer groups to establish a truly independent television service, and in 1991 the Independent Television Service (ITVS) was born.

PRODUCING FOR PUBLIC BROADCASTING (PBS)

The focus at PBS is on their returning strands and their icon series, with less focus on limited series programming, and even less on single documentary programming. While PBS does schedule one-off programming, 80% of their schedule is reserved for the major multi-part series (strands), which typically run four to six episodes. The strands also command the greater part of the PBS budget.

There is an up side and a down side to working with PBS. When you bring PBS a program with a $1 million budget it will end up coming in at $1.5 million because of all of the required ancillary elements. This includes all of the activities surrounding promotion and advertising, such as on-air promos and the development and maintenance of a website, as well as those activities that are integral to PBS's philosophy, such as educational programs, audience outreach, and closed captioning. These expenses must be covered in addition to normal production expenses, so if you're going to produce with PBS, you must raise extra funds. The good news is that PBS raises funds too.

Even projects that receive significant funding from PBS usually only end up with one-fourth to one-third of the production budget, which means producers working with PBS are usually required to seek additional funding from outside sources. The program producer is also responsible for managing all aspects of a project's development and production. PBS will consider allocating finishing funds for one-off programs, though they usually do not make that decision until a project has reached the rough-cut stage of production.

PBS children's programming has a significant infrastructure with anywhere from $10 million to $20 million raised for weekday programs. These multi-million dollar productions typically run about 45 episodes per season, which places children programming beyond the scope of most independent filmmakers.

PBS accepts proposals on an ongoing basis. Proposals are evaluated according to the quality of the proposal, the credentials of the production team, PBS's schedule needs, and the financial commitment required by PBS. PBS wants quality programs that are journalistically sound and will reach a broad spectrum of people. If you have a project in mind, you need to make sure that your project is in sync with PBS's goals for your particular target audience.

If your proposal meets the PBS criteria it is forwarded to the senior director for the appropriate genre, who will present your proposal to a content team. Together they will evaluate your proposal and make specific recommendations regarding your project. Your funding plan and your list of possible donors will be forwarded to PBS's underwriting department so that each of your potential funding sources can be verified as an acceptable donor. The senior programming team then reviews recommended proposals and makes the final decision on whether or not to green light the project. This team includes PBS's president and CEO and PBS programming executives in Virginia, Florida and California.

There are other ways of getting on PBS. Some producers distribute their films on a market-by-market situation by contacting each PBS station. PBS Plus feeds programs to local stations to be picked up and scheduled on an ala carte basis. These programs are completely underwritten so they come to PBS fully funded. Producers should also consider other funding sources available for PBS through ITVS and the CPB Minority Consortia, which covers contemporary issues that fall within the five minority consortia including: Latino Public Broadcasting, National Black Programming Consortium, Native American Telecommunications Association, the National Asian American Telecommunications Association, and the Pacific Islands Telecommunications Association.

If you are even thinking about producing for public television you need to visit the respective website and carefully review their guidelines. They have very strict guidelines on who can underwrite programs and if they feel even one of your underwriters has any real or perceived influence regarding the content of your project they will not accept it.

On the PBS website is a page called Resources for Producers: *pbs.org/prv/ utils/forproducers_resources.html*

It lists the following sources of funding for three categories: funding sources, PBS series, and minority consortia. Here are the links to their websites:

A. Funding Sources

1. Public Broadcasting Service (PBS) *www.pbs.org*

2. Corporation for Public Broadcasting *www.cpb.org*

    a. America at the Crossroads

    b. New Voices, New Media Fund

3. Independent Television Service *www.itvs.org*

    a. LINCS

    b. Open Call

    c. Independent Lens Series — co-created with PBS

B. PBS Series

1. American Experience *www.pbs.org/wgbh/amex*

2. American Masters *www.pbs.org/wnet/americanmasters*

3. Frontline *www.pbs.org/frontline*

4. Wide Angle *www.thirteen.org/wideangle*

5. Independent Lens *www.pbs.org/independentlens/submissions.html*

C. Minority Consortia

1. Latino Public Broadcasting *www.lpbp.org*

2. Native American Public Telecommunications *www.nativetelecom.org/*

3. National Asian American Telecommunications Association *www.naatanet.org*

4. National Black Programming Consortium *www.nbpc.tv*

5. Pacific Islanders in Communication *www.piccom.org*

II.

1. PBS/CPB Challenge Fund *www.pbs.org/producers/funding.html*
   Full proposals and project budgets must be submitted to both PBS
   (see Submitting a Proposal at *www.pbs.org/producers/proposal.html*) and
   CPB (see Submission Instructions at *www.cpb.org/grants/challengefund/*)

2. P.O.V. *www.pbs.org/pov/utils/forproducers.html*

AMERICAN PUBLIC TELEVISION (APT)

APT is the main distributor for thousands of quality series and single programs in all genres, including: children's, drama, performance, comedy, music,
documentaries, news and public affairs, and how-to series. They offer a wide
array of marketing and distribution services and will provide promotion and
ongoing carriage reports for a fee.

APT works with all 349 public television stations to help shape content,
program design and pledge formats. APT has developed some of the most successful public television fundraising programs, such as The Moody Blues in
Concert at Red Rocks and the Dr. Andrew Weil specials.

ITVS

ITVS was designed to open the door to independent producers by acting as a bridge between producers and public television. They are interested in subject matter that may be controversial and would not have been funded without their support.

Programs that air on ITVS are utilized beyond the initial broadcast, through the public education system and various public programs designed to stimulate group discussions. They want films that will promote healthy dialogue; therefore, the ITVS judges will consider your film's potential for promoting stimulating conversation as one of the most important criteria during the evaluation process.

ITVS encourages emerging producers to bring their projects. While they do not sponsor student works, they are looking for individuals who want to be professionals. ITVS will embrace filmmakers who are just on the doorstep, and will accept the responsibility of nurturing emerging filmmakers as they make their way into the industry.

ITVS will be involved throughout your entire project as your executive producer. This is a full service organization. Services include funding, creative development, feedback during production, and a comprehensive public television launch which includes marketing, publicity, website, station relations and outreach support. They have 13 grassroots staff members who take new projects around the country into local communities where they work on building an audience.

They have two open calls a year, with deadlines in February and August of each year. It takes judges about four months during each round to read and evaluate submitted proposals. One recent round included 640 proposals. The rounds operate in either two stages or three stages. Usually there is an internal cut followed by a second phase, then the third phase, which goes to a panel.

During the re-application stage, filmmakers who are selected for the last round will have an opportunity to address certain issues brought up by the judging panel. Filmmakers submit a detailed budget during this re-application period. The panel will discuss and evaluate each proposal before deciding which ones will be considered for funding.

The most crucial phase in the selection process is the orientation. During this phase, producers whose projects have been selected so far travel to San Francisco where they will undergo two and a half days of intense meetings filled with essential information about ITVS's role during production. (For more personal information on ITVS, read the chapter with Jilann Spitzmiller's interview for her experience with ITVS funding *Shakespeare Behind Bars*.)

ITVS also features LINCS (Linking Independents and co-producing stations) a joint proposal between producers and local public television stations that provides matching production funds. LINCS is considered a very important project because it promotes the collaborative effort and allows projects to reach smaller stations that do not have a competitive edge. See *www.itvs.org/producers/funding.html*.

ITVS has a Diversity Development Fund which seeks talented minority producers to develop projects for public television. They want "to support minority artists to tell their stories and reach audiences often overlooked by conventional programming. Projects must be in the research or development phase, and cannot have begun production." See this site: *www.itvs.org/producers/ddf_guifelines.html*.

ITVS has another fund called Research and Development/Commissioning Funding. They state that "ITVS accepts proposals on an ongoing basis for production funding for projects that do not fit within the parameters of its standing initiatives (open call, LINCS and DDF), including limited series." Website: *www.itvs.org/producers/funding.html*.

When ITVS funds a project they require a licensing fee for U.S. broadcast. This license gives them copyright over the project during the duration of broadcasting, which usually covers six releases in four years; or four releases in three years, after which all rights revert back to the producer. The producer will control the international rights, home video rights, domestic and international rights, educational domestic rights, and the international theatrical domestic rights while ITVS will enjoy domestic rights for television broadcast.

If ITVS is the full funder they will take 50% of the royalties of other funding, which is their back-end share for the funding they put in, which can be considerable compared to what is available. Some of this funding comes from the Corporation for Public Broadcasting (CPB), which is ITVS's funder. There is a back-end share of revenues earned, which is put back in the production fund for future funding of other projects. If ITVS puts in 100% of the budget, they get a 50% return; if they put in 50% of the budget, they get a 25% return. They get 50% return for whatever percentage they put into the budget.

ITVS participates in foreign co-production partnerships with ZDF

Germany, ARTE France, the BBC in England, and many other international distributors. This partnership allows several organizations to share the responsibility of funding, and creates a wider distribution base for films, which encourages more production.

If ITVS offers something to NPS and they turn it down they can offer it to PBS Plus. PBS Plus does not have national carriage and you can work with the individual stations. They also work with strands (such as Frontline) which have timeslots that can accommodate additional programs. ITVS will also take programs to presenting stations such as Nebraska Educational Telecommunications (NET) or Oregon Public Broadcasting (OPB). If these options do not work out, ITVS will send the program out via satellite and will send notification out to local stations letting them know when they can download the program. These stations can then air the program according to their scheduling needs. Sometimes if you work station by station you can get as much coverage as a national broadcast.

ITVS has additional calls on a year-to-year basis that address specific topics that may emerge throughout the year. For example, they commissioned 30 producers to do a one-minute piece on the aftermath of 9/11. When digital technology exploded onto the film scene, ITVS put out a special call for programs produced on DV. ITVS wanted to explore the different ways this technology would impact the industry and they encouraged filmmakers to submit applications for their DV projects. Keep watching the ITVS website for these types of calls.

ITVS, INDEPENDENT LENS

Independent Lens started out as a series of ten docs that previously aired on PBS for about three seasons. In 2003 they established a 29-week national PBS series that showcases independent documentaries, dramas, experimental films, and shorts. Independent Lens is a partnership between ITVS and PBS that is designed to give independent programs a year-round presence on PBS, and is part of the program service ITVS provides to the stations. They fully expect that a large number of programs that ITVS chooses to fund will be a part of this series, and hope to use this series to showcase work that is distinctive in content. This is good news for all documentary filmmakers.

Independent Lens wants programs that are "innovative, provocative, character driven, and well crafted." Most programs are scheduled in one-hour time-slots.

WNET AND WIDE ANGLE

Thirteen WNET is New York's PBS flagship station. Each department features one or more strands that are the core of PBS programming.

The news department at WNET launched Wide Angle, a weekly series of one-hour international documentaries that recently filled the time slot vacated by Frontline. WNET rarely looks at proposals for single documentaries for Wide Angle unless they have a solid international or current affairs appeal. If they receive a proposal that has a good science spin, or might be good material for Frontline they will send the proposal off to the respective producers of these programs.

Because WNET is based in New York City, they are the most watched station in the public broadcasting system. This puts them in a very strong position at the international markets when producers are searching for foreign distribution and foreign co-production deals.

Program producers at WNET have only included six or seven single one-hour or 90-minute docs in the last few years. They occasionally acquire individual programs for the New York City market; however, this is not a place to find significant funding, as the acquisition prices are in the low few thousands of dollars. They encourage producers to bring projects with some funding already attached. Visit *www.thirteen.org* for additional information on submission guidelines and how to pitch to WNET program producers.

Other important links are Wide Angle: *pbs.org/wnet/wideangle* and Stage on Screen *www.pbs.org/wnet/stageonscreen*.

OREN JACOBY

Oren Jacoby of Storyville Films made it through the PBS maze with *Topdog Diaries*, a documentary that follows playwright Suzan-Lori Parks during the creation and production of her hit play, *Topdog/Underdog* According to Oren, "When you are accepted you are told that your film will find a place in the public television system." *Topdog Diaries* was lucky enough to find its way on the PBS national schedule through Stage on Screen, one of WNET's strand projects.

The story of how Oren got his film on national television is one of perseverance, determination, and instinct. Part of Oren's success story involves

ITVS's belief in his cinema vérité–style film; however, like many other documentary filmmakers who start out without a broadcasting station and end up with one, Oren made his share of good luck along the way.

ITVS had never really funded money for development before. But, as luck would have it, when Oren picked up the phone to call ITVS to pitch his idea, he reached David Liu, the executive in charge of program development at ITVS. Oren wanted to tell a story that would show the playwright's process of bringing words to life. When David heard Oren's pitch he believed in the story and gave him some seed money.

When Oren set out to find a central character he started at the Eugene O'Neill workshop, but after sitting through 20 plays he still did not find what he was looking for. Then he heard about a new writer named Suzan-Lori Parks. He read her script for *Topdog/Underdog* and approached her with the idea of documenting her journey as she went through the creative process of producing her play. Parks agreed and that is when WNET came into the picture.

Suzan-Lori Parks was a great character from the very first day of filming. Her play was good, but there was something else about her that Oren noticed. His original idea was to produce a documentary that would concentrate on several different playwrights, but his instincts told him to concentrate on Parks. If he was going to be true to his original idea of showing the creative process of a playwright, Oren knew that he would have to stick with one writer and get inside this writer's head. He went to David Liu and explained what he wanted to do and Liu encouraged him to follow his instincts.

Up until this time Suzan-Lori Parks was relatively unknown, but true to Oren's instincts she managed to pull off a successful off-Broadway run, followed by an extended Broadway run, and eventually took the 2002 Pulitzer Prize for Drama.

ITVS are excellent people to work with. They certainly supported Oren through his entire process, and because of their faith in Oren and his project they created a great documentary.

These are wonderful people behind ITVS and PBS. Just know they are there to help you create. Now you know why I want you to perfect your pitch so you can pitch your ideas to anyone, anywhere, at anytime. Oren called ITVS and when David answered the phone he pitched his idea immediately. It must have been a good succinct pitch for David to follow up with Oren and eventually fund him. You may have only three to five minutes to make your pitch and answer any questions about your film so you must always be prepared for any chance meeting.

ARTHUR DONG

Arthur Dong is one of the most well respected documentary filmmakers in the industry today. He is a graduate of the Film School at San Francisco State University (1982, Summa Cum Laude) and the American Film Institute's Center for Advanced Film and Television Studies (Directing Fellow, 1984). He served on the Board of Governors of the Academy of Motion Pictures Arts and Sciences, representing the Documentarsey Branch, and currently represents the Academy on the National Film Preservation Board. He also served on the FIND (Film Independent, formerly IFP/Los Angeles) Board of Directors' Executive Committee. Arthur has won numerous film awards, including a George Foster Peabody Award, three Sundance Film Festival awards, an Oscar nomination, and five Emmy nominations.

His documentary, *Family Fundamentals*, explores the emotional issues that envelop three conservative Christian families with gay and lesbian children. The film, which was an official selection of the 2002 Sundance Film Festival, "is a deeply personal look at the 'cultural wars' over homosexuality that are being fought in families, communities, and the social/political public spheres of our nation."

Throughout production, Arthur collaborated with a diverse panel that included both gay and lesbian advisors and conservative Christian advisors. He challenged members of the panel to engage in healthy dialogue by resisting the temptation to polarize into two opposing groups. This supported one of the major goals of participating foundations, to support projects that involved an extensive community partnership.

Arthur's film got off the ground when he won In the Works, a grant sponsored by Kodak and P.O.V./American Documentary, Inc. The grant, which offered $10,000 in products, services, or cash, supplied Arthur with the resources to start shooting. With this win under his belt, he forged ahead embracing a proactive strategy for funding. He completed grant applications, networked, and spent quality time taking one-on-one meetings with potential funders. His strategy worked.

In addition to subsequent finishing funds from American Documentary, Inc., primary grants came from the Guggenheim Fellowship in Filmmaking and the Theophilus Foundation, with additional support from numerous sources, including the Soros Documentary Fund (now the Sundance Documentary Fund),

Eastman Kodak Company, Hugh M. Hefner Foundation, National Asian American Telecommunications Association with funds from the Corporation for Public Broadcasting, Los Angeles Cultural Affairs Department, Paul Robeson Fund, Unitarian Universalist Funding Program, California Arts Council Visual Arts Fellowship, Columbia Foundation, Lear Family Foundation, Durfee Foundation, Theophilus Fund, Lewy Gay Values Fund, Gill Foundation, and the Jay Cohen Philanthropic Fund of the Horizons Foundation.

Arthur's final budget for the project came in under $200,000. Funding took about two years from the onset of his original concept to its premier at Sundance. He decided early on that the project would be formatted for an art house theatrical release alongside a campus college tour, feeling confident that even a tour's limited distribution could generate much needed revenue.

P.O.V. was instrumental in helping Arthur complete his film. They respond to Arthur because he is a filmmaker who steps out and tackles complex issues that encourage communication between diverse groups. Executive Director of P.O.V./American Documentary, Cara Mertes, describes Arthur as the kind of filmmaker who "takes the film out and engages people who don't have a language to talk about their very human experience and how they live that from whatever perspective they are in. We believe this is a great gift." Arthur refuses to preach to the converted.

Arthur kept *Family Fundamentals'* production cost down by shooting and editing his own footage and distributing this and his other films through his company, Deep Focus Productions, Inc. "This is a good way to build a company," Cara explained, "you are not always waiting for funds to start your project. You can be generating money on your own and paying yourself and your crew back."

Arthur is truly the quintessential solo filmmaker. He did not sit around waiting for his dream to come true. He took control of his own destiny and came up with ideas and strategies that empowered him to create one compelling film after another. He is currently in postproduction on The Chinese in Hollywood Project (working title).

For more information and clips from Arthur's films, please visit his website at *www.deepfocusproductions.com.*

CHAPTER 12

MISSION, VISION, AND VALUES:

A CONVERSATION WITH MORRIE WARSHAWSKI

On Morrie Warshawski's homepage he describes himself as a consultant, facilitator and writer. He is being far too modest. Morrie is one of the best-known film finance gurus in the industry. His list of clients includes the Corporation for Public Broadcasting, Independent Feature Project, the John D. and Catherine T. MacArthur Foundation, the California Arts Council, the St. Louis Art Museum, and the New Orleans Video Access Center. He is the author of several fundraising books including *The Fundraising Houseparty: How to Get Charitable Donations from Individuals in a Houseparty Setting* and *Shaking the Money Tree: How to Get Grants and Donations for Film and Video Projects*.

Morrie provides individual consultations with film and video makers, focusing either on long range career planning or on a specific project. The advice he offers comes from years of hard-earned experience in the fundraising world. For more information on Morrie Warshawski's consulting services and his books visit his website at *www.warshawski.com*.

What advice do you have for filmmakers?

My major advice to every filmmaker is to step back from all of this and really try to understand why you are doing this work at all. This is why my consulting is so very different, and why when I begin a relationship with a filmmaker I make them go through this thing I call an initial consultation. I believe the major part of my consultation with the filmmaker means understanding, clarifying and committing to a mission statement before they can go on with the film.

What is your mission statement as a filmmaker? Why are you making films? Corollary to this is the question of vision. What do you see yourself doing in five years? The third thing is have you identified your set of values?

Mission, vision, and values. Those three things are at the very heart of my work with everyone I work with.

I say to the beginning, the emerging, the seasoned, the veteran filmmaker, "Have you clarified these things first? Because until you do and unless you do, you will not be as effective at filmmaking as you could be!"

When I tell filmmakers this before we consult, they scratch their heads and wonder what I am talking about. Then I say, "Well, either we can talk about these, and you work with me, or we don't."

This is the way I work. I guarantee if you speak to 99% of the people I work with, they will verify how beneficial this work is.

Why is it important for filmmakers to know what they will be doing in five years?

How else can you decide what you want to do between now and then? The three rocks that are the basis of all my work — mission, vision and values — each have a different function in keeping the filmmaker or any professional productive, strategic, and forceful in their career.

You asked abut the vision portion and the importance of vision is it tells you what you need to do next because you decided in the future what you really want. The issue for a filmmaker, especially, is that they have to put a lot of time, energy, and resources in the project they are working on right now. It is truer of a filmmaker than many other types of artists. The work they will do will take years to create and it will eat up their lives during that time. If they can't step back and have a perspective on how that one film is a piece of a larger puzzle, then they miss many opportunities for maximizing everything they do while they are making the film.

For example, if they were searching for grants, they should be keeping records on each funder even if the funder does not fit this film but may fit a future film.

Right, but it is actually much bigger than that. They are trying to say to themselves as they are making this film, "how can I set myself up for the next two, three or four pieces I want to make." "How can I maximize the contacts I am making now so they will help me in the future?" It also makes them step back and think whether or not they should actually be making the film that they think they should make now.

I will give you an example. Occasionally I will meet a filmmaker and we will go through the work. They have decided they want to make a documentary. When we start talking about the vision, they will say to me, "You know five years from now what I really want to do is to be making independent feature films." So the first thing I will say to a filmmaker is why are you bothering to make a documentary? Why don't you start making feature films now?

This is a real wake-up call for a filmmaker. Because for some reason they have it stuck in their mind that they have to get this documentary out. Really, lots of times they don't. They could shift it, change it and turn it into a fiction work. See, the filmmaker thinks if I complete this documentary and it is successful then it will help me in my career as a feature filmmaker and that's not true.

When this filmmaker starts looking for money for their narrative feature the funders and investors will say, "Let me see your script." "Have you ever written a script?" "Let me see the work you have done with actors, have you worked with actors before?" The documentary hasn't done either one of those. So they are better off making a short now and just turning the documentary into a work of fiction.

You believe knowing what is in their heart allows people to move to the future with a clear direction?

That's right. They can be much more strategic and intentional. I try to get all my clients to be strategic and intentional.

You want your filmmakers to have a mission; can you give me an example of a mission statement?

Yes, the mission has a completely different function. The function of the mission is that it is the filmmaker's raison d'etre. It is why they are doing anything. It is the heart of the work. Until or unless they can identify the mission, I see my clients floundering. Getting a mission statement from filmmakers is actually the first thing I do with them. In fact, I just sat down with a filmmaker yesterday and I had to walk them through creating it.

The first thing I ask a filmmaker is, "What is your mission as a filmmaker?" It may be different than their mission in life or their mission as a husband or their mission as a daughter. I tell my clients they will be much more effective in each of their roles in life if they create a mission for it. But the only mission that I am interested in is their mission as a professional. I will give you a mission statement one of my clients wrote yesterday. She said the mission of her production company is "to promote non-violent social change through amplifying women's voices."

That's a very clear mission statement.

Yes, that's very clear and it took us an hour to find it. Some filmmakers might take six months to a year to find a mission. Her original mission statement was ten times longer than this. That's a good clear, simple mission statement. My next question to her is, "If that is your mission," and this is very important, "then what makes you think that filmmaking is either the only way or the best way to exemplify this mission in the world?"

This means you have to clearly define your mission and clearly forecast your future.

Yes, and this is what drives the future. With the mission and the vision you can see what you want to do in five years. The mission is what drives you towards it because you say to yourself, "Oh, this is what I am about." And you know why it is really important for non-commercial films to locate their mission is because they are going through tremendous sacrifices to create the work. There is no way around it.

You are going to have to bleed and bleed and bleed to make everything count. And if you don't have a strong reason for doing this, a mission, then it ain't gonna happen. Those are the ones who fall by the wayside, people who don't have a strong mission, a strong driving force, a reason to make the work. Every client I ever work with has to clarify their mission the first thing.

We have the mission and we have the vision and do you ask them for a set of their values?

Yes, I do, absolutely! My task is to help them as much as I can. And what I found — and it took years to discover this — is that I couldn't really help the filmmaker in a significant, qualitative way until these things were cleared up. It seems stupid to start talking about fundraising until these things are straight. If you don't then you are not going to get the money.

Yes, and you will be so much clearer when you write your proposal.

That's right, and the funder appreciates it because now they know they are dealing with a serious person, a person with a backbone, a person that is on a mission. They may not like the mission but they will respect you for having one.

What suggestions would you give to filmmakers on creating their proposal?

The most important thing is to really understand what it is you want to make and why you want to make it. Those are the two big things and everything else flows from that. It is the journey of figuring that out that begins the proposal writing process. If you can articulate those two things, you can sit down next to somebody and say it, and a good grant writer could create a good proposal for you. Of course there is a lot more that goes into it but at the very center, the very heart of the proposal is, "Why am I doing this and what is it?" A lot of filmmakers haven't clarified these things when they start looking for money.

Right, I hear it in their pitches and don't you think potential donors realize they don't have a handle on their film?

Absolutely. Now you know of course, there are things that you can't know about the film before you make it, especially if you are a vérité filmmaker. That's okay, everybody understands this. But people have to know, what is it you are trying to accomplish with this, why are you doing it? What's it likely to look like once you have created it? Those things you really have to clarify. Then, of course, there are other things that are very important once those are done but there are subsets. One subset is, "Who is it for?"

A subset of that, which is a crucial one, is now that you have articulated who it is for, how are you going to get to them, in other words, distribution, how will you do your distribution? It is amazing how many proposals I see that don't address this issue.

When you were teaching in L.A., you made a statement that knocked me off my seat. You said, "I can tell you within 30 seconds of listening to a pitch, which films will be funded and which won't."

Well if you have been around the business long enough and you have met enough filmmakers, you can tell. But see, that's the role of funders, funders can tell. They get pitched all the time, they know. The beauty of getting your mission, vision, and values together is that it is so much easier and quicker for you to articulate everything you want to do. That's why that ground work pays off in spades because then you can hone in on the thing you are trying to make. It is like the mission I gave you, when I first met this filmmaker, she couldn't articulate her mission. She had written literally paragraphs and paragraphs trying to say what she was about and that showed me there was a lot of confusion. I know that every funder that looked at her material said, "There is confusion here, what is she really about?" You have got to get down to the nub and really hone in on the thing that is driving you and this work. You have to be able to articulate this to everyone in a very succinct, quick manner, because if you can't everybody's going to know it. That's true of the funder and the listener.

You've got 20 or 30 seconds and after that they are either with you or they are gone. That's what I find, I know within 20 seconds if I want to hear any more. Absolutely, and after that it is all commentary. I get approached by film-makers all the time, at conferences, on the street, on the phone, and I might ask them what they are doing or they may just be telling me what they are doing. Quite often they will just go on and on and on about the work and really they don't need to. They could give you a good 20 or 30 seconds at the most and see if I am interested. Because after that, they can keep talking but if I have lost my interest, it is wasted time.

I tell filmmakers they have to pause after they give you a bit of information for the listener to absorb it; to remember they have been carrying the film for years and this person is just hearing it for the first time.

Yes, and they have to articulate it like they are saying it for the first time.

Yes, with the same passion and enthusiasm as they had when they first got the concept.

Now, if you sit with that for a moment and you say, "What would it take to keep me enthused and excited about this pitch?" The secret is the mission. That's one of the practical ways the mission works. You go back into your heart and it gives you the energy to get excited and you know why you are excited about the film

Is that because you know your long-term goal?

Right and that brings the passion out every time. You might have to give a pitch a hundred times a day and every time you have to sound enthusiastic and passionate. The little energy nugget that keeps the flame alive, that keeps the flame hot, is your mission.

When someone has an idea for a film, how to you recommend they test it to see if it will have an audience?

I recommend they test the idea by starting at square one. They need to do basic research to see if anything like the film they want to do has already been created. It is surprising how many people don't do that work. This is just as important for someone doing a fiction narrative as it is for documentaries. It is imperative because if this has already been done then no one will fund it.

Once you have this settled, the second thing is to open it up. I think independents are too isolated. I say go out and talk to these kinds of people. One is distributors, people who know the marketplace. They know these works. Find a distributor who specializes in the kind of picture you are making.

Next, you want to talk to your potential audience. Ask yourself who are you making this for and then go talk to them. Tell them about the film you want to make and ask, "What do you think about this?" The whole process is just a lot healthier. Otherwise you may end up with a film that no one wants.

What I find is that many times filmmakers are passionate about the project but are not good writers.

Do you recommend filmmakers hire someone to write the proposal?

What I recommend is when they create the proposal it must be perfect. So my recommendation is do whatever it takes to make it perfect. If that means having to hire someone, then so be it. Typically filmmakers, even if they are not good at writing, can find a partner who can help them write, or they can write a rough first draft and get someone who knows about writing to create a final draft. Most of my clients have the capacity to actually create a good proposal on their own with some assistance. Sometimes it just means having someone like me look at the proposal and make suggestions for change. Occasionally if they need it, and especially if they can afford it, having a professional grant writer is fine.

Where do you find good professional grant writers?

The question is really where you find professional grant writers that know about film and video. This can be hard. There are thousands of people in the U.S. who are grant writers, take a look at the Association of Fundraising Professionals, the AFP. Everyone on this list is a professional grant writer and this is a good place to find grant writers.

The whole reason I wrote my book, *Shaking the Money Tree*, is that none of them literally know anything about film and why writing a proposal for a film grant is so different than writing any other proposal. You almost have to have been around filmmakers yourself or have done a few of them to begin to understand the process.

How you find those people is more difficult. I think the best way is to go to the media art centers around the country and see who they recommend. They are all listed at the National Alliance for Media Arts and Culture at *www.namac. org.* You can go to the website and look by state for a media art center near you. All of the media arts centers are members of NAMAC. You can also talk to other filmmakers for names of people who are good at writing grants.

Once filmmakers have their proposal written can they submit them to you for your guidance?

Yes, I have written over 500 grants myself. I stopped writing grants a few years ago. With my hourly rate it is too expensive to write for people and grant writing is just not that interesting to me anymore!

An effective way to use my time is just send me the grant package. Then with my critiques almost anyone can write a second draft that will be totally effective.

I noticed in the chapter headings of the current edition of *Shaking the Money Tree* you have small businesses listed under funding possibilities. Can you elaborate on this?

Yes, I love small businesses because they are easy to tap for support and they are very informal. They are all around you. You are probably no more than a few blocks away from some small business that you can get support from. That is the upside.

The downside is they never give you money. They are a good source for products. For example, I worked with a filmmaker/client of mine in Chicago. She told me the story of a project she was doing with students in the neighborhood. They walked around the neighborhood with a one-page description of the project. They asked the local businesses for things they needed for the film that they normally would have had to pay for. They got free meals every day for the crew from KFC, Pizza Hut and local restaurants.

They needed walkie-talkies and they couldn't find them and the local cell phone company let them have unlimited use of five cell phones for a week. For the script, the local Kinko's let them have free photocopies. I tell filmmakers all the time to look through their budgets and pick out things small businesses can donate to you. It is as good as money.

These small businesses are very easy to approach. You just literally walk through the door and ask for the manager and you can talk to them right there. They can make a decision very quickly. What you may give them in return is a credit on the film, or they might want an invitation to the film or a free video copy when it is released.

What about larger corporations? For example, corporations that are yielding between $12 and $20 million a year that may not have an established foundation, but are starting to get involved in the industry, perhaps advertising on PBS?

When you are dealing with a corporation and want to ask them for money, then you have to jump through a completely different set of hoops than with a small business. This is much, much harder. Most of my clients have not had much luck with corporations. I would say there are some general things to keep in mind that are true about corporations.

One thing to consider, unlike a private foundation, there is usually more than one door you can go through and it is not always clear which one you should go through. For instance, one door might be human resources, or another door that is a lot more usual is the marketing door, or the community relations door. There is another door that no one talks about and that is the CEO's door. If the CEO has a personal interest in the topic of the film, or knows someone you know, well, then that door might open to you. You need to think of all these doors before you approach the corporation.

Another thing about corporations that is difficult is that if they don't have a formal giving program or foundation it is hard to do the research. They might have given to a film before but it may not be found on the paperwork. Unlike a private foundation that has to list everything, they may have just expensed the money, as they do not have to list it separately. This makes the research difficult.

The basis of all good fundraising is savvy research. So what is a good film-maker to do? The answer is obvious. You need a personal contact. You almost always need someone who will walk you through one of the doors if you want to get corporate money.

Let's say you decide to go for corporate money. What type of package would you need to take them?

That's the other bug-a-boo. A normal grant proposal won't work in a corporation because they never really give you the money outright. If you get a donation from a corporation it is almost always a marketing buy. Filmmakers can call it whatever they want, but as far as the corporation is concerned they are buying something. That means when you go to them you have to talk to them in a way that is very different from talking to any other donor.

With corporations you have to have a lot of demographic data and psycho-graphic data. You need to tell them essentially who the audience is that will want to see the film. You have to show them the psychographic data. Here is the age group; here is where they live, and here is how much they spend on these kinds of products.

The corporation is thinking, "I want more good will from people who buy my products. How will your film help me impact those people I want to reach?" You have to make this connection for them.

Where do you think is the best place for filmmakers to go for funding?

Your mother, your father! You know Carole; it is too big of a question to answer generally. It depends on several factors. One factor is what type of piece are you making? Some work is more appropriate for some venues of fundraising than others. If you are making an independent narrative feature film you probably don't want to go to private foundations. On the other hand, if you are making a social issue documentary then you absolutely do want to go to private foundations.

I am recommending that everyone go to individuals as much as they can. It is an underused resource of funding for most filmmakers. It is so proactive and there is a lot of money available but there are some instances where individuals would be impossible, like short experimental work.

You may be stuck paying for it yourself, or there are a handful of foundations that are interested in this type of film, but you won't get money from individuals.

Then you feel individuals are a good untapped resource?

Oh, yes, absolutely.

How many ways do you work with people, and how do they reach you?

The easiest way is to go to my website at www.warshawski.com. On my page called "Workshops" there is a detailed description of my initial consultation service. That is the fastest way to find out how I work. I am very clear and detailed about what I want from a filmmaker before we talk, and then what they will get during that initial consultation. That is how I begin every relationship with every filmmaker. After that I am very flexible. I work on a retainer by the hour or by the day if the filmmaker and I both agree we are a good match. That is one thing we discover in our initial conversation.

What do most of your clients want help with?

The filmmaker always comes to me because they are desperate for money. The reason they have called me is they have hit the wall and are desperate for funds. Then they get the good news and bad news from me. The bad news is I can't help them with the money until they work on these things with me. The good news is if they can get these other things straightened out they will absolutely increase their effectiveness as a fundraising filmmaker. But whether or not we will continue to work together depends on a lot of factors. For one thing, usually the initial consultation gives the filmmaker enough work to keep them busy for a year without me.

On the other hand I have had relationships that went on for years afterward where I kept working on a couple of tracks. One of these is career development. What I can do is help someone keep in context how their current project is just a piece of a larger puzzle. Filmmakers can wear blinders. They can get so involved in their projects they can't see the forest for the trees. I help to keep bringing them back to the larger picture and that way they can make more powerful strategic decisions.

Then another track we work on is fundraising. I don't do the fundraising or write the grants, but I help keep them on course, spot check, and look at proposals. But I am much more interested in the entire life of the filmmaker.

This must be very rewarding work for you, Morrie.

Yes, it is. I love the work I do.

CHAPTER 13

SPONSORSHIP IS DEAD!
PARTNERSHIPS ARE ALIVE AND WELL!

BY DANIEL SHERRETT

Daniel Sherrett is the Founder of *beep!* (branded entertainment equity partners), branded entertainment and sponsorship consultants who work with producers and corporate America to bring a variety of television, film, entertainment and cultural projects to fruition via corporate/brand partnerships.

The following was written by Daniel Sherrett.

"Sponsorship Is Dead" is how I addressed a large group of television and film producers at a conference in New York City.

The obvious reaction from the crowd was a deep breath and an "oh no!" as so many producers have relied on sponsorship to help fund their projects.

I partially relieved the tension in the room by announcing, "Partnerships are alive and well." But, there was still a lot of explaining to do.

When I say, "sponsorship is dead," what I mean is that sponsorship, and the way it has been presented, is yesterday's way of approaching corporations for production and promotional funding.

"Sponsorship" is now perceived by potential corporate partners as "a lot of money for very little return."

Let's take a look at the definitions of Sponsorship and Partnership:

Sponsorship: "One that finances a project or an event carried out by another person or group, especially a business enterprise that pays for radio or television programming in return for advertising time" (dictionary.com).

Partnership: "A relationship between individuals or groups that is characterized by mutual cooperation and responsibility, as for the achievement of a specified goal" (dictionary.com); "a contract between two or more competent persons for joining together their money, goods, labor, and skill, or any or all of them, under an understanding that there shall be a communion of profit between them" (online plain English dictionary).

Note the major difference: Sponsorship — return — advertising; Partnership — return — ROI (return on investment).

ROI, or return on investment, is what the new breed of marketing executives at corporations are looking for. The old "sponsorship model" could offer a sponsor little more than opening and closing program billboards and maybe a commercial spot or two within a program. The sponsor could buy the same media exposure or media value from a television broadcaster for a mere fraction of what the producer needed in funding to bring their project to fruition.

Corporate Partnership Model

As previously stated, corporations are looking for tangible returns on their investments. The old days of "let's sponsor this because we like it" or "because the CEO is particularly interested in that subject matter" are gone.

The new breed of marketing/communications executive is looking out for the best interests of the company and has been mandated to make sure that getting involved with a television program or film is in line with the company's current marketing, sales and communications strategies.

Now that many people who are looking for funding have heard that partnership has replaced sponsorship as the latest buzz-word to get in the door, most are simply approaching potential corporate partners with the same old sponsorship package, masking it as a partnership. That won't fly!

Corporations are looking for true business partnerships. Again let's look at the definition of a partnership: A contract between two or more competent persons for joining together their money, goods, labor, and skill, or any or all of them, under an understanding that there shall be a communion of profit between them. Aha! There's that ugly word profit. This could just as easily say that there shall be a return on investment.

In order for those of us who on the "asking for funding" side to better understand what return on investment means to our potential corporate partner(s), we are going to have to do some research and find out how they run their businesses.

Return on investment will mean different things to different companies, based on many varying factors: type of business, products' demographic target, company mission statement and philosophy, business location(s), distribution, etc.

ROI isn't always about selling more goods. In the case of the insurance and financial services industries, corporate partnerships will likely be more about creating good will in the community and seeing longer-term benefits. It will be particularly important to these industries to have more local grass-roots involvement, via their branches, agents, etc.

Let's take a look at a typical corporation and the working groups within that corporation that should be affected by the company's decision to enter into a corporate partnership with a film, TV series/special, event, etc.

TRADITIONAL MEDIA BUYS	⬥ Brand Partnership
	⬥ Brand Exposure
⬥ TV	⬥ Product Placement
	⬥ Consumer Promotion Corporate
⬥ Print	⬥ Communications/ PR
⬥ Outdoor	⬥ Internet
	⬥ Hospitality, etc.
Sponsorship, Consumer Promotion, PR, Internet, Hospitality, etc.	TRADITIONAL MEDIA BUYS

XYZ Corp.
Marketing
Advertising
Website — online strategy
Sales — sales force
Consumer/Trade Promotion — contests, sampling, etc.
Corporate Communications/PR
Retail partners (if products sold at retail).
Agents (if products or services sold through agents).

Trade shows

Hospitality — hosting

Employee relations — incentives

Merchandising — books, posters, apparel, etc.

Donations/Cause Marketing (supporting charities).

Now, when crafting and pitching the corporate partner's benefits package, there are a lot more "hot-buttons" to push and a greater opportunity for the corporate partner to see a return on investment. Developing a partnership that gets many areas of the corporation involved creates excitement within the company and a healthy competitiveness between the divisions to get as much out of the partnership as possible.

Money for corporate partnerships (sponsorship as many may still call it) is available; we on the asking side just have to work harder to get it and earn it.

Keeping the corporate partner satisfied is key. Fulfillment is the most important aspect of the process. We promised that we were going to do this and that for the money/funding so we'd better come through. There's no question that this is a lot more work than the old "sponsorship model", but, if well executed, the new "partnership model" will keep corporate clients coming back for the "next big project."

Because the new process is a lot more work, many producers/property rights holders will look to a specialist that is experienced in marrying corporations with media properties and one that has a good track record within the industry. Most producers want to produce and simply do not have the time to research, create, pitch, and fulfill a corporate partner relationship.

Now is as good time as ever to be looking for a corporate partner because as traditional media and its audiences become more fragmented and the cost of media less efficient, many corporations are looking for more creative and tangible ways to reach their customers and potential customers. Some people call it niche marketing, others one-on-one marketing, but whatever you call it there is a trend to move budgets away from traditional mass media advertising. The old "shotgun" approach doesn't work anymore, it's too inefficient. That's why we've seen such a proliferation of "specialty" TV networks, magazines, websites, etc.

To take this several steps farther, a corporation can now partner with targeted media properties (TV programs, films) that will deliver the exact audience they're looking for and be able to leverage their partnership investment by integrating many aspects of their business.

Many producers are nervous that by bringing on a corporate partner they might be giving up some creative freedom around their projects. In most cases, the senior marketing/communications staff at corporations are very "media savvy" and do not want to interfere with the content of a program or film. They're "buying in" because they like the content that was presented.

They also realize that the general public is now more media savvy than ever and they don't want to do anything that might turn the audience off.

In developing the corporate partner's package, creativity is more about what can be done, (leveraged) outside the program/film than within. This can be a big win for the producer, especially if the corporate partner is directed to spend a portion of the partnership funds on promoting the program or the film. This usually results in bigger audiences for the producer and the corporate partner. Everybody wins!

Product placement can be an important element of the partnership. The partner's product should only be placed within the program/film if and when appropriate. Again, most corporations understand this, but if the shot calls for a car to drive by, "Why can't it be a Ford?"

When pitching potential corporate partners, challenge the point person (should be a senior marketing or communications exec) to invite as many senior managers as possible from as many departments as may be positively affected by the partnership. Your chances of securing a deal will be greater if two or three of the departments see a benefit to their area.

Let's not forget that we're in "Show Biz" — that's how the corporate partner is going to view the meeting. This should be the best meeting these people have had in a long time. Because we're in "Show Biz," the corporate partner presentation meeting should be compelling and entertaining. Without going over-the-top, we should be using the latest in presentation technologies. Both electronic and print copies of the presentation should be left behind.

The presentation needs to be scripted and rehearsed, allowing time for lots of comments and questions. We should also be asking questions. No question is a dumb question. Most executives love to talk about what they do and how they do it. This will give us, on the asking side, more insight into the workings of the corporation and will better enable us to satisfy the needs of our corporate partner.

For more information on the subject, contact:

Daniel W. Sherrett, Founder & CEO Beep!
Toll-free: (866) 410-7066
Email: *dsherrett@beepgroup.com*

CHAPTER 14

FEDERAL TAX LAWS AND STATE INCENTIVES FOR FUNDING FILMS:

AN INTERVIEW WITH ATTORNEY HAL (CORKY) KESSLER

Corky has donated time to my seminars teaching filmmakers how to package their films and use these new laws for funding. He is dedicated to supporting filmmakers, and he has a good knowledge of the federal tax laws and stays current with state funding incentives.

Since you are an attorney and you have also been an executive producer, tell us why you think this American Jobs Creation act is beneficial to filmmakers.

I want all filmmakers to know that in October of 2004, President Bush signed into law the American Jobs Creations Act of 2004. The act itself is about 1,500 pages, section 181 relates to how investors can now take their investment as a total loss when the money is spent and therefore certainly get a relief from their taxes in the year or years that their investment in the film is spent. Section 199 also affects the film industry. It says that when revenue is returned, instead of paying taxes on 100% you get a slight deduction for each year the investment is returned or on any income received on a film.

Please tell us about section 181 and how it relates to film investors.

The pertinent part of section 181 states that any taxpayer in the United States such as any individual, company, or pass-through organization like an LLC corporation or a sub S corporation, that invests in a qualifying film or TV project whose budget is less than $15 million for film and $15 million per episode for television (with a cap of 44 episodes) can take a 100% loss against their income in the year or years the money in spent. There is no floor — it could be a $1,000 movie, it could be a $10,000 movie, it could be a $500,000 movie — and it just has a ceiling that says it can't be greater than $15 million. The one exception is that the budget could go up to $20 million if more than 50% of your expenses in your budget are spent in a low-income or depressed area. If all these qualifying matters are met and if the film or TV project is not sexually explicit and 75% of the wages in the budget are performed and paid in the United Sates, the taxpayers who invest can take 100% loss in the year or years the money is spent.

What if the film is made over two years, say starting in December and finishing in February of the following year?

What you spent in the first year you can write off and what you spend in year two you can write off. Section 181 expires at the end of 2008 unless it is extended. The Department of Commerce wants a report as to the impact that section 181 has had in the film and TV industry in the USA.

So the more people who take advantage of this program, the better our chance to have it extended?

Exactly. That's why I am talking to filmmakers and I am encouraging them to take advantage of this new program. I am involved in giving data for this report and I want to have the greatest amount of data that I can to encourage its extension.

What Section 181 does not clearly state has created confusion in the industry among filmmakers, producers, accountants and attorneys. It does not state whether the loss is an ordinary loss against your income or whether it is a passive loss to be written off only against passive income. All of the indicators in the legislative intent and history behind this Section and all that has happened since the act was enacted, have indicated that you can take the loss as an ordinary loss and thereby substantially reduce or even wipe out the investor's tax liability in the year or years the money has been spent.

Can you give me an example, say someone had a liability of $100,000 in tax and the shooting was completed in the year they needed the write off, can they get the full $100,000?

If the $100,000 was spent in 2006 and if they were a 35% income tax bracket payer then the net result of their $100,000 being written off against ordinary income would be a $35,000 tax credit against actual taxes paid. However, you can not carry forward the loss to subsequent tax years. If you have a greater credit than your tax liability then you forfeit the difference.

That's when it would benefit you if the film was shot over two years.

Yes, people are taking a look at how to maximize the benefits for the investors. But sometimes they can't, sometimes the film has to be in the can by a certain period of time and they can't carry these projects over. 2005 was the first year this law was used. As I understand it, a couple of taxpayers filed their returns for investment and used it as an ordinary loss, not a passive loss and said they were entitled to a refund and they got their refund.

The accountants who want to be ultra-conservative say since there are still no tax regulations yet on how to apply Section 181 losses or tax forms to any such losses, the loss is only a passive loss. This should not be a reason not to take advantage of the loss against your income. The taxpayer should get a K 1 form from the production company showing what money was invested and what money was spent. You should also get a letter from the production company stating what the taxpayer's investment was and what was spent in that tax year. The taxpayer should then attach these two documents and a copy of section 181 to the tax return and take it as a loss against income.

I want to caution everyone to know that I am not giving tax advice. I want everyone to know that under IRS circular 230, attorneys and accountants cannot give tax advice without a disclaimer that simply says under circular 230 that you should not rely on what is stated, you have to check with your own tax advisors for the full information. I am not substituting for your tax advisor. I am just giving you some personal opinions supported by my firm.

Okay, Corky, we understand that each filmmaker needs to have his/her investors check with their accounts for specific information on their personal deductions.
Tell us if a filmmaker can use both state incentives and this federal incentive?

You can use the federal tax benefits in conjunction with state benefits. They are not mutually exclusive, they are mutually inclusive. You can pick a state that has wonderful state incentives and get benefits from that state as well as the federal tax benefits. I'll give you an example. In the state of Illinois new legislation was passed in May 2006 and currently runs until May 2007; it is revisited each year. This means that a production company that spends money in the state of Illinois gets a 20% tax credit on all money spent on production in the State of Illinois.

That is a generous discount. Can you give me an example?

A production company on a $2 million project could amass a few hundred thousand dollars of actual Illinois tax credits. Since the production company probably will not pay much, if any, Illinois state taxes it is of little use to them. You can sell unused tax credits to Illinois taxpayers. The State of Illinois Film Office has a bank that provides buyers that will pay up to 90% for those tax credits.

That's incredible!

Yes, you can get money after your film is shot and certified by the State of Illinois. This money can be used to repay your investors. This can be in addition to the federal benefits that Illinois taxpayers might have if they have invested in the film. They would get both federal and state benefits.

Filmmakers should continuously check out the state tax laws for their benefits, right?

The thing that a filmmaker needs to do is to pick out those states that best fit the climate of their movie and call or check each film office online and see what the incentives are. The filmmaker can also call an attorney that is well versed in this area and secure this information. I would encourage any filmmaker to talk to the film offices of the state or states where they might consider filming. If the city within the state has its own film office, they should check with that office too.

Filmmakers sometimes make the error that they don't feel comfortable talking to the state, city or municipal film offices. This can be exceptionally useful in their planning stages for their film project.

Do you think the states compete for filmmakers' business?

Yes, states are competing and state incentives change almost yearly. It is a very encouraging time to have filmmakers go forward with their films because they have a wider venue of potential investors and ones who have never invested in film before.

Can you tell us about section 199?

Section 199 is the income section; it is called the manufacturing section of the American Jobs Creation Act of 2004. Film production has been defined as a manufacturer but television is not. Section 199 does not apply to television. This section says that any manufacturer (film production) can have some tax relief on money returned to the investor.

◈ from 2005 till 2007 the taxpayer is entitled to a 3% deduction

◈ from 2007 to 2010 they get a 6% deduction

◈ And from 2010 on they get a 9% deduction.

So for example, Carole, if I give you $1 back on your investment in a movie after you have already written off 100%, then you will only be taxed on 97 cents if I give it back before 2007. If I give it back to you from 2007 to 2010 you are only taxed on 94 cents and if you are given that same dollar from 2010 on then you get to pay taxes only on 91 cents and it stays at this 9% rate.

This is a little-known benefit, right?

Yes, this benefit is separate from the other investment benefit. It says that if you earn a return of $1, you only have to show the return at the rates mentioned above.

To wrap up these new tax laws, would you say this is a magnificent time for emerging and established film and TV producers?

Yes, this is a great time for filmmakers to find new investor opportunities for people and companies who may never have invested in film before.

Attorney Hal (Corky) Kessler can be reached at:
Funkhouser Vegosen Liebman & Dunn Ltd.
55 West Monroe, Suite 2410, Chicago, IL 60603
phone: (312) 701-6889
email: *ckessler@fvldlaw.com*
website: *www.fvldlaw.com*

Disclaimer. This advice does not constitute legal or tax advice. This information is not intended or written to be used by any taxpayer for the purpose of avoiding penalty that may be imposed on the taxpayer under the internal revenue code of 1986, as amended. A taxpayer should seek advice based on taxpayer's particular circumstances from an independent tax advisor.

CHAPTER 15

LIGHTS, CAMERA, ACTION!

Studio & Lighting: Interview with Britt Penrod, Raleigh Studio

Britt, we all want to know how to approach a studio for the best price for stage and light rental.

You really need to be prepared to get down to brass tacks, quickly. It starts with a phone call to a facility to check on rates and availability. Calls are better than email because you have an opportunity to form some kind of memorable bond with someone in studio operations that helps filmmakers for a living, by proxy alone. Emails don't give you that human connection and that connection is the beginning of a positive relationship.

Those of us whose job is to fill sound stages and provide as much of the necessary services to production as we can are under pressure to accomplish that goal while attempting to handle a multitude of studio projects that always happen simultaneously. The absolute last thing anyone wants to hear in the midst of phone calls, emails, and deadlines is a synopsis, followed by a log line, followed by dialogue from the script and the number of people who agreed to work for free to get it in the can. There are plenty of seasoned UPMs on well-funded projects who are going to beg for the whole kit and caboodle for whatever they found in their wallet that morning and even they won't make you listen to excerpts from the screenplay before getting right down to it.

One of the greatest things we can say, and always do say, is "What can we do for you?" You should be prepared to answer that question. When you think about it, how many people would ask a filmmaker that question and then listen to see if they can do something to help get the project done?

You should have an idea of everything you're going to need, would like to have, and at least some funds allocated to that portion of the project. Do you need a sound stage? When, and for how long? Do you need production office space? When, and for how long? What is your budget? Do you have your pre-production, materials, postproduction, equipment and services secured?

At Raleigh Studios, one of my primary responsibilities is to supply bids for goods and services other than stage and offices. If a filmmaker is able to utilize the studio for all their production needs, the better deal they're able to negotiate for each individual expense, including stages and offices. Once you know what you need, check with the studio for everything you need to spend money on. It will give you bargaining power. Obviously, if you've gotten a free editing system that came with your editor, you're going to take it. However, if there's any item, whether it's digital storage or tape decks, that are ancillary to that part of the project, let the studio know you are interested in getting a quote for those items. It lets them know you're trying to keep your project within their family of businesses. You have to do what's in the best interest of your project, but don't count out the studio. I know first hand, when the studio is able to save a filmmaker some money, it can be a lot of money.

Everyone I work with at Raleigh will do everything they can to make it work. We all take great pride in working to give you what your need for your budget, and that's any budget. There doesn't have to be a bottom-line number. I've had people call and say they only have $250 and they need an exterior shot inside the studio. If there is nothing going on and they can do it on a Sunday at four o'clock in the afternoon when no one is around, we might be able to make that happen.

When I was on the other side as a filmmaker I thought if I tell them the story and how it will better society, change the world as we know it, feed the hungry, house the homeless, etc., all doors would magically open at no cost to me. After working in studio operations I've become acutely aware of the need to keep the studio operating successfully. Free stuff doesn't keep it operating long. Everyone's story is worth telling… okay, that might be a stretch, but hopefully you've convinced your investors that you're the only one ready, willing and able to tell it. Keep reading Carole's book on funding (I've read it a few times) for a little insight on how to make that happen. Once you have some kind of budget, please give us a call.

What facilities does Raleigh have and how does that compare to other stage rental places?

Raleigh Studios currently consists of 12 stages and production support space at Raleigh Studios, Hollywood, 14 stages and production support space at Raleigh Studios, Manhattan Beach, and has recently taken over the management of the Stages at Playa Vista. The cost varies with the size of space necessary for each production. However, negotiations always take place for studio facilities and services. Raleigh is great for many reasons, especially the mindset of a family-owned business that is extremely service oriented. The last few years has seen the development of the studios Production Services Department, made up of numerous production-related, reputable companies that provide goods and services to production. Raleigh now packages services for every aspect of production, from preproduction through postproduction. Raleigh has a vested interest in the success of these companies and is selective in what companies they want to refer to their client base. Most of the services we provide are not mandatory when shooting at the studio. However, given the opportunity to bid on a production, we're confident the rates and service provided will beat any competing studio facility. Raleigh's independent status also provides a more tolerant environment for union and non-union productions. I would strongly suggest a tour and brief meeting to find out just how much the studio can assist in getting a project completed. There should be no reason to go outside the studio for production-related services.

How does that differ from the major studios?

The well-known major studios vary in their requirements for in-house services, and do open their doors for independent union production, albeit at a much higher cost to production. If your budget provides for that environment you're in good hands. But you can house a union or non-union production at Raleigh, rent the same state of the art equipment and stages, utilize the same crews, and have all the services you may need provided for you, all at a much lower cost to the project.

The reach of Raleigh's Production Partners is nationwide, including Hollywood Rentals, a major provider of grip and electric equipment, with branches in Charlotte and Orlando. Under the direction of Michael Moore, the President of Raleigh Film & Television Studios, we have also begun work on a studio facility in Baton Rouge, Louisiana. There are other locations on the horizon.

We're confident in our ability to provide options in any part of the country, and with any luck, facilities in Eastern Europe as well.

If I was a producer and needed a medium-size stage, I would come in and say this is my budget and I need a stage, lights and grip equipment, then would I rent my camera and bring it on the set?

You do have to use the studio grip and electrical equipment so no one can bring a lighting package into the studio. The way to stretch your dollar is to use any service the studio can provide and this is the pitch I use, from major TV shows to a small independent feature. If you rent the sound stage for two weeks and you also agree to rent video gear from a partner company, we are able to reduce rates for big ticket items, like sound stages — and you wouldn't be paying any more for the video gear either. On one occasion a Digital Intermediate bid for a feature was $50,000 less than any outside bid, so the money saved was substantial, and the stage rate was reduced as well. The same production received financial considerations for location fees, a swing stage, and their location grip and lighting package from Hollywood Rentals. That kind of savings wouldn't be possible at a major studio.

I really couldn't tell you how hard we try to make it work when presented with requests and at least some kind of budget.

$50,000 is an incredible savings!

Yes, and the next time that filmmaker goes to shoot their higher budget film, the production will come back to our studio — and they do. We've been hovering at close to 100% occupancy for over a year in all our facilities, at a time when multiple stages are empty at the major studios. A testament to our sincere efforts.

My advice to beginning producers is to be sure you know what you need, how long you need it, and the money you have to spend. This saves a lot of time. If you need people to assist in determining your needs, be it a construction coordinator, UPM, special effects supervisor, or post supervisor, we can refer you to some of the best in the business. Take a tour of the studio, ask for introductions, shake hands and say hello to people you would like to work with and see everything a studio has to offer.

Do you rent to short films?

Absolutely. We just accommodated a short films request for an interior shoot and all he could afford was the insurance and the studio guard. The film-maker was polite, to the point, and professional. The shoot is happening this coming Sunday, when there's no other activity at the studio. See! I'm tellin ya, if we are able to help you make your film, we will.

What if a short wanted to shoot over the weekend, came in Friday and was out by Sunday night?

As long as there is some kind of budget and the studio activity for that period is accommodating, we will do our best to work with a professional and considerate group. There is no guarantee that every weekend will be available, but the request will be taken as seriously as any large budget production.

What about documentary filmmakers who need a small set with a black screen for interviews?

That is not an uncommon request. Raleigh's screening rooms are frequent-ly utilized for interviews for major television networks and independent docu-mentaries alike. It's an affordable soundproof alternative. We've even arranged film shoots in adjacent properties for productions that didn't necessarily need, or have the budget for, a sound stage.

Even if we don't have it at Raleigh, we either make phone calls to other businesses we know or put you in contact with someone that can help find rooms available for you. I have done this numerous times when we were too full or when I knew someone else had what they needed at a very low cost. Someday when they are on a higher budget they will come back to us because of the favor.

I find this industry to be full of people like you, Britt, who sincerely care about filmmakers.

Maybe so — but to make a film, a short film, or a documentary, that's the real contribution to society. Both you and I revere that desire and will do what-ever we can to facilitate those artists, their ideals, their expressions and their shot at telling a story worth telling. If it's not worth telling you are probably shooting at a major studio and wish you had read this first!

Film Benefits: Interview with Robert Mastronardi, Sr., Regional Account Manager for Kodak's Entertainment Imaging

Bob began his career in the motion picture business in 1980 as a supervisor for Du Art Laboratory in New York City. In his 11 years with Du Art he managed the postproduction needs for independent filmmakers, television networks and studios. He joined Kodak in 1992 and is currently responsible for managing the sales and technical support for television primetime drama accounts and documentary productions.

Robert, I notice a lot of feature filmmakers are choosing to shoot in Super16 over Hi Def and I would like to know why.

Experienced producers are finding that they have gone down that road of making digital films and realized that while they saved money up front in the production budget, when they needed to go out to 35mm from a digital capture medium they encountered a lot of postproduction costs they did not anticipate. The thing is, it is more difficult to follow the path from a digital capture to a 35mm negative and I think we are seeing over the last four to five years a trend of choosing Super16 over digital capture devices. Because producers know the money they are saving up front will be spend in post to get back to 35mm film.

In conjunction, this trend to 16mm also coincided with the introduction of our Vision 2 technology which really took the 500 speed, for example, into a whole new realm in terms of an imaging tool. Now we have the entire product line in place and the acceptance in the market has been so favorable and these new emulsions make such fantastic images that it is really hard to argue against the benefits you get from shooting film over any affordable digital capture devices.

What ASA does Vision 2 come in?

From 50 daylight up to 500 tungsten, a 250T and 250D, we even have a unique film of 500T lower contrast film which has become very popular especially in 35mm. The identification number is 5229 and we are seeing a big upswing of usage in that product in features and TV work.

What does 5229 look like?

It has a different look than what you would associate with the Kodak look, which is a very saturated, rich, juicy look. This stock has a reduced contrast look so you don't really lose, in terms of the vibrancy, and you gain in terms of seeing more shadow detail. You have less contrast in the frame, which a lot of Directors of Photography actually prefer, especially when they are going to an electronic postproduction.

Are there any technical benefits on shooting 16mm over Hi Def?

Film inherently has a better color pallet in terms of color saturation and color reproduction than Hi Def. Hi Def has a very distinctive look and there is another distinctive look called "the film look" which is hard to emulate with electronic capture because of its nature. Producers are starting to recognize that when you are shooting digitally, because tape is cheaper, you are not spending money on film processing and transfer costs, then you tend to be perhaps less disciplined and want to roll the camera longer and do more takes and I think this translates to a less disciplined style of filmmaking which doesn't necessarily always turn out to be a bad thing.

However, when you are going into a production knowing you are shooting film, you tend to plan ahead and be more disciplined in your planning so that you know you don't want to go above a 5 to 1 or 8 to 1 ratio in shooting as opposed to planning a digital shoot in Hi Def or one of the other forms of digital capture where you wouldn't be worried about how much tape you are rolling. I think that discipline translates sometimes into the final product.

Yes I understand this from watching digital works-in-progress from documentary filmmakers that can be very long and sometimes not focused.

That's particularly true in documentaries and documentaries are a completely different world from feature films where you have a script that you can sit down and really plan shot by shot. Most documentaries, unless you are doing historical recreations where you can actually plan, like in a theatrical production, are sort of point-and-shoot and capture as much as you can. In years past there were some great documentarians that shot film and continue to shoot film.

Film shoots seems to involve a certain discipline of knowing when to pull that trigger as opposed to just setting up two or three cameras and shooting everything which becomes a monster editing task, plowing through eight hours of video tape as opposed to two 400-foot rolls of film.

Exactly, I remember speaking to a filmmaker who was shooting Kodak film inside of a government office and he wanted to get the workers at their job under a relaxed, natural condition and stay within his budget. He took his camera in and set it up and pretended to shoot for the first two days until everyone relaxed and when they became comfortable with the camera he put the film in the camera and actually began to shoot.

Yes, that's an old trick. I have heard that from other documentarians who did this to get people used to having a camera around because it can be intrusive in your environment. But today people are so used to seeing cameras pointed at them it is not as much of an issue now with so many reality-based shows.

Was Spike Lee's documentary *When the Levies Broke* shot on Kodak?

Most of it, there was newsreel footage, footage that had been captured during the aftermath of Katrina that was video, but most all of the interviews and many of the shots of the city after the Katrina disaster were shot on film. Spike shot a lot of film on that project.

What stock did Spike Lee use?

He shot in 16mm and he used primarily 7217, which is a 200 tungsten film, along with 50 and 250 daylight and some of the 500 tungsten.

The film had a beautiful look, especially when viewed on Hi Def television sets. Can viewers see the difference between digital recording media and film on the newer TV sets?

There is a difference. The difference inherently in video vs. film is that video has a sharp, clear, crisp image that people sometimes say looks electronic as opposed to film that has a softer overall look. There's been a lot of time and effort put into defining the term "film look," why it is different from the electronic look of video. I think it has to do with the randomness of the film from frame to frame as opposed to a digital chip where you are dealing with a grid of information that replicates one video frame to the next.

In film, in any given frame you have a slight difference between the grain structures where you have captured the image as opposed to this locked-down grid thing you have in the digital capture. I think that has something to do with the difference. Years ago people used to attribute the difference to the speeds of recording, thirty frames per second (fps) as opposed to film's 24fps. Now a lot of the cameras are emulating that 24fps, the film look, and still not getting it. So there is something else intangible that has not been well defined.

I remember hearing a famous Director of Photography speak about the benefits of using film and he said that film audiences become co-creators with the picture. He explained that our eyes are so fast they pick up the black line between each frame on the film, that split second when the camera advances each frame, we see. He explained that our minds compensate and recreate the vision we just saw in the prior frame, hence his description of co-creators. He said this is why you can be so personally touched by a movie and you can feel so moved by characters in films, especially when viewed in a proper theatre setting. Whereas video at that time was moving 60fps, which he said was the maximum movement the eye can absorb so you are just a receiver when you view video and there is less personal connection.

That is an interesting theory and somewhat in line with Marshall McLuhan's hot and cold medium that he defined so many years ago.

I have lived in three or four places in my professional career and I always seemed to live next to teachers. In my conversations with teachers, we discussed years ago when they showed 16mm films in class. Now, they show videos on the TV monitor, and some teachers remember the old days where they threaded up the 16mm projector, turned off the lights and closed the blinds to view the film. They said there was something distinctly different between the attention span of kids in a classroom watching a film print projected on a screen rather than kids in a classroom watching a TV with a video playing.

Yes, I like to believe there is some truth to this co-creator concept with film.

Going back to documentaries, I think another essential part of this move towards digital is there are lots of benefits to this renaissance of digital tools for documentarians. I am a big documentary fan and I think the more points of view we have for our society, the better. So it is a wonderful thing to pick up a very small camera and go out and start documenting your subject.

Hand-in-hand with that is the economic reality of money going to support film documentaries where over the last five to six years the budgets have been squeezed down so much so that it is difficult to support a film production unless you are an experienced documentarian who has shot film before. There's a comfort level for putting together a film budget. Yet I get lots of calls at Kodak from younger documentary filmmakers who are thinking of shooting film. As I take them through the process, during the conversation we discuss what they are planning and then when I ask what the shooting ratio is they often say "25 or 30 to 1." That's when I stop them and say, "You may need to rethink this."

This goes back to what we talked about earlier, i.e., the discipline and preplanning and how when your are working with film it actually works for you on the back end because you are more efficient in capturing your story and consequently more efficient in the editing room.

I have seen some magnificent docs shot on Kodak and usually they are Academy nominations and have had film screenings.

That's another thing, going back to independent films, we hear from distributors when they have a pile of submissions for acquisitions on their desk, they tend to gravitate towards the ones shot on film first because film portends there is a higher production value to begin with.

What future plans does Kodak have for new or improved film stocks?

We spend an enormous amount of money on research and development and we are totally committed to the future of film and motion picture technology. Even though the consumer side of the business has gone to digital conversion, here in the motion picture division we work to improve our products. Because as we keep raising the bar it becomes more difficult for the digital technologies to approach what we can do with a film emulsion so, yes, we have things planned, not necessarily changing ASAs but improving and upgrading our current films.

Robert, I want to thank you and Kodak for the many donations Kodak makes to emerging and established filmmakers. We see your name sponsoring film festivals, film grants, supporting organizations with large donations; Kodak is a major donor in our industry. I always tell filmmakers that their Kodak rep is the best friend they can find in the industry. Your

Kodak rep is always well informed, friendly and will gladly consult with you on the possibility of shooting film. We especially appreciate the generous student discount Kodak gives.

And I thank you for recognizing that. It is not always that people realize how much of a commitment we have to student and young, emerging filmmakers for which Kodak's support is spread around the world to promote their efforts.

Camera Equipment: Interview with Craig Ellefsen, Rental Accounts Manager of AbleCineTech, Professional Motion Picture Equipment Rental Company (New York City and L.A.), *www.abelcine.com*

Craig, I often find AbelCine's name marketed by filmmakers and I see your name on proposals from well known Line Producers. What type of service are you giving to create this "word of mouth" among documentary and independent filmmakers?

It's hard to say, but I think it's predominantly for two reasons:

First, we've been around for a long time and with our Aaton background, we have our roots in the doc and Indie industry. As technologies change, I think it's comforting for producers to rent from a source that they are familiar with, even if what they are renting is not a film package, but any one of a number of new digital formats.

Secondly, I think it's because we understand how tricky the transition to new technologies can be. We take the time to walk filmmakers through new equipment and new post workflows.

What are the most popular cameras and why do people like them?

Just like in the heyday of Super16, filmmakers get most excited when a new camera can give them better quality at a more economical price. Today, both film and digital cameras are delivering better images at a lower cost.

So what was at one time a 35mm project is now requesting Aaton XTRprod's shooting Super16. We also see a lot of HD business using the Panasonic VariCam, HDX900 and Sony F900R for projects that used to shoot 16mm film.

An Interview with Craig Ellefsen

Our budget-challenged Indie clients are favoring little high-performance HD cameras like the Panasonic HVX200, which takes P2 cards. We anticipate that this trend will continue.

What are the most economical cameras to rent?

Besides the HVX200, the Sony Z1U and the Panasonic DVX100A, which rent for approximately $250–$300 per day, are still very popular with our clients.

What advice can you give filmmakers that can save them money?

I think today, more than ever, a filmmaker needs to really understand the image quality that can be achieved with all the affordable formats on the market, as well as their pitfalls and limitations.

What may appear to save money on the front end, like a low-cost camera, may cost more in post to meet your requirements. The adverse can be true as well. An HD camera like the Panasonic VariCam or Sony F900R may be more expensive to rent, but the streamlined workflow and dynamic range of these cameras will often save you time and money in post.

The best case is to select the right tool for the creative intent of the project and have all aspects of your post workflow strategy in place. In this way, you are maximizing the camera's performance and reducing the potential for "unpleasant" surprises in post.

I think this type of consultation with clients is what we do best at Abel.

In all cases, we also recommend that filmmakers shoot sparingly. Just because tape or re-recordable media like P2 is less expensive than film raw stock shouldn't change the discipline of economy on set. More footage means more for storage and edit decision work for the editor — which costs time and money.

What future trends do you see emerging from the marriage of electronics and motion pictures?

I think we are at the stage where clients are more open minded about digital imaging in general, and mixing mediums and tools to their advantage.

We're beginning to see these worlds coming together with camera packages as well. Convenient electronic equipment that you wouldn't often find on a film set, like ENG style servo-driven lenses and lighter weight video accessories, are now much more prevalent because of their cost and convenience.

Is AbelCineTech noticing more production of the low-budget digital indie films?

Clearly. It's hard to say how much it has grown because most of the clients shooting ultra-low-budget independent projects are doing so with digital equipment that they can afford to own outright, but since so many new young filmmakers are purchasing these cameras from Abel, we're well aware of this renaissance.

We do see an increase in higher end independent productions; and for content creation across the board. This includes content for new media, like Internet-based industrials, streaming content and in-store content for retail outlets.

I notice on your site, www.abelcine.com, that you sponsor many events for the film community. Is that part of AbelCine's direction, to share its profits with the filmmaking community?

The reason we do so many of these seminars and workshops is because, today, production technology is changing so quickly and filmmakers need to disseminate new products and information on the fly.

We find that it's one of the best ways to share information and open up interesting dialogues. You'll be surprised how mush we learn from our clients as well. This, in turn, makes us more informed as a resource and, as a result, even more valuable to our clients.

Thank you, Craig, we appreciate your support of documentary and independent filmmakers.

PRODUCTION RESOURCES
FOR PUBLIC TELEVISION

American Public Television Producer's Handbook
http://www.apton-line.org/aptweb.nsf/vProducers/Index-Producers

Enhancing Education, a Producer's Guide
http://enhancinged.wgbh.org/
If you are going to get funding for your public television program, you will need to have an educational outreach plan. This site is essentially a producer's guide on how to maximize the educational impact of their projects. The guide will give you a deeper understanding of how public broadcasting approaches educational theory. You can see what other projects have developed as educational enhancements, and how they've done it, and discover the basics of educational outreach by exploring various educational formats.

Public Broadcasting Service (PBS)
http://www.pbs.org/
1320 Braddock Place
Alexandria, VA 22314-1698
Tel. (703) 739-5000 Fax: (703) 739-0775

Producing for PBS
http://www.pbs.org/producers/

Independent Television Service (ITVS)
http://www.itvs.org/
501 York Street
San Francisco, CA 94110
Tel. (415) 356-8383 Fax: (415) 356-8391
Email: itvs@itvs.org

Latino Public Broadcasting (LPB)
http://www.lpbp.org/
Marlene Dermer, Executive Director

6777 Hollywood Boulevard, Suite 500
Los Angeles, CA 90028
Tel. (323) 466-7110 Fax: (323) 466-7521

National Black Programming Consortium
http://nbpc.tv/
145 East 125th Street, Suite 220
New York, NY 10035
Tel. (212) 828-7588 Fax: (212) 828-7930
Email: *nbpcinfo@blackstarcom.org*

National Asian American Telecommunications Association (NAATA)
http://www.naatanet.org/
145 9th St, Suite #350
San Francisco, CA 94103
Tel. (415) 863-0814 Fax: (415) 863-7428
Email: *naata@naatanet.org*

Native American Public Telecommunications, Inc. (NAPT)
http://www.nativetelecom.org/
P. O. Box 83111
Lincoln, Nebraska 68501
Tel. (402) 472-3522 Fax: (402) 472-8675
Email: *fblythe@unlinfo.unl.edu*

Pacific Islanders in Communications (PIC)
http://www.piccom.org/home.php
1221 Kapiolani Blvd Suite #6A-4
Honolulu, Hawaii 96814
Tel. (808) 591-0059 Fax: (808) 591-1114
Email: info@piccom.org

National Science Foundation (NSF)
http://www.nsf.gov/
4201 Wilson Boulevard
Arlington, VA 22230
Tel. (703) 306-1234 Fax: (703) 306-0250
Email: *info@nsf.gov*

National Endowment for the Arts (NEA)
http://www.arts.endow.gov/
1100 Pennsylvania Avenue
Washington, D.C. 20506
Tel. (202) 682-5400

National Endowment for the Humanities (NEH)
http://www.neh.gov/
1100 Pennsylvania Avenue
Washington, D.C. 20506
Tel. 1-(800) NEH-1121 / (202) 606-8400

U.S. Department of Education
http://www.ed.gov/

The Carnegie Corporation of New York
http://www.carnegie.org/

The Ford Foundation
http://www.fordfound.org/

MacArthur Foundation
http://www.macfound.org/

The Pew Charitable Trusts
http://www.pewtrusts.com/

Rockefeller Foundation
http://www.rockfound.org

Understand the PBS Greenlight Process:
Getting PBS to Yes, by Jackie Conciatore
http://itvs.org/producers/pbstoyes.html

WNET
http://www.thirteen.org

INTERNET SEARCH TOOLS

About.com (*http://about.com*)

ListOfLists.com (*http://listoflists.com*)

Metacrawler (*http://www.metacrawler.com*)

Northern Light (*www.northernlight.com*)

Search Engine Watch (*www.searchenginewatch.com*)

DATABASES, RESOURCES & TOOLS

Free Databases

Action Without Borders
http://www.idealist.org
Searchable index to more than 21,500 nonprofit and community organizations in more than 150 countries, search by organization name, location, or mission keyword.

Charles Steward Mott Foundation
http://www.mott.org/news/detail-preview.asp?newsid=187
Detailed fact sheets on every grant made by the foundation since 1995. Updated quarterly.

European Foundation Centre

http://www.efc.be

Established in 1989 by seven of Europe's leading foundations, the EFC today serves a core membership of more than 200 members, associates and subscribers; 250 community philanthropy initiatives; as well as a further 48,000 organizations linked through a network of information and support centers in 37 countries worldwide.

FastWeb

http://www.fastweb.com/

Searchable database of more than 400,000 private sector scholarships, fellowships, grants, and loans from more than 3,000 sources for all levels of higher education.

Ford Foundation

www.fordfound.org

http://www.fordfound.org/grants_db/view_grant_by_keyword.cfm

Includes three years of grants made by the foundation, updated quarterly. Search by program or keyword. A good place to check out who got funded!

Foundation Finder (Foundation Center)

http://lnp.fdncenter.org/finder.html

Search by name for basic information about foundations, it has more than 70,000 private and community foundations in the U.S.

Foundations On-Line

http://www.foundations.org/index.html

Browse the foundation directory, pick a listed foundation, search any foundation's information page or search any foundation's home page. Foundation home pages may contain downloadable information such as grant applications, periodical and financial reports, and email capabilities.

GrantSmart

http://www.grantsmart.org

Find private foundations with areas of support that match your needs. You can also determine if an organization specifically excludes proposals in a particular area. This can save you time and effort when applying for grants.

Kellogg Foundation Online Database of Current Grants

http://www.wkkf.org

To access database select "grants" then "search database." Includes all of Kellogg's grants since 1991.

Pew Charitable Trusts Grants Database

http://www.pewtrusts.com

Includes every grant awarded since 1995.

GuideStar

http://www.guidestar.org/

The GuideStar website is produced by Philanthropic Research, Inc., a 501(c)(3) public charity founded in 1994. GuideStar's mission is to revolutionize philanthropy and nonprofit practice with information. Search grantmakers' websites by keyword. Also view grantmakers' tax return forms.

FEE-BASED DATABASES

Foundation Grants for Individuals on CD-ROM

Located at most major city libraries for free! Offers high-speed searching of foundations and public charities that provide support for individuals. 4,200 foundations and public charities that support education, research, arts, general welfare, and more. Search fields include: fields of interest, types of support, geographic focus, company name, school name, grantmaker name, grantmaker city, grantmaker state, and text search.

GrantSelect

http://www.grantselect.com/

GrantSelect is the online version of the GRANTS Database, produced by Oryx Press, containing over 10,000 funding opportunities provided by over 3,400 sponsoring organizations. Michigan State University faculty, staff, and students can identify additional funding opportunities related to film by searching this database. You can fill out the form for a free, no obligation seven-day trial.

GrantsWeb
http://www.srainternational.org/newweb/grantsweb/index.cfm

RESOURCES & TOOLS

Chamber of Commerce
www.chamber.com/

DMA Nonprofit Federation
www.the-dma.org/nonprofitfederation/index.html

Directory of Financial Aids for Women

NetLibrary. Available via World Wide Web
Access may be limited to NetLibrary affiliated libraries
(check with your local library).

Edgar Database (U.S. Securities & Exchange Commission)
http://www.sec.gov/edgar/searchedgar/webusers.htm

Fundraising and Foundation Research
http://www.usc.edu/dept/source/found.htm

Fundraising Forum
http://www.raise-funds.com/forum.html

Fundraising.com
http://www.fund-raising.com

Fundsnet Services Online
www.fundsnetservices.com/

Nonprofit Guides
http://npguides.org Database of grantwriting tools for nonprofits

Idealist.org
www.idealist.org/

Internet Movie Database
http://us.imdb.com/

Internet Nonprofit Center
http://nonprofits.org/

Internet Prospector
www.internet-prospector.org/found.html

National Alliance for Media Arts and Culture
http://www.namac.org/

National Endowment for the Arts
www.arts.endow.gov

Nonprofit Gateway
http://www.firstgov.gov/Business/Nonprofit.shtml

Online Fundraising Resources Center
www.fund-online.com/

Philanthropy News Digest (PND)
www.fdncenter.org/pnd/index.jhtml

The Grantsmanship Center
www.tgci.com/

Virtual Foundation
www.virtualfoundation.org/

GrantsNet
http:www.grantsnet.org/
Welcome to GrantsNet, your one-stop resource to find funds for training in

the sciences and undergraduate science education. Through the support of HHMI and AAAS, this service is completely free.

Grantmakers in the Arts
www.giarts.org/

ONLINE ARTICLES

Contract Law as a Remedy for Story Theft
Excerpt from *Contracts for the Film & Television Industry* (2nd Edition)
by Mark Litwak (*http://www.marklitwak.com*)
http://www.marklitwak.com/articles/general/contract_law.html

Copyright Registration of Scripts & Films
by Mark Litwak
http://www.marklitwak.com/articles/general/copyright_registration.html

Filmmaker's Bill of Rights
by Mark Litwak
http://www.marklitwak.com/articles/general/bill_of_rights.html

Grantwriting 101: Tips for Novice Proposal Writers
by Julie Seewald Bornhoeft, CFRE
http://charitychannel.com

How to Throw a Fundraising Houseparty
by Morrie Warshawski. Book available at
http://www.warshawski.com/books.html

Movie Merchandising
by Mark Litwak
http://www.marklitwak.com/articles/general/movie_merchandising.html

Obtaining Music for a Motion Picture Soundtrack
by Mark Litwak
http://www.marklitwak.com/articles/general/obtaining_music.html

Protecting Film Investors
by Mark Litwak
http://www.marklitwak.com/articles/general/protecting_film_investors.html

Tips for Winning Federal Grants
by Lawrence H. Trachtman (*http://charitychannel.com*)
http://charitychannel.com/publish/templates/?a=367&z=0

PRINT RESOURCES

The Art of Manifesting: Creating Your Future by Carole Lee Dean
(Oxnard, CA: Dean Publishing, 2006)

Contracts for the Film and Television Industry (2nd edition) by Mark Litwak
(Los Angeles: Silman-James Press, 1999)

Corporate Foundation Profiles (12th edition) by Francine Jones, Michele Kragalott
and Georgetta Toth (New York: Foundation Center, 2002)

Dealmaking in the Film and Television Industry: From Negotiations Through Final Contracts (2nd edition) by Mark Litwak (Los Angeles: Silman-James Press, 2002)

Directing Feature Films: The Creative Collaboration Between Directors, Writers, and Actors by Mark Travis (Los Angeles: Michael Wiese Productions, 2002)

The Directory of Corporate and Foundation Givers
(Rockville, MD: Taft Group, 2004)
Directory of Grants in the Humanities (Westport, CT: Oryx Press, 2003)

Directory of International Corporate Giving in America and Abroad
(Rockville, MD: Taft Group, 2004)

Excuse Me, Your Life Is Waiting: The Astonishing Power of Feelings
by Lynn Grabhorn (Charlottesville, VA: Hampton Roads Publishing Company, 2000)

Filmmakers & Financing: Business Plans for Independents by Louise Levison
(Burlington, MA: Focal Press, 2006)

Foundation Grants to Individuals (15th edition) by Phyllis Edelson
(New York: Foundation Center, 2006)

The Four Agreements: A Practical Guide to Personal Freedom by Don Miguel Ruiz
(San Rafael, CA: Amber-Allen Publishing, 1997)

The Fundraising Houseparty: How to Get Charitable Donations From Individuals in a Houseparty Setting by Morrie Warshawski
(Los Angeles: Michael Wiese Publications, 2003)

Grant Finder: Arts & Humanities (New York: St. Martin's Press, 2000)

Guide to Private Fortunes (Rockville, MD: Taft Group, 2004)

Guide to U.S. Foundations, Their Trustees, Officers, and Donors by David Jacobs
(New York: Foundation Center, 2006; in three volumes)

Litwak's Multimedia Producer's Handbook by Mark Litwak
(Los Angeles: Silman-James Press, 1998)

National Directory of Corporate Giving (12th edition), edited by David L. Clark
(New York: Foundation Center, 2006)

The Perfect Pitch by Ken Rotcop
(Los Angeles: Michael Wiese Productions, 2001)

Producer's Business Handbook (Book & CD-ROM) by John J. Lee
(Burlington, MA: Focal Press, 2000)

Reel Power: The Struggle for Influence and Success in the New Hollywood
by Mark Litwak (Los Angeles: Silman-James Press, 1994)

Shaking the Money Tree: How to Get Grants and Donations for Film and Television
(2nd edition) by Morrie Warshawski
(Los Angeles: Michael Wiese Publications, 2003)

WRITING RESOURCES

The Elements of Style by William Strunk, Jr.
http://www.bartleby.com/141/

Purdue University's Online Writing Lab
http://owl.english.purdue.edu/

The Writer's Handbook: A Guide to the Essentials of Good Writing
by John B. Karls and Ronald Szymanski

The Writer's Journey: Mythic Structure for Writers
by Christopher Vogler (Los Angeles: Michael Wiese Productions)

Writing a Better ITVS Treatment
http://itvs.org/producers/treatment.html

Grant/Proposal Writers

Cathrine Ann Jones, Story and Writing Consultant
Website: *www.wayofstory.com*

JanEva Hornbaker (Grant & Proposal Writing, Script Revision,
Film Treatments, Editing)
Phone: (602) 274-1666
Email: *eva@SNAFUfilms.com*

BUSINESS PROMOTION/PUBLIC RELATIONS

Branwen Edwards
BranwenEdwards@aol.com
Life coach to Carole Dean: Branwen's mission is to have people expand beyond their wildest dreams.

Morrie Warshawski, Arts Consultant/Writer
Phone: (734) 332-9768
Website: *www.warshawski.com*

Tony Estrada, Line Producer for independent films
Phone: (469) 471-4241
Email *TexasFilmGuy@yahoo.com*

Louise Levison, President of Business Strategies in Sherman Oaks, California (*www.moviemoney.com*) specializing in creating business plans for films and film companies as well as financial consulting. Levison is the author of Filmmakers and Financing: Business Plans for Independents, publisher and editor of The Film Entrepreneur: A Newsletter for the Independent Filmmaker and Investor.

ORGANIZATIONS

American Film Institute
http://www.afi.com

American Film Marketing Association
http://www.afma.com/

Archive of American Television (from the Academy of Television Arts & Sciences)
http://www.emmys.org

Business Committee for the Arts, Inc. (BCA)
http://www.bcainc.org/
Center for Entertainment Data
http://www.ceidr.org/

DirectorsNet
http://www.directorsnet.com/index.html

Documentary Educational Resources
http://www.der.org/

Documentary Films.Net
http://documentaryfilms.net/

Filmmakers Alliance
http://www.filmmakersalliance.com/

HollywoodU.com, Dov S-S Simens, Founder
http://hollywoodu.com
Email: *info@webfilmschool.com*
1223 Olympic Blvd, Santa Monica, CA 90404
Phone: (800) 366-3456 / (310) 399-6699

Independent Feature Project
http://www.ifp.org

International Documentary Association
www.documentary.org

MIPCOM World TV market
http://www.mipcom.com

Motion Picture Association of America
http://www.mpaa.org/

National Association of Theatre Owners
http://www.natoon-line.org/

New England Film Archives
http://www.newenglandfilm.com/
On-line magazine & resource for 38,000+ local filmmakers & video makers.

Screen Actors Guild (SAG)
http://www.sag.com

Write News
http://www.writenews.com/

FUNDERS

911 Media Arts Center
http://www.911media.org
Offers access to media-making tools for artists at a low cost

J. Muste Institute
339 Lafayette St., New York, NY 10012
Phone: (212) 533-4335 Fax: (212) 228 6193
Email: *ajmusteinst@igc.org*
Website: *www.ajmuste.org*
Funds for projects that promote social change.

Academy of Motion Picture Arts & Sciences
8949 Wilshire Boulevard, Beverly Hills CA 90211-1972
Phone: (310) 247-3059 Fax: (310) 859-9351
Richard Miller Phone: (310) 247-3000
Email: *ampas@oscars.org*
Website: http://www.oscars.org
Send legal-size SASE after January 1 to receive entry form for $2,000, $1,500
and $1,000 awards in dramatic, experimental, documentary, animation.

Agape Foundation Fund for Nonviolent Social Change
1095 Market St., Suite 304, San Francisco, CA 94103
Phone: (415) 701-8707 Fax: (415) 701-8706
Email: *info@agapefn.org*
Website: *www.agapefn.org*
Western states only, funds films/videos that promote the use of nonviolence,
they support films/videos that are unable to secure funding from traditional
sources.

Akonadi Foundation

488 Ninth Street, Oakland, CA 94607

http://www.akonadi.org/index.html info@akonadi.org

They support a variety of programmatic approaches including research, policy work, advocacy, litigation, organizing, media, arts, diversity training, education and other tools in their anti-racism work.

American Antiquarian Society (AAS)

Contact: Artists and Writers Fellowships American Antiquarian Society
185 Salisbury St., Worcester, MA 01609-1634

Phone: (508) 471-2131 or (508) 471-2139 Fax: (508) 754-9069

Email: *jmoran@mwa.org www.americanantiquarian.org/artistfellowship.htm*

Calling for applications for visiting fellowships for historical research by creative and performing artists, writers, filmmakers, journalists and other persons whose goals are to produce imaginative, non-formulaic works dealing with pre-twentieth-century American history.

American Film Institute

P. O. Box 27999

2021 N. Western Avenue, Los Angeles CA 90027

Phone: (213) 856-7691 Fax: (213) 476-4578

http://www.afi.com

Call, write or check website for application instructions.

Three-week training program for mid-career women in the media arts to learn about narrative directing and to apply for production grant positions.

American Public Television (APT)

120 Boylston Street, Boston, MA 02116

http://www.apton-line.org

Phone: (617) 338-4455

Acquires finished programs and develops/produces original programming concepts. Undertakes the distribution of programming that is tailored to specific interests or demographics.

Annie E. Casey Foundation
Attention: Office of the President
701 St. Paul Street, Baltimore, MD 21202
http://www.aecf.org/about/grantguidelines.htm
Fosters public policies, human service reforms, and community supports that
more effectively meet the needs of today's vulnerable children and families.

Arthur Vining Davis Foundations
Dr. Jonathan T. Howe, Executive Director
111 Riverside Ave., Ste. 130, Jacksonville, FL 32202-4921
Phone: (904) 359-0670
Email: *arthurvining@msn.com*
Website: *www.jvm.com/davis.*
Provides partial support for major educational series assured of airing nationally
by PBS. The Foundations prefer proposals for "capstone" grants which assure
completion of production funding.

Artists' Television Access
992 Valencia St., San Francisco CA 94110
Email: *ata@atasite.org*
Website: *http://www.atasite.org*
Phone: (415) 824-3890 Fax: (415) 824-0526
They have equipment access available at subsidized rates to artists, community
organizations, and people on limited incomes.

Astraea Foundation
116 East 16th Street, 7th Floor, New York, NY 10003
Phone: (212) 529-8021 Fax: (212) 982-3321
Email: *info@astraea.org*
This supports cultural/media film/video on issues involving lesbian, gay,
bisexual, and transgender issues.

Barbara Deming Memorial Fund
P. O. Box 40-1043, Brooklyn, NY 11240-1043
Offers up to $1,000 per grant, open to women whose projects speak for peace
and social justice.

Bay Area Video Coalition

2727 Mariposa Street, 2nd Floor, San Francisco, CA 94110

Phone: (415) 861-4328 Fax: (415) 861-4316

Email: *awards@bavc.org*

Website: *www.bavc.org/resources/grants*

San Francisco Bay Area only, with the exception of the Phelan Award, which is available to artists born in California, regardless of current residence.

Bogliasco Foundation

http://www.liguriastudycenter.org/

Accepting applications for fellowships during the academic year and their deadlines are normally January 15 for residencies during the fall–winter semester beginning in September and April 15 for the winter-spring semester beginning in February. They grant semester-long fellowships for scholars or artists to work at the Liguria Study Center in Bogliasco, Italy, near Genoa. The Fellowship is designed for advanced creative work or scholarly research in archaeology, architecture, classics, dance, film or video, history, landscape architecture, literature, music, philosophy, theater, or visual arts.

Boston Film/Video Foundation

1126 Boylston St. #201, Boston, MA 02215

Phone: (617) 536-1540

Email: *info@befvf.org* Website: *www.befvf.org*

Various funding for New England film/video makers.

California Arts Council

1300 I Street, Suite 930, Sacramento, CA 95814

Phone: (916) 322-6555 Fax: (916) 322-6575

Offers grants & programs for film & media makers.

California Documentary Project

Los Angeles office: (213) 623-5993

San Francisco office: (415) 391-1474

San Diego office: (619) 232-4020

Email: *info@calhum.org* Website: *www.calhum.org*

It is designed to encourage documentarians of the new millennium to create enduring images and text of contemporary California.

Carnegie Endowment for International Peace

Email: *info@ceip.org* Website: *http://www.ceip.org*

Private, nonprofit organization dedicated to advancing cooperation between nations and promoting active international engagement by the United States. Founded in 1910, its work is nonpartisan and dedicated to achieving practical results.

Carole Fielding Student Production & Research Grants

http://www.ufva.org

Competitive awards presented annually to students whose research and production projects meet rigorous standards of academic scholarship. Up to $4,000 is available for film, video, or multimedia production and up to $1,000 is available for research projects in historical, critical, theoretical or experimental studies of film or video.

Catchlight Films

www.catchlightfilms.com/directory.html

Invests in eligible films through all unfinished stages of postproduction: editing, music scoring or clearance, post-supervision, deliverables, negative cut, lab fees, etc.

Center for Alternative Media and Culture

P. O. Box 0832, Radio City Station, New York, NY 10101

Phone: (212) 977-2096

Email: *tvnatfans@aol.com*

Supports independent media projects in post-production that address the economy, class issues, poverty, women, war and peace, race, and labor.

Center for Independent Documentary

1608 Beacon St., Waban, MA 01268

Phone: (508) 528-7279

Email: *info@documentaries.org* Website: *www.documentaries.org*

Multiple Grant Programs. Also provides services on a sliding scale and may select one or two projects a year to receive services for free. Seeking proposals on an ongoing basis from independent producers for the production of documentaries on contemporary issues.

Change, Inc.

P. O. Box 54, Tapiva, FL 33924

Phone: (212) 473-3742 Fax: (212) 995-8022

Emergency grants for artists in all disciplines needing help with rent, medical expenses, utility bills, fire damage, etc and grants up to $1000.

Charles and Lucille King Family Foundation

http://www.kingfoundation.org/

Provides scholarships to outstanding undergraduate students in television and film production and postproduction Grants for outstanding MFA projects at the University of California, Los Angeles and the University of Southern California.

Chiapas Media Project (CMP)

http://www.chiapasmediaproject.org

A bi-national partnership that provides video equipment, computers and training, enabling marginalized indigenous and campesino communities in Southern Mexico the opportunity to create their own media.

Chicago Resource Center

104 S. Michigan Ave., Ste. 1220, Chicago, IL 60603

Phone: (312) 759-8700

Awards grants to nonprofits that serve the gay/lesbian community.

Chicago Underground Film Fund

3109 North Western Ave., Chicago, IL 60618

Phone: (773) 327-FILM Fax: (773) 327-3464

Email: *info@cuff.org* Website: *http://www.cuff.org*

Promotes works that pushes the boundaries, defies commercial expectations and transcends the mainstream of independent filmmaking.

Columbia Foundation

One Lombard Street, Suite 305, San Francisco, CA 94111

Phone: (415) 986-5179

Email: *carolyn@columbia.org* Website: *http://www.columbia.org/index.htm*

The foundation gives priority to Bay Area film makers; to films or videos that will be used by Columbia Foundation-funded public-interest organizations to further their work in human rights and sustainable communities and economies; and to projects for which a grant of $5,000 to $25,000 makes a difference in getting the project started or completed.

Compton Foundation
http://www.comptonfoundation.org
There are no cut-off dates for discretionary grants, they focus most of their grant-making in the areas of Peace & World Order, Population, and the Environment. Most of the Foundation's grants for Culture & the Arts are discretionary grants ranging in size from $200 to $10,000.

Corporation for Public Broadcasting
901 E St. NW, Washington, DC 20004-2037
Phone: (202) 879-9734 Fax: (202) 783-1019
Email: *askus@cpb.org* Website: *www.cpb.org.*
Accepting proposals for the Public Television Future Fund and are open to any project that addresses large-scale opportunities to increase non-federal revenues, create new operating efficiencies and improve the quality of service that stations provide to their communities.

Creative Capitol
65 Bleeker St 7th Floor, New York NY 10012
Phone: (212) 598-9900 Fax: (212) 598-4934
Email: *info@creative-capital.org* Website: *www.creative-capital.org*
Provides grants to individual artists for specific projects, with an emphasis on experimental work. Disciplines rotate, meaning that media grants are given every other year.

Dance Film Association, Inc.
48 West 21st Street, #907, New York, NY 10010
Phone/Fax: (212) 727-0764
Website: *http://www.dancefilmsassn.org*
Postproduction grant up to $2,000 for films about dance.

Delaware Humanities Forum
100 West 10th St., Ste. 1009, Wilmington, DE 19801
Phone: (302) 657-0650 Fax: (302) 657-0655
Email: *dhfdirector@dhf.org* Website: *www.dhf.org*
Supports humanities programs for the public sponsored by nonprofit
organizations. Projects should foster an understanding of the humanities
disciplines or apply the humanities to topics of public concern.

Digital Media Education Center
Kate Wolf
5201 SW Westgate Dr., Ste. 114, Portland, OR 97221
Phone: (503) 297-2324

The Durfee Foundation
1453 Third St., Ste. 312, Santa Monica, CA 90401
Phone: (310) 899-5120 Fax: (310) 899-5121
Email: *admin@durfee.org* Website: *www.durfee.org/contact/index.html*
Deadline: November 5, yearly and provides ARC (Artists' Resource for
Completion) grants which provide rapid, short-term assistance to individual
artists in Los Angeles County who wish to complete work for a specific,
imminent opportunity that may significantly benefit their careers.

Empowerment Project
8218 Farrington Mill Rd., Chapel Hill, NC 27517
Phone: (919) 928-0382
Email: *media@empowermentproject.org* Website: *http://www.empowermentproject.org/*
Provides facilities, training and consultation for independent filmmakers,
producers, artists, activists and organizations working in video and other
electronic media; as well as produces and distributes its own documentary
films. Academy Award–winning directors Barbara Trent and David Kasper are
available for presentations and screenings.

Experimental Television Center
109 Lower Fairfield Road, Newark Valley, NY 13811
Phone: (607) 687-4341
Email: *etc@servtech.com* Website: *http://www.experimentaltvcenter.org/*

Finishing funds (up to $1,500) awarded to individual artists and has presentation funds (up to $1,000) to organizations. Media Arts Technical Assistance Funds (Up to $2,000) to organizations.

Film Arts Foundation
145 Ninth St. # 101, San Francisco, CA 94103
Phone: (415) 552-8760
Email: *info@filmarts.org*
Wonderful organization with great support for filmmakers and offers comprehensive training, equipment, information, consultations, and exhibition opportunities to independent filmmakers.

Film/Video Arts
462 Broadway, Suite #520, New York, NY 10013
Phone: (212) 941-8787 Fax: (212) 219-8924
Email: *info@fva.com* Website: *http://www.fva.com/aboutfva/funders_main.htm*
Offers multiple programs and grants; offers programs that encourage interaction between producers of narrative features, documentaries, nontraditional work, shorts, industrials, cable programs, music videos or student projects, by offering them affordable services essential to the creation of their work and the development of their careers.

Filmmakers Foundation
5858 Wilshire Blvd. Suite 205, Los Angeles, CA 90036
Phone: (213) 937-5505 Fax: (213) 937-7772
Website: *http://members.aol.com/newfilmkrs/*
They offer low- or no-cost, high-level programs to give industry professionals the skills and experience to move their careers forward quickly, yet with the confidence that they are building on a solid foundation of knowledge and experience.

Ford Foundation
Director, Media Arts and Culture
320 E. 43rd St., New York, NY 10017
Website: *www.fordfound.org/grant/guidelines.html.*
Supports public broadcasting and the independent production of film, video and radio programming, and supports efforts to engage diverse groups in work related to the media and to analyze the media's effect on society.

Foundation for Hellenic Culture
7 West 57th Street, New York, NY 10019-3402
Phone: (212) 308-6908 Fax: (212) 308-0919
Website: *http://www.foundationhellenicculture.com/*
The Foundation sponsors art and visual art exhibitions, film screenings, concerts, lectures, theatrical productions, readings, and educational programs.

Foundation for Middle East Peace (FMEP)
1761 N St. NW, Washington, DC 20036
Phone: (202) 835-3650 Fax: (202) 835-3651
Email: President: *pcwilcox@fmep.org* Editor/Analyst: *jeff@fmep.org*
Website: *http://www.fmep.org/*
Committed to "informing Americans on the Israeli-Palestinian conflict and assisting in a peaceful solution that brings security for both peoples." The grantmaking program provides support for organizations and individuals working toward a solution of the Israeli-Palestinian conflict.

Frameline
http://www.frameline.org/
Supports lesbian, gay, bisexual, transgender, visibility through media arts.

Fund for Jewish Documentary Filmmaking
Phone: (212) 629-0500 ext. 215
Email: *Grants@JewishCulture.org*

Parent organization: **National Foundation for Jewish Culture**
Phone: (212) 629-0500 Fax: (212) 629-0508
Email: *nfjc@jewishculture.org*
Established by Steven Spielberg, this fund is designed to support the creation of original documentary films and videos that promote thoughtful consideration of Jewish history, culture, identity, and contemporary issues among diverse public audiences.

Fund for Women Artists
Website: *http:// www.womenarts.org*
The Fund for Women Artists is a nonprofit arts service organization dedicated to increasing the diversity and employment of women in the arts.

Glaser Foundation
P. O. Box 91123, Seattle, WA 98111
Email: *grants@glaserfoundation.org*
Focuses on three program areas: progress definition and measurement; animal advocacy; and socially conscious media. In each of these areas, the Foundation develops and pursues its own initiatives and also provides funding support to other nonprofit organizations.

Harburg Foundation
225 Lafayette Street, Room 813, New York, NY 10012
Phone: (212) 343-9453
Email: *yipharburg@choreographics.com*
Advances and promotes new works of American political art, especially those efforts which speak to cultural and societal issues and include television, videos, shows, concerts, radio programs, and all artistic media.

Harvestworks
Website: *http://www.harvestworks.org*
Contact Director Carol Parkinson for more information: (212) 431-1130
Deadlines vary. New Works Residencies deadlines November. Offers a Digital Media Arts Center to cultivate artistic talent using electronic technologies. Also offers various programs, production studios, grant opportunities, education, communal lab practice and distribution.

Haymarket People's Fund
42 Seaverns Avenue, Boston, MA 02130
Phone: (617) 522-7676 Fax: (617) 522-9580
Email: *haymarket@igc.org* Website: *http://www.haymarket.org/index.htm*
Support for New England film/video makers for films with strong connection to community organizing work.

HBO America Undercover
Send proposal or tape to Greg Rhem, HBO
1100 Sixth Ave., NY, NY 10036
Phone: (212) 512-1670 Fax: (212) 512-8051
Provides production funds for American indie docs; Cinemax Reel Life acquires completed docs or offers finishing funds for partially completed projects.

Hermes Foundation

13600 Shaker Blvd. #802, Cleveland, OH 44120

Phone: 216-751-1100

Email: *senex@msn.com*

They are especially interested in gay/lesbian issues. Grants up to $1,000.

Hollywood Film Foundation

433 N. Camden Dr., Ste. 600, Beverly Hills, CA 90210

Website: *www.hff.org/grants/application.html*

Experimental, digital moviemaking, postproduction, and partial budget grants for up to 50% of budget. Projects must have a first or second-time feature director and/or producer and must be budgeted under $5 million; 75% of the production must take place in the State of California.

IFP/Chicago Production Fund

Phone: (312) 435-1825 Fax: (312) 435-1828

Email: *infoifpmw@aol.com* Website: *www.ifp.org*

Win an in-kind donation of production equipment and services, valued at up to $85,000 for your next short film. Applicants must be IFP/Chicago members, and the film must be shot in the Midwest region.

IFP/Los Angeles Project

Mentoring and training program that provides young people with exposure, experience, and connections in the film industry. The program supports film-makers from traditionally under-represented communities through mentor-ships, workshops, and screenings.

Illinois Humanities Council Media Grants

203 N. Wabash Ave., Ste. 2020, Chicago, IL 60601-2417

Phone: (312) 422-5580

Email: *ihc@prairie.org* Website: *www.prairie.org*

Funding for development (up to $4,000) or production (up to $10,000). Projects must relate centrally and unambiguously to the humanities, have clear potential for reaching a large public audience and be made by producers whose work demonstrates imagination and technical skill.

Independent Television Service (ITVS)

51 Federal St., 1st Floor, San Francisco, CA 94107

Phone: (415) 356-8383 Fax: (415) 356-8391

Email: marlene_velasco@itvs.org Website: www.itvs.org

Various programs and support for video and filmmakers.

Institute of Noetic Sciences

475 Gate Fire Road, Suite 300, Sausalito, CA 94965

Phone: (415) 331-5650 Fax: (415) 331-5673

Email: ions@well.com

Deadline for applications is usually March 1 and they offer an annual Hartley Film Award of $10,000 for production of a film or video which addresses subjects of relevance to the Institute's mission, including consciousness research, mind-body health, meditation, creative altruism, and other areas.

Jane Morrison Memorial Film Fund

P. O. Box 7380, Portland, ME 04112

Phone: (207) 761-2440

Website: http://www.mainecf.org

The annual submission deadline is May 15. Offers a fellowship and various support, including educational opportunities for filmmakers who are in the early stages of career development. Preference given but not restricted to those residing in Maine.

Jerome Foundation

125 Park Square Ct., 400 Sibley St., St. Paul, MN 55101-1928

Phone: (651) 224-9431 Fax: (651) 224-3439

Grant program for individual media artists living and working in New York City serving primarily film and video artists.

John D. and Catherine T. MacArthur Foundation
Letters of inquiry only (2-3 pages).
Requests for proposals by invitation.
The John D. and Catherine T. MacArthur Foundation
140 S. Dearborn St., Chicago, IL 60603
Phone: (312) 726-8000
Email: 4answers@macfdn.org Website: www.macfdn.org.
Key executives: Partial support for selected documentary series and independent
films intended for national and international broadcast; community outreach
related to media; community-based media centers; and public radio. Projects
are selected from those that focus on issues that fall within one of the
Foundation's two major programs: Human and Community Development or
Global Security and Sustainability.

John M. Olin Foundation
330 Madison Avenue, 22nd floor, New York, New York 10017
Phone: (212) 661-2670 Fax: (212) 661-5917
Website: http://www.jmof.org/index.html
Provides support for projects that "reflect or are intended to strengthen the
economic, political and cultural institutions upon which the American heritage
of constitutional government and private enterprise is based." Provides grants
in the areas of American institutions, law and the legal system, public policy
research, and strategic and international studies through support of various
programs including on occasion, television and radio programs.

John Simon Guggenheim Foundation
90 Park Avenue, New York, NY 10016
Phone: (212) 687-4470 Fax: (212) 697-3248
Website: http://www.gf.org.
Application deadline is October 1 for U.S. and Canadian citizens fellowship,
December 1 for Latin American and Caribbean citizens fellowship. Fellowship
competitions: one open to citizens and permanent residents of the United
States and Canada, and the other open to citizens and permanent residents of
Latin America and the Caribbean. Film and video makers are eligible to apply.
The average grant is $28,000

Kentucky Foundation for Women, Inc.
1215 Heyburn Bldg., 332 W. Broadway, Louisville, KY 40202
Phone: (502) 562-0045 Fax: (502) 561-0420
Email: kfw@kfw.org Website: http://www.kfw.org/
Grants to Kentucky feminist film/video artists.

KQED TV
Scott Dwyer
2601 Mariposa Street, San Francisco, CA 94110-1426
Phone: (415) 553-2147
Email: inview@kqed.org
They are interested in presenting challenging independent dramas and
documentaries to the Bay Area, looking for works that are truly independent,
unique and fulfill a personal vision and they encourage Independent Producers
to approach the station with their projects in development.

Latino Public Broadcasting
Marlene Dermer, Executive Director
6777 Hollywood Blvd., Ste. 500, Los Angeles, CA 90028
Phone: (323) 466-7110
Open call for proposals for programs to air on public television. The projects
should center on themes and issues that are relevant to Latinos. LPB's mission
is to provide a voice for the Latino community throughout the United States
with an equitable and accessible funding and distribution mechanism.

LEF Foundation
Website: http://www.lef-foundation.org
Funds are given for projects, programs, and services that encourage "a positive
interchange between the arts and the natural urban environment", and may
involve visual, media, performing and literary art.

Lucius & Eva Eastman Fund
P. O. Box 470, Westwood, MA 02090
Phone: (781) 329-2473
Contact: Lucius R. Eastman, Pres.
5926 Fiddletown Pl., San Jose, CA 95120
Phone: (408) 268-2083
Supports film/video on social issues.

Lyn Blumenthal Memorial Fund for Independent Video
P. O. Box 3514 Church St. Station, New York, NY 10007
Awards grants for criticism and production.

Maryland Humanities Council
Executive Plaza One, Ste. 503, 11350 McCormick Rd.
Hunt Valley, MD 21031-1002
Phone: (410) 771-0650 Fax: (410) 771-0655
Email: pweber@mdhc.org Website: www.mdhc.org.
Any nonprofit organization may apply for a grant. The council does not fund
individuals or for-profit organizations. The project must be a public program,
the disciplines of the humanities must be central to the project, humanities
scholars must be involved in the project, and funding must support projects
that would not normally occur without council support.

Massachusetts Foundation for the Humanities
Email: *ekrothman@mfh.org* with a brief summary of your proposed project.
Media proposals are accepted only at the November and May deadlines. Makes
grants to support radio programs, films, and videos that explore humanities themes.
In FY 2003, media grants were available for preproduction and distribution only.

Massachusetts Foundation for the Humanities
66 Bridge St., Northampton, MA 01060
Phone: (413) 584-8440 Fax: (413) 584-8454
Website: *www.mfh.org*
Deadline: October 1. Makes major grants each year to support radio programs,
films and videos that explore humanities themes. Media grants are available in
three categories: pre-production, production and distribution, in amounts over
$5,000 and up to $15,000.

Media Alliance
c/o WNET
356 W. 58th St., New York, NY 10019
Phone: (212) 560-2919
Assists NYC artists and nonprofit organizations in using state-of-the-art
equipment and post-production facilities at reduced rates.

MediaRights

104 W. 14th St., 4th Floor, New York, NY 10011

Phone: (646) 230-6288 Fax: (646) 230-6328

Email: *info@mediarights.org* Website: *www.mediarights.org*

A community website that helps media makers, educators, nonprofits, and activists use documentaries to encourage action and inspire dialogue on contemporary social issues.

Minnesota Humanities Commission

Humanities Education Center

987 East Ivy Ave., Saint Paul, MN 55106

Phone: (651) 774-0105 Fax: (651) 774-0205

Email: *mnhum@thinkmhc.org* Website: *www.thinkmhc.org*

Grant applications are reviewed on a rolling basis, so applicants who submit proposals early in the year enhance their likelihood for funding. Provides Media Grants to support humanities projects in radio, film, video and multimedia.

Moving Image Fund

P. O. Box 382866, Cambridge, MA 02238-2866

Phone: (617) 492-5333

Email: *kathryn@lef-foundation.org* Website: *www.lef-foundation.org*

Support for New England filmmakers.

National Alliance for Media Arts and Culture (NAMAC)

A nonprofit association composed of diverse member organizations who are dedicated to encouraging film, video, audio and on-line/multimedia arts, and to promoting the cultural contributions of individual media artists.

National Asian American Telecommunications Association (NAATA)

145 9th St, Suite 350, San Francisco, CA 94103

Website: *http://www.naatanet.org/index.html*

Seeks engaging and provocative project proposals from independent media producers. Encourages works that address contemporary issues, reflecting the growth and change in our communities.

National Black Programming Consortium
4802 Fifth Avenue, Pittsburgh, PA 15213
Phone: (412) 622-6443 Fax: (412) 622-1331
Email: *nbpcinfo@blackstarcom.org* Website: *www.blackstarcom.org*
Nonprofit national media arts organization dedicated to the funding, promotion, presentation and distribution of quality Black film and video projects. Through their annual Request For Proposals (RFP), NBPC seeks contemporary films about the Black experience for the National PBS Schedule.

National Endowment for the Arts
1100 Pennsylvania Avenue NW, Washington, DC 20506-0001
Phone: (202) 682-5742
Email: *webmgr@arts.endow.gov* Website: *www.arts.gov*
NEH is an independent grant-making agency of the U.S. government, dedicated to enriching American cultural life by promoting knowledge of human history, thought and culture. Priorities include subjects of national significance, projects geared to diversified audiences, collaboration with other cultural organizations, and the use of multiple formats or interactive media technology. implementation and production.

National Endowment for the Humanities (NEH)
1100 Pennsylvania Ave, NW, Washington, DC 20506
Phone: 1-800-NEH-1121 Fax: (202) 606-8400 TDD: (202) 606-8282
Email: *info@neh.gov* Website: *http://www.neh.gov*
Offers grants for independent filmmakers and digital media producers whose work addresses significant subjects in the humanities; reaches broad public audiences; grows out of sound scholarship; and uses imaginative, engaging formats.

National Foundation for Jewish Culture
Fund for Jewish Documentary Filmmaking
330 Seventh Avenue, 21st floor, New York, NY 10001
Phone: (212) 629-0500 Fax: (212) 629-0508
Email: *Grants@JewishCulture.org* Website: *http://www.jewishculture.org/film.htm*
The Fund is designed to support the creation of original documentary films and videos that promote thoughtful consideration of Jewish history, culture, identity, and contemporary issues among diverse public audiences. Grant size: $20,000–$30,000.

National Science Foundation

4201 Wilson Blvd., Arlington, VA 22230

Phone: (703) 292-5090

Email: *info@nsf.gov* Website: *www.nsf.gov*

Supports media projects designed to deepen the appreciation of science and technology and the understanding of the impact science and technology has on today's society. Projects generally develop materials and programs that reach large audiences and have the potential for significant regional or national impact.

National Video Resources

73 Spring Street, Suite 403, New York, NY 10012

Phone: (212) 274-8080 Fax: (212) 274-8081

Email: *nvrinfo@nvr.org www.nvr.org* Website: *www.nvr.org/*

This fund is to assist in increasing the public's awareness of and access to independently produced media & film and video as well as motion media delivered through new digital technologies. Commissions and publishes research on issues of concern to independent media makers, distributors, educators, activists and individuals.

Native American Public Telecommunications

1800 N. 33rd St., Lincoln, NE 68583

Email: *native@unl.edu* Website: *http://www.nativetelecom.org*

They supports program ideas that bring new perspectives on Native American cultures to public television audiences, increasing the quality and quantity of Native American television programming on a national and international scale.

New Filmmaker Equipment Grant Program

Oppenheimer Camera

666 S. Plummer St., Seattle, WA 98134

Phone: (206) 467-8666 Fax: (206) 467-9165

Email: *filmgrant@oppenheimercamera.com*

Website: *http://oppenheimercamera.com/grant2.html*

Oppenheimer supports new filmmakers in producing their first serious film project. The grant awards the use of their Grant Program Arriflex 16SR camera package to senior and graduate thesis students and to independent filmmakers for a scheduled period of time. Proposed projects may be of any non-commercial nature: dramatic, narrative, documentary, experimental, etc.

Next Wave Films

Phone: (310) 392-1720

Website: *www.nextwavefilms.com*

Company of the Independent Film Channel, provides finishing funds and serves as a producer's rep helping filmmakers implement festival and press strategies and secure distribution and has expanded its focus to include documentaries.

Nextpix

295 Greenwich St., Ste. 348, New York, NY 10007

Phone: (212) 465-3125 Fax: (212) 658-9627

Email: *info@nextpix.com* Website: *www.nextpix.com.*

Deadline: September 15. This New York City–based production company, is offering postproduction grants to first-and second-time filmmakers. The projected budget cannot exceed $250,000, and principal photography must have been completed after January 1, 2000. Production must be completed and the project must be in postproduction.

Open Meadows Foundation

P. O. Box 150-607, Van Brunt Station, Brooklyn, NY 11215-0150

Phone: (718) 768-4015

Email: *openmeadows@igc.apc.org* Website : *www.openmeadows.org*

Projects that have limited financial access which reflect the cultural and ethnic diversity of our society and promote the empowerment of women and girls; and projects for social change that have encountered obstacles in their search for funding. Grants: up to $2,000.

Pacific Islanders in Communication

1221 Kapi'olani Blvd., #6A-4, Honolulu, HI 96814

Phone (808) 591-0059 Fax: (808) 591-1114

Email: *info@piccom.org* Website: *http://www.piccom.org/*

National nonprofit media organization established primarily for the purpose of increasing national public broadcast programming by and about indigenous Pacific Islanders. Sponsors Open Door Completion Fund and Media Fund.

Pacific Pioneer Fund

P. O. Box 20504, Stanford, CA 94309

Phone: (650) 497-1133

Website: *www.pacificpioneerfund.com*

CA, WA, OR documentary filmmakers. Grant size: $1,000 - $10,000.

Panavision's New Filmmaker Program

6219 DeSoto Ave., Woodland Hills, CA 91367-2602

Website: *http://www.panavision.com*

Submit proposals three months before you intend to shoot. Donates 16mm ADD and 35 mm camera packages to short, nonprofit film projects, including graduate student thesis films, of any genre.

Paul Robeson Fund for Independent Media
AKA Funding Exchange

Ms. Trinh Duong, Program

Officer Funding Exchange

666 Broadway, Suite 500, New York, N.Y. 10120

Phone: (212) 529-5300 Fax: (212) 982-9272

Email: *fexexc@aol.com* Website: *www.fex.org/robeson*

Preproduction funds & distribution funds for projects by organizations & indipendemt artists. Topics of interest: AIDS and other health issues, racial & gender justice, reproductive rights, homelessness, welfare reform, women, gays, lesbians, disabled persons. Artists from communities of color and people with little recourse to other funding are encouraged to apply.

PEW Charitable Trusts

2005 Market Street, Suite 1700, Philadelphia, PA 19103-7077

Phone: (215) 575-9050 Fax: (215) 575-4939

Email: *info@pewtrusts.com*

Support nonprofit activities in the areas of culture, education, the environment, health and human services, public policy and religion and makes strategic investments that encourage and support citizen participation in addressing critical issues and effecting social change.

Playboy Foundation
Playboy Foundation
680 North Lake Shore Dr., Chicago, IL 60611
Phone: (312) 751- 0001
Website: *www.playboy.com/pd-foundation.*
Supports media projects that help to foster open communication about and
research into human sexuality, reproductive health and rights; protect and foster
civil rights and civil liberties in the U.S. for all people, including women,
people affected and impacted by HIV/AIDS, gays and lesbians, racial
minorities, the poor and the disadvantaged; and eliminate censorship and
protect freedom of expression. Projects must have nonprofit fiscal sponsorship
to be eligible.

Potrero Nuevo Fund Prize
1246 Folsom St., San Francisco, CA 94103
Phone: (415) 626-5416
Website: *http://www.newlangtonarts.org/*
Bay Area only and gives up to four $12,500 awards for artist's projects on urban
and social environmentalism.

Princess Grace Foundation
150 East 58th Street, 21st Floor, New York, New York 10155
Phone: (212) 317-1470 Fax: (212) 317 1473
Email: *pgfusa@pgfusa.com* Website: *http://www.pgfusa.com/index.html*
They are dedicated to identifying and assisting young talent in theater,
dance and film through grants in the form of scholarships, apprenticeships and
fellowships.

Puffin Foundation
20 East Oakdene Avenue, Teaneck, NJ 07666-4198
Phone: (201) 836-8923 Fax: (201) 836-1734
Email: *puffingrant@mindspring.com* Website: *www.angelfire.com/nj/PuffinFoundation*
Grants to encourage emerging artists whose works, due to their genre and/or
social philosophy, might have difficulty being aired. Grants: up to $2,500.

Regional Arts Organizations
Website: *http://www.arts.gov/artforms/RAO_SAAs.html#RAOs*
Works with the Arts Endowment utilizing funds mandated by the Congress as well as funds from state governments and other sources.

Resist, Inc.
259 Elm Street, Somerville, MA 02144
Phone (617) 623-5110
Email: *resistinc@igc.apc.org* Website: *http://www.resistinc.org*
Distribution costs of film and video linked to social justice organizing.

Retirement Research Foundation
Website: *http://www.rrf.org/welcome.html*
Operates a general grants program, two award programs (ENCORE and the Congregation Connection Program) open to Chicago-area nonprofits only, and the National Media Owl Awards, a national film and video competition.

Robert Flaherty Film Seminar
Website: *http://www.flahertyseminar.org*
Various educational and grant opportunities to artists in film and video.

Robert Wood Johnson Foundation
Website: *http://www.rwjf.org/index.jsp*
RWJF's mission is to improve the health and health care of all Americans. The Foundation has goals and interest areas related both to health and health care. We rarely make grants for publications or media projects, except those that grow out of one of our grant programs.

Roy W. Dean Grants
From The Heart Productions
1455 Mandalay Beach Road, Oxnard, California 93035-2845
Phone: (805) 984-0098
Email: *CaroleEDean@.att.net*   Website: *www.fromtheheartproductions.com*
LA Film and LA Video Grants; NYC Film Grant; Editing Grant; Writer/
Researcher Grant that takes you to New Zealand to write. Multiple grant
programs for docs, shorts and low-budget digital indie films. We are looking
for film and video projects that are unique and make a contribution to society.
New projects, works-in-progress, length is not a consideration. We want strong
character-driven stories and $500,000 is the top budget we allow in the grant.

Schott Foundation
678 Massachusetts Avenue, Suite 301, Cambridge, Massachusetts 02139
Phone: (617) 876-7700 Fax: (617) 876-7702
Website: *http://www.schottfoundation.org*
Focuses on the development of: universal and accessible high quality early care
and education, excellent public schools in underserved communities, gender-
healthy public schools. The Foundation is always interested in learning about
the programs and projects like-minded organizations are doing and it also
funds research and media campaigns for public awareness.

Scottish Screen
Isabella Edgar
Information Manager
Phone: 011-141 302 1730 Fax: 011-141 302 1778
Website: *http://www.scottishscreen.com/*
Scottish Screen develops, encourages and promotes every aspect of film,
television and new media in Scotland. Working with the Scottish Executive,
our mission is to establish Scotland as a major screen production center and
project our culture to the world.

Sister Fund
116 East 16th St., 7th Floor, New York, NY 10003
Phone: (212) 260-4446 Fax: (212) 260-4633
Email: *sisterfund@aol.com*
Support for programming that fosters women's and girls' economic, social,

political, and spiritual lives with a primary emphasis on national advocacy and media strategies to heighten public consciousness around issues affecting women and girls.

Southwest Alternate Media Project (SWAMP)

1519 West Main, Houston, TX 77006

Phone: (713) 522-8592 Fax: (713) 522-0953

Email: *info@swamp.org*

Promotes film, video and new media through education, information and presentation activities. Provides a nonprofit umbrella for established media artists seeking grants and contributions to develop and produce film and video.

Standby Program

P. O. Box 184, New York, NY 10012-0004

Phone: (212) 219-0951 Fax: 212- 219-0563

Provides artists access to quality video postproduction services at reduced rates. It is a nonprofit media arts organization dedicated to providing artists and independent makers access to broadcast quality video post-production services at extremely discounted rates.

State and Jurisdictional Arts Agencies

Website: *http://www.arts.gov/artforms/RAO_SAAs.html*

They works with the Arts Endowment utilizing funds mandated by the Congress as well as funds from state governments and other sources.

State Humanities Councils

Website: *http://www.neh.gov/whoweare/statecouncils.html*

A total of 56 humanities councils located in U.S. states and territories support local humanities programs and events.

Sundance Documentary Fund

8857 West Olympic Blvd., Beverly Hills, CA 90211

Email: *sdf@sundance.org* Website: *www.sundance.org*

No deadlines and supports international documentary films and videos focused on current and significant issues and movements in contemporary human rights, freedom of expression, social justice, and civil liberties. Development funds up to $15,000 and production/postproduction to $50,000, though most will be around $25,000.

Texas Filmmakers' Production Fund

Phone: (512) 322-5192

Website: *www.austinfilm.org*

The Texas Filmmakers Production Fund is an annual grant awarded to emerging film and video artists in the state of Texas with grants for $5,000.

Thanks Be to Grandmother Winifred Foundation

P. O. Box 1449, Wainscott, NY 11975

Phone: (516) 725-0323

Two deadlines annually (postmarked): March 21 and September 21. Provides funding for women over 54 years of age to create and manifest into reality, ideas and concepts that will improve the lives of women in one or more aspects.

Third World Newsreel

545 Eighth Avenue, 10th Floor, New York, NY 10018

Phone: (212) 947-9277 Fax: (212) 594-6417

Website: *http://www.twn.org*

They are committed to the creation and appreciation of independent and social issue media by and about people of color, and the peoples of developing countries around the world.

Unitarian Universalist Funding Program/Fund for a Just Society

P. O. Box 40, Boston, MA 02117

Phone (617) 247-6600 Fax: (617) 247-1015

Email: *uufp@aol.com* Website: *http://www.uua.org/uufp/*

Funds film/video only if it is an integral part of a strategy of collective action for social change. Grants to $10,000; most in the $5,000 to $7,000 range.

Visual Studies Workshop Media Center

Phone: (716) 442-8676

Accepts proposals on an ongoing basis for its media access program for artists, independent producers, and nonprofits working on noncommercial projects; awards reduced rates for production and postproduction equipment.

Wallace Alexander Gerbode Foundation
Thomas C. Layton, President
470 Columbus Ave., #209, San Francisco, CA 94133-3930
Phone: (415) 391-0911
Email: *maildesk@gerbode.org* Website: *www.fdncenter.org/grantmaker/gerbode/*
Their applications are accepted on an ongoing basis and they are interested in
programs and projects offering potential for significant impact. The primary
focus is on the San Francisco Bay Area (counties of Alameda, Contra Costa,
Marin, San Francisco and San Mateo) and Hawaii. To qualify for support, an
organization must be a tax-exempt public charity, as determined by Internal
Revenue Code Section 501(c)(3).

WebCinema
Website: *http://www.webcinema.org*
A nonprofit organization dedicated to the independent filmmaker using
Internet and new media technologies to finance, create, produce, distribute
and market independent film.

Women in Film and Television
8857 West Olympic Blvd., Suite 201, Beverly Hills, CA 90211
Phone: (310) 657-5144 Fax: (310) 657-5154
L.A.: *http://wif.org/home/index.html*
New York: *http://www.nywift.org/Women In Film*
Offers various programs.

Women in Film Foundation
Website: *http://www.wifti.org/*
Various programs including completion funding and in-kind contributions to
independent producers and nonprofit organizations for documentary, dramatic,
educational, animated and experimental film and videos.

Women in the Director's Chair
941 W. Lawrence #500, Chicago, IL 60640
Phone: (773) 907-0610 Fax: (773) 907-0381
Email: *widc@widc.org* Website: *http://www.widc.org/*
Various Programs.

Women Make Movies
462 Broadway Suite 500, New York, NY 10013
Phone: (212) 925-0606 Fax: (212) 925-2052
Email: *info@wmm.com* Website: *http://www.wmm.com/*
Major distributor of film and videos by women, they offer fiscal sponsorship programs. They give proposal writing workshops, networking opportunities with other women media makers, and discounts at labs and equipment facilities.

PRODUCTION LIST

These companies donate to the Roy W. Dean film grants. Use this as your production list for quality products at excellent prices. Say you found their names in this book and were referred by Carole Dean of From the Heart Productions. Email me if you need services not on the list as we are always acquiring new donors. These corporations will service your needs and treat each of you the same as they treat the major production houses whose budgets are much larger.

Los Angeles

Ace Rentals Generator
Generator rentals
Los Angeles, CA
Phone: (626) 584-1201

Acey Decy Equipment Rentals
Moving lights, special effects
200 Parkside Dr.
San Fernando, CA 91340
Phone: (818) 408-4444 Fax: (408) 2777
sales@aceydecy.com
www.aceydecy.com

Airstar Lighting Balloons
Unique balloon lighting
10950 Burbank Blvd.
North Hollywood, CA 91601
Phone: (800) 217-9001
www.airstar-light.net

Alan Audio Works
Jeff Alan, film music composer
5602 Hazelbrook Ave.
Lakewood, CA 90712
Phone: (562) 408-6821

Copywrite Duplication
Duplication for all formats
1554 18th St.
Santa Monica, CA 90404
Phone: (323) 461-4151
info@copyrightvideo.com
www.copyrightvideo.com

Coufal-Isley Sound
Audio equipment rental
665 North Lillian Way
Hollywood, CA 90004
Phone: (323) 871-9288

Carole Joyce Photography
Stills and head shots
1455 Mandalay Beach Rd
Oxnard, CA 93035
Phone: (805) 984-0098
authenticvisions@yahoo.com

Claire Papin
Voice-over talent
Phone: (713) 812-7461 Fax: (713) 812-7461
www.lightedpaths.org
Claire@lightedpaths.org

David Raiklen
Full symphony film music composer
Los Angeles, CA
Phone: (310) 699-0361
www.davidraiklen.com

Divertimento Productions
Documentary trailer specialist
Studio City, CA
Phone: (818) 763-1505
www.divertimento-prod.com
Bill@divertimento-prod.com

Documentary Doctor
Fernanda Rossi, Story Development
info@documentarydoctor.com
www.documentarydoctor.com

Edgewise Film & Video
Film, video, equipment
New York & Los Angeles
Phone: (800) 824-3130 (Phillip Loving)
www.edgewise-media.com
jstolo@edgewisemedia.com

Film Arts Foundation
Services & fiscal sponsorship
145 9th St. #101
San Francisco, CA 94103
Phone: (415) 552-8760
info@filmarts.org
www.Filmmarts.org

Film Works FX, Inc.
Film processing & telecine
523 Colorado Ave.
Santa Monica, CA 90401
Phone: (310) 395-5595 Fax: (310) 395-8895
www.filmworksfx.com
info@filmworksfx.com

Go Edit
Full editing facilities
940 North Orange Dr.
Hollywood, CA 90038
Phone: (323) 337-1174 Fax: (323) 337-1440
www.goedit.tv

Howard Wexler
Director of Photography
961 Vernon Ave.
Venice, CA 90291
Phone: (310) 396-3416
howard@howardwexler.com
www.howardwexler.com

Lightning Dubbs
753 Highland Ave.
Hollywood, CA. 90038
Phone: (323) 957-9255
www.lightning-media.net

Louise Levison
Business plans
www.MovieMoney.com
LouiseL@earthlink.net

Mark Litwak
Hollywood's foremost production attorney
433 N. Camden Drive, Ste. 1010
Beverly Hills, CA 90210
Phone: (310) 859-9595 Fax: (310) 859-0806
atty@marklitwak.com
www.marklitwak.com

Digital Express, Etc.
Mazir Senehi
6404 Wilshire Blvd. #105
Los Angeles, CA 90048
Phone: (323) 402-7528
Maziar.senehi@scriptcopier.com

Michael Wiese Productions
Books, consulting, seminars
11288 Ventura Blvd.
Studio City, CA 91604
Phone: (818) 379-8799 Fax: (818) 986-3408
www.mwp.com

Morrie Warshawski
Documentarian consultant
1480 Cedar St.
Napa, CA 94559
Phone: (707) 224 4353
molrriewar@sbcglobal.net
www.warshawski.com

Michele Blood
Personal motivator
P. O. 12933
La Jolla, CA 92039
Phone: (800) 809-9705 Fax: (858) 277-0629
Michele@musivation.com
www.musivation.com

Norman C Berns
Budgeting consultant
ncberns@gmail.com

One-On-One Film Training
Jeffrey Seckendorf
info@oneononefilmtraining.com
www.oneononefilmtraining.com

Otto Nemenz Corporation
Cinematographic equipment (16mm & 35mm)
870 Vine St.
Hollywood, CA 90038
Phone: (323) 469-2774 Fax: (323) 469-1217
jnorwood@ottonemenz.com
www.otonemenz.com

Raleigh Studios
Stages, lighting & screening rooms
5300 Melrose Ave.
Hollywood, CA 90038
Phone: (323) 466-3111
YMontellano@raleighstudios.com
www.raleighstudio.com

Story Board Productions
Story Board Software
Phone: (408) 418-3935
www.powerproduction.com

Sam Dlugach Digital
Color Corrections
P. O. Box 304
Burbank, CA 91503
samdlugach@mac.com

Skullco
Website designers
16787 Beach Blvd.
Huntington Beach, CA 92647
Phone: (747) 841-3470
info@skullco.com
www.skullco.com

Smart Girls Productions
Marketing services for actors and writers
15030 Ventura #914
Sherman Oaks, CA 91403
Phone: (818) 907-6511
smartgirls@smartgirlsprod.com
www.smartgirlsprod.com

Solvent Dreams
Complete postproduction
4222 Santa Monica Blvd.
Los Angeles, CA 90029
Phone: (323) 906-9700 Fax: (323) 906-9711
info@solventdreams.com
www.solventdreams.com

Universal Studios
Sound editing & postproduction services
100 Universal City Plaza
Universal City, CA 91608
Phone: (818) 777-2211

Wilshire Screening Room
8670 Wilshire Blvd.
Beverly Hills, CA
Phone: (310) 659-3875 Fax: (310) 861-9005
michael@StudioScreenings.com
www.studioscreenings.com

Wiseman & Burke, Inc.
Business and financial management
206 S. Brand Blvd.
Glendale, CA 91204
Phone: (818) 247-1007.

New York

AAA Communications
Rental & sales: walkie-talkies, cell phones & pagers
210 Fairfield Rd.
Fairfield, NJ 07004
Phone: (973) 808-8888 Fax: (973) 808-8588
lori@aaacomm.com
www.aaacomm.com

Abel Cine Tech, Inc.
Professional motion picture equipment rental
66 Willow Ave. #201
Staten Island, NY 10305
Phone: (212) 462-0162
info@abelcine.com
www.abelcine.com

Analog Digital International
Editing suites and videotape transfers
20 E 49th Street, 2nd Fl
New York, NY 10017
Phone: (212) 688-5110 Fax: (212) 688-5405
www.analogdigitalinc.com

C'est Fou!
Special events producers
307 E. 67th St. #10
New York, NY 10021
Phone: (212) 288-6085

Documentary Doctor
Fernanda Rossi Story Development
www.documentarydoctor.com
info@documentarydoctor.com

Eastman Kodak Company
Sales of motion picture film and print stocks
360 West 31st St., Suite 710
New York, NY 10001
Phone: (212) 631-3400
www.kodak.com

Edgewise Media
All your production needs
630 9th Ave.
New York, NY 10036
Phone: (800) 444-9330
www.edgewise-media.com

Film/Video Arts
Filmmaking training & non-profit center
236 E. 3rd Street
New York, NY 10009
Phone: (212) 941-8787
www.fva.com

Magno Sound & Video
Audio, video & film postproduction
729 Seventh Avenue
New York, NY 10019
Phone: (212) 302-2505 Fax: (212) 819-1282
www.magnosoundandvideo.com

Metro Access
Mr. Jim Chladek
204 East 23rd St.
New York, NY 10010

Unilux Inc.
Lighting for film & video productions
59 North 5th
Saddle Brook, NJ 07663
Phone: (201) 712-1266

ABOUT THE AUTHOR

Thirty years ago Carole Dean took a $20 bill and turned it into a $50 million a year industry when she reinvented the tape and short-end industry with Studio Film & Tape in Hollywood, New York City and Chicago. Carole coined the phrase "short ends" and began buying and selling film ends left from production. She was instrumental in the birth of the Hollywood independent film community because she offered film to indies at prices they could afford, allowing many producers to go on to great success; customers like Cassavetes took chances with her raw stock and succeeded. She ran this business for 33 years and sold it in 2000.

As president and CEO of From the Heart Productions since 1992, Carole produced over 100 television programs, including the popular cable program, *HealthStyles*, where she interviewed some of the biggest names in the industry including Dr. Deepak Chopra, Dr. Andrew Weil and Dr. Caroline Myss, and the historical show, *Filmmakers*, now housed in the National Archives.

A sought-after international speaker, Carole is currently touring the U.S. with her popular book, *The Art of Film Funding: Alternative Financing Concepts*, teaching filmmakers how and where to find funding. Her newest book, *The Art of Manifesting: Creating Your Future*, was created to enrich lives and expand awareness of your personal potential. This book and seminar bring important information from leading physicists on the new studies that support your ability to create your reality, attract what you want and manifest your future. Carole says, "You are manifesting daily, the trick is to manifest what you want, not what you don't want."

In 1992 Carole created the Roy W. Dean Grant Foundation, which she currently manages, in honor of her late father. To date Carole's grant and mentorship programs have provided filmmakers with millions of dollars in goods and services and have played an instrumental role in creating important films and establishing the careers of some of the industry's most talented filmmakers.

From the Heart has given close to $2 million in over 25 grants. Carole has helped these filmmakers pursue their dreams from the original donation of raw stock, lights and camera to the current New York Film, LA Film and LA Video grants and her writing grant. The writing grant is a four week sojourn in New Zealand. This allows serious screenwriters and documentary filmmakers to work on their projects in a serene, quiet setting on the Wye River.

Completed films sponsored by the Roy W. Dean grants are: *All Power to the People* on Starz; *A Chance to Grow*, Discovery; *Save A Man to Fight*, History; *The Flute Player*, PBS; *Stolen*, Court TV; *Salvages Lives*, Discovery; *Homeland* and *Shakespeare Behind Bars* both on ITVS; *In My Corner*, PBS; *The Tomato Effect*, *Halstead Street*, PBS; *Hempsters Plant the Seed*, *Double Dare*, *Tahara*, *American Chain Gang*, *Bam 6.6*, *Wakefield Convicted: Sentenced to Die* and *Hopilavayi*, given to the Hopi Indians to distribute. For current films see *www.fromtheheartproductions.com*

For more information on Carole Dean see *CaroleDean.com* and *Who's Who.*

A NOTE FROM THE AUTHOR

Dear Filmmakers,

The Art of Film Funding was created by questions from filmmakers like you. The purpose of the book is to give you as much information as possible to help you create your pitch, your proposal and to use some new concepts along with the standard ones for funding your films. I sincerely hope you found this book helpful.

The goal of the Roy W. Dean film grants and my personal goals are to see more documentaries and independent films created that "are unique and make a contribution to society." I want my books to give you the guidance to make your artistic journey joyful.

I take my hat off to all of you. I see so many applications that say writer/director/producer. I just wonder if you realize how creative you really are. Many people in this world would give anything to have just one of those talents.

Please let me know what you want in the next edition of Film Funding. *You can email me at caroleedean@att.net and, if possible, I will be happy to include it.*

For current interviews, new funding ideas and the latest tax laws, keep checking our website, www.fromtheheartproductions.com.

It is a pleasure to work with and for such talented people. Keep up the good work; you are raising the consciousness of all of us.

Best Regards,

Carole Dean
1455 Mandalay Beach Rd.
Oxnard, CA 93035
caroleedean@att.net

MICHAEL WIESE PRODUCTIONS

Since 1981, Michael Wiese Productions has been dedicated to providing both novice and seasoned filmmakers with vital information on all aspects of filmmaking. We have published more than 70 books, used in over 500 film schools and countless universities, and by hundreds of thousands of filmmakers worldwide.

Our authors are successful industry professionals who spend innumerable hours writing about the hard stuff: budgeting, financing, directing, marketing, and distribution. They believe that if they share their knowledge and experience with others, more high quality films will be produced.

And that has been our mission, now complemented through our new web-based resources. We invite all readers to visit www.mwp.com to receive free tipsheets and sample chapters, participate in forum discussions, obtain product discounts — and even get the opportunity to receive free books, project consulting, and other services offered by our company.

Our goal is, quite simply, to help you reach your goals. That's why we give our readers the most complete portal for filmmaking knowledge available — in the most convenient manner.

We truly hope that our books and web-based resources will empower you to create enduring films that will last for generations to come.

Let us hear from you at anytime.

Sincerely,
Michael Wiese
Publisher, Filmmaker

www.mwp.com

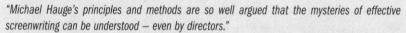

DIGITAL FILMMAKING 101
2ND EDITION

AN ESSENTIAL GUIDE
TO PRODUCING LOW-BUDGET MOVIES

DALE NEWTON & JOHN GASPARD

America's top two gurus of low-budget independent filmmaking are back with the second edition of their popular bestseller.

From script to screen, every aspect of low-budget digital feature production is covered in this updated classic. This second edition provides additional detail on new business structures for the independent filmmaker, looks at camera and editing system options that are available for budgets as low as $8,000, examines new trends in film festivals and distribution, and provides a wealth of information for anyone who has the passion and the zeal to bring their cinematic dreams to life.

"These guys don't seem to have missed a thing when it comes to how to make a digital movie for peanuts. It's a helpful and funny guide for beginners and professionals alike."
    – Jonathan Demme, Academy-Award®-Winning Director, *Silence of the Lambs*

"Gaspard and Newton are the undisputed champs of straight talk when it comes to moviemaking."
    – Timothy Rhys, Publisher and Editor, *MovieMaker* Magazine and *MovieMaker.com*

"Simply put, this is the best book on digital moviemaking I've yet read."
    – *Screentalk* Magazine

"Strong, smart, funny advice for independent filmmakers from people who've gone through the process more than once — and lived to tell about it."
    — Peter Tolan, Co-Creator and Producer, *Rescue Me*;
      Screenwriter, *The Larry Sanders Show*, *Analyze This*, *My Fellow Americans*

"The book is a vast storehouse of ideas of acquiring capital, preproduction, casting, finding a crew, the production process, special effects, post and distribution. *Digital Filmmaking 101* will almost certainly change your perception of getting your project off the ground."
    — *Videomaker* Magazine

When it comes to producing successful movies on a shoestring, JOHN GASPARD and DALE NEWTON, know of what they speak. Together they created the award-winning digital feature, *Grown Men*, as well as *Resident Alien* and *Beyond Bob*, two critically acclaimed ultra-low-budget feature films. The first edition of *Digital Filmmaking 101* has been a bestseller, racking up sales of over 15,000 units worldwide.

$26.95 · 309 PAGES · ORDER NUMBER 124RLS · ISBN: 1932907238

THE WRITER'S JOURNEY
3RD EDITION

MYTHIC STRUCTURE FOR WRITERS

CHRISTOPHER VOGLER

BEST SELLER
OVER 170,000 COPIES SOLD!

See why this book has become an international best seller and a true classic. *The Writer's Journey* explores the powerful relationship between mythology and storytelling in a clear, concise style that's made it required reading for movie executives, screenwriters, playwrights, scholars, and fans of pop culture all over the world.

Both fiction and nonfiction writers will discover a set of useful myth-inspired storytelling paradigms (i.e., "The Hero's Journey") and step-by-step guidelines to plot and character development. Based on the work of Joseph Campbell, *The Writer's Journey* is a must for all writers interested in further developing their craft.

The updated and revised third edition provides new insights and observations from Vogler's ongoing work on mythology's influence on stories, movies, and man himself.

"This book is like having the smartest person in the story meeting come home with you and whisper what to do in your ear as you write a screenplay. Insight for insight, step for step, Chris Vogler takes us through the process of connecting theme to story and making a script come alive."
> – Lynda Obst, Producer, *Sleepless in Seattle, How to Lose a Guy in 10 Days;* Author, *Hello, He Lied*

"This is a book about the stories we write, and perhaps more importantly, the stories we live. It is the most influential work I have yet encountered on the art, nature, and the very purpose of storytelling."
> – Bruce Joel Rubin, Screenwriter, *Stuart Little 2, Deep Impact, Ghost, Jacob's Ladder*

CHRISTOPHER VOGLER is a veteran story consultant for major Hollywood film companies and a respected teacher of filmmakers and writers around the globe. He has influenced the stories of movies from *The Lion King* to *Fight Club* to *The Thin Red Line* and most recently wrote the first installment of *Ravenskull*, a Japanese-style manga or graphic novel. He is the executive producer of the feature film *P.S. Your Cat is Dead* and writer of the animated feature *Jester Till*.

$26.95 · 300 PAGES · ORDER NUMBER 76RLS · ISBN: 193290736x

Cinematic Storytelling: *The 100 Most Powerful Film Conventions Every Filmmaker Must Know* / Jennifer Van Sijll / $24.95

Complete DVD Book, The: *Designing, Producing, and Marketing Your Independent Film on DVD* / Chris Gore and Paul J. Salamoff / $26.95

Complete Independent Movie Marketing Handbook, The: *Promote, Distribute & Sell Your Film or Video* / Mark Steven Bosko / $39.95

Could It Be a Movie?: *How to Get Your Ideas Out of Your Head and Up on the Screen* / Christina Hamlett / $26.95

Creating Characters: *Let Them Whisper Their Secrets* Marisa D'Vari / $26.95

Crime Writer's Reference Guide, The: *1001 Tips for Writing the Perfect Crime* Martin Roth / $20.95

Cut by Cut: *Editing Your Film or Video* Gael Chandler / $35.95

Digital Filmmaking 101, 2nd Edition: *An Essential Guide to Producing Low-Budget Movies* / Dale Newton and John Gaspard / $26.95

Digital Moviemaking, 2nd Edition: *All the Skills, Techniques, and Moxie You'll Need to Turn Your Passion into a Career* / Scott Billups / $26.95

Directing Actors: *Creating Memorable Performances for Film and Television* Judith Weston / $26.95

Directing Feature Films: *The Creative Collaboration Between Directors, Writers, and Actors* / Mark Travis / $26.95

Eye is Quicker, The: *Film Editing; Making a Good Film Better* Richard D. Pepperman / $27.95

Fast, Cheap & Under Control: *Lessons Learned from the Greatest Low-Budget Movies of All Time* / John Gaspard / $26.95

Film & Video Budgets, 4th Updated Edition Deke Simon and Michael Wiese / $26.95

Film Directing: Cinematic Motion, 2nd Edition Steven D. Katz / $27.95

Film Directing: Shot by Shot, *Visualizing from Concept to Screen* Steven D. Katz / $27.95

Film Director's Intuition, The: *Script Analysis and Rehearsal Techniques* Judith Weston / $26.95

Film Production Management 101: *The Ultimate Guide for Film and Television Production Management and Coordination* / Deborah S. Patz / $39.95

Filmmaking for Teens: *Pulling Off Your Shorts* Troy Lanier and Clay Nichols / $18.95

First Time Director: *How to Make Your Breakthrough Movie* Gil Bettman / $27.95

From Word to Image: *Storyboarding and the Filmmaking Process* Marcie Begleiter / $26.95

Hitting Your Mark, 2nd Edition: *Making a Life – and a Living – as a Film Director* Steve Carlson / $22.95

Hollywood Standard, The: *The Complete and Authoritative Guide to Script Format and Style* / Christopher Riley / $18.95

I Could've Written a Better Movie Than That!: *How to Make Six Figures as a Script Consultant even if You're not a Screenwriter* / Derek Rydall / $26.95

Independent Film Distribution: *How to Make a Successful End Run Around the Big Guys* / Phil Hall / $26.95

Independent Film and Videomakers Guide – 2nd Edition, The: *Expanded and Updated* / Michael Wiese / $29.95

Inner Drives: *How to Write and Create Characters Using the Eight Classic Centers of Motivation* / Pamela Jaye Smith / $26.95

I'll Be in My Trailer!: *The Creative Wars Between Directors & Actors* John Badham and Craig Modderno / $26.95

Moral Premise, The: *Harnessing Virtue & Vice for Box Office Success* Stanley D. Williams, Ph.D. / $24.95

Myth and the Movies: *Discovering the Mythic Structure of 50 Unforgettable Films* / Stuart Voytilla / $26.95

On the Edge of a Dream: *Magic and Madness in Bali* Michael Wiese / $16.95

Perfect Pitch, The: *How to Sell Yourself and Your Movie Idea to Hollywood* Ken Rotcop / $16.95

Power of Film, The Howard Suber / $27.95

Psychology for Screenwriters: *Building Conflict in your Script* William Indick, Ph.D. / $26.95

Save the Cat!: *The Last Book on Screenwriting You'll Ever Need* Blake Snyder / $19.95

Screenwriting 101: *The Essential Craft of Feature Film Writing* Neill D. Hicks / $16.95

Screenwriting for Teens: *The 100 Principles of Screenwriting Every Budding Writer Must Know* / Christina Hamlett / $18.95

Script-Selling Game, The: *A Hollywood Insider's Look at Getting Your Script Sold and Produced* / Kathie Fong Yoneda / $16.95

Selling Your Story in 60 Seconds: *The Guaranteed Way to get Your Screenplay or Novel Read* / Michael Hauge / $12.95

Setting Up Your Scenes: *The Inner Workings of Great Films* Richard D. Pepperman / $24.95

Setting Up Your Shots: *Great Camera Moves Every Filmmaker Should Know* Jeremy Vineyard / $19.95

Shaking the Money Tree, 2nd Edition: *The Art of Getting Grants and Donations for Film and Video Projects* / Morrie Warshawski / $26.95

Sound Design: *The Expressive Power of Music, Voice, and Sound Effects in Cinema* / David Sonnenschein / $19.95

Stealing Fire From the Gods, 2nd Edition: *The Complete Guide to Story for Writers & Filmmakers* / James Bonnet / $26.95

Storyboarding 101: *A Crash Course in Professional Storyboarding* James Fraioli / $19.95

Ultimate Filmmaker's Guide to Short Films, The: *Making It Big in Shorts* Kim Adelman / $16.95

Working Director, The: *How to Arrive, Thrive & Survive in the Director's Chair* Charles Wilkinson / $22.95

Writer's Journey, – 2nd Edition, The: *Mythic Structure for Writers* Christopher Vogler / $24.95

Writer's Partner, The: *1001 Breakthrough Ideas to Stimulate Your Imagination* Martin Roth / $24.95

Writing the Action Adventure: *The Moment of Truth* Neill D. Hicks / $14.95

Writing the Comedy Film: *Make 'Em Laugh* Stuart Voytilla and Scott Petri / $14.95

Writing the Killer Treatment: *Selling Your Story Without a Script* Michael Halperin / $14.95

Writing the Second Act: *Building Conflict and Tension in Your Film Script* Michael Halperin / $19.95

Writing the Thriller Film: *The Terror Within* Neill D. Hicks / $14.95

Writing the TV Drama Series: *How to Succeed as a Professional Writer in TV* Pamela Douglas / $24.95

DVD & VIDEOS

Field of Fish: *VHS Video* Directed by Steve Tanner and Michael Wiese, Written by Annamaria Murphy / $9.95

Hardware Wars: *DVD* / Written and Directed by Ernie Fosselius / $14.95

Sacred Sites of the Dalai Lamas – DVD, The: *A Pilgrimage to Oracle Lake* A Documentary by Michael Wiese / $22.95